MANY KINDS OF
COURAGE

MANY KINDS OF
COURAGE

AN ORAL HISTORY OF WORLD WAR II

BY RICHARD LIDZ

G.P. PUTNAM'S SONS · NEW YORK

General Publishing Co. Limited, Toronto.
PRINTED IN THE UNITED STATES OF AMERICA
Library of Congress Cataloging in Publication Data

Lidz, Richard.
Many kinds of courage.
Includes index.
SUMMARY: A collection of personal narratives
describing the London Blitz, the attack on Pearl Harbor,
the Normandy invasion, and other events of World War II.
1. World War, 1939-1945—Juvenile literature.
2. World War, 1939-1945—Personal narratives—Juvenile
literature. [1. World War, 1939-1945. 2. World War,
1939-1945—Personal narratives] I. Title.
D743.7.L5 1979   940.53   79-1031
ISBN 0-399-20690-6
Second Impression

CONTENTS

ACKNOWLEDGMENTS

A great many people aided me in this project. I particularly want to thank Shirley Blumenthal, Stuart Dworeck, Marc Goldbaum and Monica Lange for their help in researching, setting up and conducting some of the interviews; Les Waffen and the staff of the audiovisual section of the National Archives for their help in locating the recordings of Irving Strobel's last message from Corregidor, the Nuremberg testimony of Marie Claude Vaillant-Couturier and Dr. Franz Blaha and Miss Palchikoff's account of the atomic bombing of Hiroshima; and Dr. John T. Mason, Jr., director of oral history at the U.S. Naval Institute, for permission to use the Pearl Harbor portion of his interview with Capt. Charles Merdinger. Thanks also to Cindy Feldner, Susan Gordon, Sharon Hubbard and Linda Perrin for their many contributions during the manuscript preparation and editing phases of this project. Charles Mercer, Jan Meyer and William J. West are particularly to be thanked for their encouragement, patience and understanding. Most important of all, I am grateful to the people who were interviewed for allowing their stories to be told.

R.L.

INTRODUCTION

Forty years have passed since Adolf Hitler's legions of darkness marched into Poland to start what was unquestionably the most destructive war in all of human history. More than 33 million people were killed in World War II, of whom at least half were civilians. This is a far greater loss of life than in any military conflict ever. More than 400,000 Americans alone were killed in action or died in service, almost ten times the number of Americans killed in Vietnam. It is unquestionably true that because of its global scope and long duration, World War II had an impact on more lives than any other event ever to have taken place.

Yet most of the people alive today were not born when World War II was fought. For them the war is only a few pages in a history book; some general statements about why and how it was fought. Many of their impressions come from seeing high-adventure films and television series that glamorize, or romanticize or parody the war. It is not hard to understand why popular perceptions of World War II grow ever more at variance with the reality of the event. These media treatments may be engrossing and amusing, but they have little to do with the truth.

Historians, generals, statesmen, and national leaders have written many excellent books giving accounts, interpretations and analyses of World War II. Some of these cover the vast panorama of the war as a whole, others examine critical moments and movements in detail, still others analyze the political, social, economic and military interactions and consequences of the war. But most of these works were written by people who could, in some way, influence events as they were going on, or who studied them after they occurred. Their perceptions are invaluable, but they are not, and cannot be, the same as those of the millions of ordinary people who were engulfed by the war, who were swept along by events over which they had absolutely no control. What actually happens in war is felt most keenly not by the generals and statesmen, but by those soldiers and civilians who chance to be in the wrong place at the wrong time.

Many Kinds of Courage is about such people. It presents the experiences of individuals who, in the face of overpowering circumstances, did what they had to do and survived. The essential truths about war seem to be found more clearly and more vividly in the living, human experiences of such people than in the memoirs of the great and the mighty. But most people know what they know and carry their stories inside themselves. Few write them down. When they are gone their experiences and their insights are lost. Many who survived the war are no longer living. For others, still alive, the sharp reality of events has begun to dim.

Much of the truth about war, or at least about World War II, will be lost to us if we fail to preserve the accounts of those who lived through it. By using a technique known as oral history, *Many Kinds of Courage* records the experiences of at least a few of these people. The oral history technique involves locating individuals who participated in, or witnessed, events of particular interest (and who remember them in sufficient detail that their recollections can be verified against documentary evidence), interviewing them and recording what they have to say.

In some cases other oral materials have been used, either because they are particularly vivid or because it was not possible to locate and interview an eyewitness of a particular event. Thus, Irving Strobing's account of the fall of Corregidor and Miss Palchikoff's description of the atomic bombing of Japan, as well as Mme Vaillant-Couturier's and Dr. Blaha's Nuremberg War Crimes Trial testimony about the concentration camps were found in the audio section of the National Archives. Many of the people who were interviewed have permitted us to use their real names, others have requested anonymity. Their wishes have been observed.

In oral history the people interviewed tell their own stories. The author is simply the conduit through which the stories pass. It is hoped that these accounts will move readers through time and space so that they become eyewitnesses of the actual events and experience the war as it really was—full of tension, deception, horror, fear, fatigue and, most of all, courage.

—RICHARD LIDZ

In memory of my parents, Adelaide and Sam,
from whom I learned that there are many kinds of courage.

1

BERLIN:
1933-1938

Kurt Lange

If anybody tries to find out whether people can be brainwashed, they don't need to do any experiments because the example is already there. The German nation was brainwashed.

—Kurt Lange

Berlin: 1933–1938

At the end of World War I a new and democratic government, the Weimar Republic, was created in Germany. But the new government found it difficult to cope with postwar conditions. Germany had been disarmed and forbidden to rearm, stripped of her foreign colonies, and forced to give up territory which she claimed as her own. She also had to pay the Allies heavy reparations for damages caused by the war.

For these and other reasons the German economy was depressed, there was high unemployment, and inflation was so rapid that money had virtually no buying power. The political scene was also unsettled, as a growing Communist movement—at times in conflict with right-wing Nationalists, and at times together with them—encouraged strikes and civil unrest.

Onto this scene came Adolph Hitler, a bitter and volatile nationalist who was strongly anti-Communist and an outspoken opponent of the Versailles Treaty. His party, the National Socialists, or "Nazis," gained increasing support, and in 1933 Hitler became Chancellor of Germany. It did not take him long to consolidate his power. Within a month he suspended the Constitution of the Weimar Republic. Then, over the next few years he eliminated all political opposition, initiated heavy use of political propaganda and censorship, and openly planned for the re-militarization of Germany. Hitler also had a blind and virulent hatred of Jews; either irrationally, or because he needed a scapegoat against which to unify the German people, he blamed them for all of Germany's economic, social and cultural ills, and imposed increasingly restrictive and punitive policies against them.

As a medical student and young professional in Berlin, Kurt Lange observed at first hand the demise of the Weimar Republic and Hitler's rise to power. As a Jew he experienced directly the increasing harshness of Nazi persecution. On *Kristallnacht* ("Crystal Night," or "The Night of Broken Glass"), in November, 1938—when full-scale destruction of Jewish homes, stores, and synagogues began—he narrowly escaped being among the thirty thousand German Jewish men who were rounded up and sent to concentration camps. Most of these men were never heard from again. Relying on their wits and their nerve, Kurt Lange and his wife managed to survive, and to escape from Nazi Germany just before it was too late. Today he is professor of medicine and professor of pediatrics at New York Medical College. He is a noted internist with a specialty in nephrology.

Kurt Lange:

In order to understand the rise of Hitler and National Socialism in Germany, one has to go back to the end of World War I. At that time I was a schoolboy and I remember clearly that the German people felt the war was not really lost. Very little damage had been done to Germany itself, and there originated the *Dolchstosslegende*—the legend of the "stab in the back"—that many Germans felt had caused the end of the war. On the other hand, the Communist movement was growing very rapidly and certain segments of the working classes saw the Communist leaders as heroes. However, the majority of people despised these leftist movements.

There were strong Jewish leaders in the Communist movement.

This touched a sensitive spot in the German, for whom anti-Semitism had been a tradition for centuries. There was no word meaning "anti-Semitism" in the German language, but not far under the surface, and in the old tradition of the German Army, there was an underlying feeling against the Jews. There was no free mixture of Jews with other groups, but this kind of social segregation began to disappear in the ten or twelve years following World War I and led to an almost complete assimilation of the Jews in Germany. The prejudices that were previously quite open became covered up.

With the end of the First World War, a massive inflation started in Germany which lasted for three or four years and hurt the economic situation of the people very deeply. Only a few people were able to recover from this setback completely. The former military caste was especially hard hit. After the First World War, when the army ceased to exist, they took whatever jobs they could find. Those people who before the war were drinking champagne, were now forced to sell it. There was a strong feeling that this officer clique was not going to tolerate this economic deterioration. The first sign was an attempt on the life of the then Chancellor of Germany, Walter Rathenau, who was a Jew of high intellectual qualities and also the president of one of the greatest German industrial firms. Although a nationalistic German, Rathenau did understand that Germany, having lost the war, would have to adapt to new circumstances. This seemingly realistic view made him a traitor in the eyes of the clique of former officers, who tried to murder him. Fortunately, their attempt was unsuccessful.

In the meantime, a somewhat moderate group of political leftists—representatives of the working class called the Social Democrats—had taken over the government in combination with the Democratic Party under President Ebert. This was in 1920–21. Many of the leading Social Democrats and Democrats of this time were highly qualified intellectuals who came from the working classes. This leadership, because of its background, was strongly influenced by university professors and theoreticians, and did not have the sympathetic support of the masses in Germany. On the other hand, intellectual life was flourishing at this time to a degree that I have never seen before or since. The years between 1923—

after the massive inflation had stopped—and 1931 were a period of incredible intellectual and artistic growth. Theaters, concerts, the creative arts, the sciences were blossoming to an unprecedented level. Out of this period came many of the basic cultural and scientific advances that today still shape the world. The basis of the atomic bomb was created in the German institutes of physics. Einstein developed his basic theory at this time. The expressionist artists and painters of this period were of tremendous influence on the development of art all over Europe and in America.

All this intellectual activity, however, was regarded by the great mass of the German people with little understanding and a great deal of mistrust. After the end of the First World War the Allies had imposed on Germany heavy reparation requirements. That is, Germany had to pay huge amounts of money to the Allies. The Rhineland was demilitarized. These measures were deeply resented by those in Germany with the old militaristic spirit, at least those who later provided the popular support for National Socialism. This clear-cut cleavage between the political right and left was very much reflected in the student bodies of the universities in Germany and Austria. Vienna, especially, became the hotbed of nationalistic student unions. The so-called *Burschenschaften* (dueling societies) became the base for an anti-Semitic and supernationalistic tradition. Many former graduates, who had once also been members of these rapidly swelling societies, were now leaders of industry. They brought these young men with their supernationalist tendencies into their industrial enterprises, where they exerted tremendous influence. On the other hand, the somewhat more democratic and socialistic student societies did not have these connections with industry and were of only moderate influence. The government shied away from supporting them too openly in order not to violate the so-called integrity of the universities.

This, then, was the background scene in Germany at the end of the 1920's: high cultural and intellectual development on the one hand, and on the other, progressively increasing unemployment. The unemployment situation became worse toward the end of the 1920's, and from year to year more people—especially young people—could not find jobs and turned to the nationalistic movements. The influence of these movements grew dramatically as those who had been thrown out of jobs and positions of leadership at the end of the First World War now joined their ranks.

There came a man who got up in an almost ridiculous way in the beer cellars of Munich and propagated a supernationalism laced with a good severe dose of anti-Semitism. What he had to say appealed to the instincts inherent in certain sizable groups of Germans. He also found support among academic youth who represented substantial groups in the student bodies of the German universities. Had the Social Democrats and Democrats then in power not been so obsessively tolerant even toward complete intolerance, this force could have been handled quickly and decisively. The nonsense of tolerance toward intolerance was the basis for the government's failure to intervene at a time when this whole movement was germinating and the government could have suppressed it by force or by legal means.

This, however, was not done. For example, on the day Karl Severing, the Weimar Republic's Minister of the Interior, was arrested by Hitler's troops, he sent word to the Workers' Unions that he did not want a general strike. The strike was set up and ready to the last detail. But he sent word that he didn't want to have any bloodshed and they should not set the strike into motion. A strike at that time would have ended the whole Hitler affair within twenty-four hours. The liberals were defeated by their own principles.

It should also be a lesson to us at the present time that tolerance against basic intolerance is nonsense that has nothing to do with the principle of tolerance. Tolerance itself is not a constitutional right; it simply permits us to deal with questions of principle and constitutional importance. If you are tolerant of those who do not want to recognize the rights of other people to speak without threat of force, then you undermine the very principle that you want to achieve, namely democracy.

I was never mesmerized by Hitler, nor were any of my friends. For our basic ideas were so far opposite to his conception of life in a civilized society that we could never have fallen under his spell. In addition, of course, from the first day anti-Semitism would have prevented you from falling under the spell even if you had the tendency to be taken in. It is, therefore, very difficult for me to say why the people at large were mesmerized. The young people were trained and indoctrinated from the age of six years on into the Nazi idea. They went through the youth groups, they went through the adolescent groups of the SS, and they went through the SS itself.

If anybody tries to find out whether people can be brainwashed, they don't need to do any experiments because the example is already there. The German nation was brainwashed. Systematically, continuously, without recourse to any other information. Whether everybody fell for it, or whether only 80 percent fell for it, or only 60 percent, is a question of very minor importance. Virtually everybody believed the junk that came over the radio, even up to the very end. The people were still hoping that the Führer would save them even though their towns were burned to the ground and bombs were still falling and it was just a few months before the end.

At the beginning the chief problem was unemployment. As it became worse and worse, the dissatisfaction of the unemployed masses pushed them toward Hitler and his National Socialist movement. Socialism was something most people wanted, especially with the unemployment situation as it was, and nationalism—even extreme nationalism—is a basic German characteristic. (Although this extreme nationalism has in my experience markedly subsided since the Second World War, but for how long only the future will show.) Using the appeals of socialism and nationalism, a demagogue like Hitler, who was also a fantastic speaker, could bring the masses to a frenzy and attract them to the National Socialist movement.

In back of all this, however, was German heavy industry. The leaders of heavy industry thought that by aiding Hitler they would get rid of the undesirable union movement, and that by using him as a puppet and supporting him financially they would gain influence with the government. Anti-Semitism was not an inherent character trait of these industrialists. But they used it as a tool in order to inflame the people and push them into Hitler's camp.

The rise of Nazism can actually be traced to the cowardice and unwillingness of the Weimar Republic's officials to defend themselves, as well as their inability to bring up the necessary strength to combat unemployment with sweeping measures of support for the unemployed. Finally it can be traced to the help of the industrialists, who thought they would get their own aims fulfilled by using Hitler as a puppet as long as they thought he could serve them.

In the beginning, the response to the Nazi movement was not very furious in most circles. For many years, even under Hitler, everybody had the idea that this spoof was soon going to be over. Initially, nobody took him very seriously. Hitler came into power through the consent of former Field Marshal Paul von Hindenburg, then President of Germany, with a minority—somewhere in the range of 30 percent—of the voting population. I want to stress that Hitler never had a majority of the votes of the German people, and the whole thing was not taken too seriously. Even among the Jews, with few exceptions, men of vision were not too alarmed initially. That is, not until Hitler was in power and the so-called Reichstag fire occurred in February, 1933. The Reichstag was the building in Berlin which housed the German Parliament. The Nazis—who were probably responsible for the fire themselves—accused, convicted, and executed an alleged Communist traitor by the name of Van der Lubbe (who was actually Dutch).

The flames of the burning Parliament building were the signal for the rapid implementation of radical measures by the National Socialists. The day after the fire Hitler got von Hindenburg to sign a decree suspending individual and civil liberties guaranteed by the Constitution of the Weimar Republic. From then on Jews throughout Germany—especially those who had played a more prominent political role—were arrested right and left. Many, among them friends of mine from student days, disappeared and were never seen again. So it became very clear that this was serious business—very serious business. Everybody realized all of a sudden that an end had to be made of the Hitler movement, but nobody lifted a finger to bring it about. Thus the Nazi movement progressed step by step, very slowly, very gradually.

Everybody, especially the Jewish population, thought, "Oh, this will soon be over, he can't do that." Or: "The Allies won't tolerate a march into Czechoslovakia." Or: "How can they permit him to march into Poland?" Or: "Tomorrow the Allies will intervene." The English and American radio supported such ideas. Many people listened to these broadcasts and said, "Ah, this is the sign of intervention which must come tomorrow. They cannot tolerate the inhumanities of Hitler's faction towards their political adversaries and towards the Jews." But soon the more intelligent people began to realize that National Socialism was something not to be shaken off lightly. The measures against the Jews rapidly increased. As soon as Hitler came into power the German universities discharged all Jewish employees. Professors, instructors, teachers of any kind were immediately discharged in spite of contracts that were unbreakable according to German tradition.

At that time I was teaching in the medical school at the University of Berlin. I got notification on the first of April, 1932, that by, I think July of '32, my contract as a tenured assistant professor was terminated. But still, those of us in the academic professions thought, "This will be over, this cannot last." It is difficult in retrospect to understand how we could have continued to delude ourselves, although those who went through the time will remember that this gradual disappearance of the floor on which you are standing was not like falling into a big hole. It was rather a slow sinking which you always hoped would stop—that you would find a way out, that you don't have to go. After all, as I mentioned before, the Jews in Germany were highly assimilated. They were in leading positions in academic and cultural fields. How could this happen after a thirty–forty year period of assimilation in Germany? One cannot, in retrospect, blame anyone for not having realized in the beginning that what was happening was to become, in its full extent, the Holocaust.

Then came the years in which economic and social restrictions against the Jews became steadily more severe. Those of us in the medical profession who had entered private practice, after being forced to leave the academic field, were now limited in our practices as well. No gentile patients could be treated by Jewish physicians anymore. Again, a blow. No gentile customers could be handled by Jewish salespeople. Another blow. No gentile servants could be kept in Jewish households. Again, a severe blow. Those who could, started to emigrate in large numbers. But where to go? Emigration was made difficult by ever greater restrictions against taking money or property along. By 1938 there was practically no property that could be taken out of Germany, and no money could be taken at all. There were death penalties threatened for those who exported German marks into foreign countries.

It has often been asked, "What became of the Communists? What became of the Socialists? What did they do with the Democrats?" The Democrats were always weak sisters. But the Social Democrats did fight against the Nazi groups in the beginning. The Berlin police, who were all to the left of center politically, did intervene at Nazi demonstrations at the University. But all this was done half-heartedly. There was no will to fight, and no recognition that one must combat Nazism right there and then. The previously mentioned decision of Severing to call off a general strike against Hitler in order to avoid having any blood spilled is symbolic of the lack of vitality in the Democratic and Social Democratic parties.

The press was very quickly suppressed. The newspapers had to report whatever the government issued as the official statement or opinion. Goebbels, the master of propaganda, became the lord of all newspapers. Anti-Semitic journals of a wildly vulgar type flooded the newsstands. Many newspapers disappeared—they were simply censored out of existence. Others were taken over very quickly by followers of the Nazi party who were imposed over the original staffs to run the newspapers. Thus, the opposition was made silent within a few months after the Nazi takeover.

Old man von Hindenburg had silently packed it in and died shortly thereafter. There are, by the way, serious questions whether von Hindenburg's consent to let Hitler become Chancellor of Germany was heavily influenced by the old man's son. Apparently Hitler had something on the son and was threatening to smear the von Hindenburg family name, which was one of the great heroic names of the First World War.

So Hitler's consolidation of power progressed with all of its terrible measures. Silently, more and more people came into the concentration camps. This was known only to relatives and to a few outsiders. Those of us who knew a little bit were actually aware of the camps right after the takeover, because some of the leaders of the Democratic and Social Democratic semi-military groups disappeared and were never seen again. They wrote occasionaly from somewhere a few notes from which it was clearly understandable, to those who wanted to understand, that they were not in a recreation home.

The real massive recognition of the existence of concentration camps came in November, 1938, after all the restrictions had already been imposed and most Jewish people had given up their apartments and others had gone into hiding. I want to stress that there were many Germans, though not enough, who protected and hid Jewish friends, often for years. But this was a small number, and the majority of them were not aware that under the boots of the SS and SA (the storm troopers) there were gruesome events taking place. How many of the German people were aware of the concentration camps, of the torture, of the murder, is a question that is difficult to answer. From my own experience I can only say that the majority of people with whom I had contact in the 1930's were not fully aware of what was going on.

The Jewish people suffered terribly. They were thrown out of their professions, and their shops and businesses were destroyed. Bands of German storm troopers rioted through villages and towns and smashed up the stores of Jewish owners. But these riots were supported by the police and other officials, and the owners were taken away, to where, nobody asked; nobody wanted to know too much. They just disappeared. The population as such certainly did not defend their Jewish co-citizens. They did not want to have anything to do with hiding them, because protecting a Jew was as much a crime as being a Jew. The same held true for Communists and Socialists.

Emigration grew to a great extent among those who had somewhere to go, but they weren't able to take anything along of any value. For anybody who was not quite young it was very difficult to visualize what their fate would be in a new country, whose language most of them did not understand, and where probably nobody would be there to help them. And so the majority of Jews were hanging on to the hope that tomorrow it would be over. Something will happen. But Mr. Chamberlain came with his umbrella to visit Hitler in September of 1938, and acquiesced to the German occupation of the Sudetenland. This sellout of Czechoslovakia in Munich was supposed to establish peace for our generation.

Meanwhile, the Nazi consolidation of power in Germany went on at an ever faster pace. The storm troopers completely dominated everything. Everybody, every leader in industry, whether Jewish, or slightly tainted with socialism, or even with good old conservatism, was replaced by one of the leaders of Hitler's horde. By that time the captains of German heavy industry realized that they had produced an egg which had hatched a monster that was strangling them. Industry was occupied with the production of war materiel. By now the regulations against producing weapons, which Germany had accepted in the treaty of Versailles, were completely ignored.

It had become clear back in early 1936 that the Nazi movement could do whatever it pleased. It was then that Hitler had marched into the demilitarized zone of the Rhineland with his troops, and nobody had moved against him. Not France, which had insisted on the demilitarized zone and was immediately concerned with the Rhineland as its neighbor, nor did any other nation (including the United States) move a finger against this clear breach of the Versailles agreement. This was actually the clearest sign to the Nazi movement that they could do what they pleased, because the world would not intervene. This was a moment when, within a day, the marching of French troops into the Rhineland would have put an end to Hitler's power then and there. But nothing happened.

Cowardice is the guiding word for the origin of the Hitler movement. Whether it was the German democratic groups, or whether it was the Allies who didn't realize what was going on, no one was prepared to stand up to the Nazis. But this could have been done, because at that time it was a fragile, noisy, amorphous movement which did not actually have the strength to fight. Had he been prevented from reoccuppying the Rhineland, Hitler's power would have been ended.

There were a few attempts by men of the German nobility, and some generals of the army, to end the Hitler spectacle, but nothing came of them. There were a few attempts on Hitler's life, especially the one much later (in 1944) by von Stauffenberg and his group, where the bomb missed Hitler by a few yards. But there was never a real popular move to depose Hitler by force. There were no groups that had power enough to do it, and what groups existed were all undermined and infiltrated by Hitler's cohorts. So there was never a serious attempt on the part of the German people to overthrow the regime, and most of them were not even so sure that National Socialism wasn't the better way.

For example, *Kraft durch Freude*, "power through pleasure," was a big movement that propaganda minister Goebbels had sold to the people, sending them on vacation trips and constantly propagandizing "Heil Hitler." The propaganda machine was unbelievably powerful, especially since anyone who spoke out against it ended almost immediately in the concentration camps. Newspapers were no longer available which could in any way oppose any of Hitler's measures. The only refuge that people had were the BBC broadcasts from Britain, which were heard clandestinely, and at great risk to the listener. In Germany there was no opposition and no news of what was going on. Everything was glorious on the radio.

Also, the problem of unemployment was partially solved by the tremendous volume of munitions production. Weapons of all kinds were produced in large amounts. While the workers were paid poorly, at least they were employed. Food was scarce, but not scarce enough to keep anybody hungry. Food was freely available—not in large quantities, and of very poor quality—but it was available. Nobody who had the money had to go hungry. So, everything was wonderful. And, in fact, it *was* wonderful, if you look at it from the viewpoint of the power-hungry Nazi movement which nobody was able, or even dared,to stop.

More and more, the conviction grew in intelligent circles that this cannot go on, this must lead to a catastrophe. But again, nothing was done. It became increasingly clear that the Nazi leadership was not doing much that was of concrete benefit to the German people. Instead they appealed to their imagination, to their nationalism, to their myth-making tendencies. "Bread and circuses" was the motto of the whole movement. Marching troops have always been one of the basic pleasures of the German people (except now, after the war, this seems to be anathema in Germany). But at the time there were brass bands marching all over: marching SS, marching SA, marching at the Olympic Games, marching at the National Socialist Congresses. This was what the people were shown, and what they listened to. They were given the voice of Hitler—which had great magnetism for the German people through his screaming, hysterical outbursts— instead of a real improvement in their economic situation.

Exports had not grown and imports were massively restricted so that the economic balance would not completely break down. In general, outside of the immediate SS, SA leaders, and the higher echelons of the Nazi party, nobody profited from Hitler and nobody got anything out of this desperate situation. The intellectuals soon realized that the only way they could escape the SS and the SA—children from the age of ten or twelve had to wear uniforms in the schools and join the block SS or SA units—was to take refuge in the army. They became physicians in the army, or joined other branches of the military wherever they could in order not to be forced into the SS or SA. But only a small group of people, mostly professionals, had the opportunity of escaping. The others were forced into these groups and indoctrinated. Indoctrination can do a great deal. All the things that the people were told were bought as pure truth, although they were nothing but fantasy and lies. In this way a figment of imagination, an illusion, was built up which everybody believed. It was only after the war that they realized that what they had seen was illusory, did not really exist.

But the leading Nazi circles lived high and exerted an unbelievable regimen of terror. Those who did not consent to their policies and methods—even members of their own group—were recklessly murdered. I remember that Röhm Putsch, in which Hitler had his best friend killed for fear that he might become a political rival. This was done under the guise that Hitler and the party could not tolerate homosexual activities.

Thus it went, worse and worse. The shouts of the storm troopers became louder and louder and there was destruction all over the place, throughout the country. Day in and day out the Nazis were stealing the property of *Volksfeinde*, that is "enemies of the people," whether they be Jewish, Socialistic or in any other way "suspicious." This went on in a completely overt manner without any concern whatever for justice. The legal system broke down completely. There was no indictment for anything that was done. Very few people would have dared to bring material to the knowledge of the courts; and, in fact, there were practically no courts which would have intervened at all.

What happened to me personally was really quite simple. I left the university, I was forced to leave the university hospital, and I started private practice and did acceptably well—until the limitation came that Jews could no longer treat any non-Jewish patients. But even then we had the daily hope that the system would break down tomorrow. You stuck together with groups that were in a situation similar to your own and everyone fired up their friends with, "Have you heard from the British Broadcasting Company that tomorrow . . . ," and on and on it went.

I personally got a contract to develop certain medical instruments for Siemens, the biggest German electrical concern. I was working in the laboratories there, completely independently, in a very pleasant atmosphere. There was a group of highly qualified people at Siemens who wanted to have nothing to do with the Nazi regime. However, they didn't say so. But just by silently doing their work and not participating in anything politically and having no prejudice, they concentrated on their work and tried to shield themselves from what was going on. Like most Germans who today say they didn't participate, they are probably telling the truth. They shielded themselves off completely, like an oyster in a shell. They didn't want to see the outside. Whether they didn't know how to handle it, or whether their decency compelled them not to handle it, they completely closed themselves off from what was happening.

I worked in this lab developing certain inventions of my own until shortly before I left Germany. In the meantime, my medical practice had practically dwindled down to nothing. We had no way out. Until a Jewish patient, a foreigner—a Dutchman—came to my office and asked me, "What are you still doing in Germany?" And I answered, "We have nowhere to go, we have nobody abroad, we have no way to go, we have no money to go." So this man said, "Let me handle that affair." And within a few days he had deposited a large amount of money in a New York bank and sent us a receipt in my name. This receipt was enough for the U.S. consul to authorize our visas, since we had capital to live on in the United States. But in the meantime, there had been *Kristallnacht* (Crystal Night).

On November 11, 1938, I got a telephone call from an American artist who was giving us English lessons since we intended to emigrate to the United States. At this point we had been promised the visa, but did not have it yet. This man called me up at 10 o'clock in the evening and said, "Doctor, tonight you have an English lesson." I asked him whether he was out of his mind to call me up at 10 o'clock—we had abandoned our apartment months before and lived in a furnished room. He said, "You come tonight for an English lesson." Again I asked him whether he had become insane. And he said most emphatically, "Don't ask, take a taxi and come." I went there, since I couldn't understand the situation, and this saved my life.

On that same night, called Crystal Night because Nazi mobs broke the glass windows in all the stores and houses owned by Jews, the Gestapo came to arrest me and practically all the Jewish men in Berlin. The American hid me in his apartment at first, and then moved me around to stay with friends at different embassies, night after night. During the day we just stayed in parks in order not to be found in any house. Sometimes we hid at the police station by just sitting in the waiting room with a book, as if we had to wait for some answer, moving from one office to another. We thought that this would be about the safest place to be until the wave of arrests was over. During the ten or twelve days of this roundup, people were caught in the streets and everywhere. Many people found ways of hiding out to avoid being arrested by the Gestapo, but a great many Jewish men were taken.

The American who saved my life has since died, blessed be his memory. He had advance knowledge of what was going to happen, for as it turned out, he was a double agent. I will ever be grateful to him for saving me. All through *Kristallnacht* Jewish stores and synagogues were destroyed and burned, and the men who were caught were thrown into concentration camps. I had one odd bit of satisfaction out of that horrible experience. The day before *Kristallnacht* I had sold my car to a gentile person, but the car still had on it the Star of David emblem that every Jew had to wear and to put on his car. The man, who had bought and paid for the car, left it on the street to pick up the next morning. The car was completely destroyed during the night. So it went.

My father and my mother, who were elderly people, were not arrested at this time, but were arrested three months later and thrown into concentration camps. So were my parents-in-law, although my father-in-law, who had been a leading Republican leftist, was hidden by some gentile friends for many months. A brother of mine had immigrated to the United States shortly before this, and finally on December 31, 1938, my wife and I got our visa, went to Amsterdam, and came to the United States.

Those were unbelievable times. Only someone who was there and went through the anxieties of daily living can imagine the courage that one had to develop in order to overcome the most impossible situations. For there were so many details from day to day that it's almost impossible for somebody who hasn't been through it to fully understand it.

The German people at large were not directly involved. They were merely silent. They didn't do anything pro, they certainly didn't do anything con. There is no excuse for anybody, except that they had families and were afraid of what would happen to them. There was no possibility of collective action, and no hope of collectively organizing anything—whether it was a bowling club, or a gathering for any other purpose. All such efforts were immediately trampled down and suppressed. Extraordinary courage would have been necessary to organize any real resistance. The backbone of the people was broken.

2

POLAND:
1939-1945

Stefan Korbonski

A great many novel methods of sabotage were devised: railway warehouses and freight cars were soaked with petrol, trains were held up and livestock let loose or grain spilled, officials were bribed to issue receipts for delivery of the same grain a number of times, receipts were forged, and cattle were concealed. But the most ingenious method of sabotaging delivery quotas was the burning of all the quota documents. The documents that served as the basis for fixing delivery quotas were kept in village offices. At the Directorate of Civil Resistance we realized that destruction of these documents would result in total confusion and disorganization, and that it would take the Germans months to reconstruct the quotas. We established a detailed plan for the burning of these records in simultaneous attacks throughout the country, so that we would have the element of surprise and the Germans would have no time to post guards at the village offices. The plan was largely successful. . . . I believe that the successful sabotage of delivery quotas . . . was a major Polish contribution to the war against Germany.

—Stefan Korbonski

Poland: 1939–1945

As Hitler's power grew, Germans living in areas that had been taken away from Germany after World War I began to agitate for the return of these territories to the Reich. Many of these areas had active and growing Nazi parties pressuring for reannexation.

In March, 1938, Hitler made his first move beyond Germany's traditional borders and annexed Austria. This was soon followed by territorial demands on Czechoslovakia, a country that had been created by diplomats at Versailles after World War I. Czechoslovakia was made up of several distinct ethnic groups, including a large German population living in a region called the Sudentenland. These Germans demanded autonomy from the Czech government and subordination of Czech interests to their own. When Hitler supported the demands of the Sudeten Germans, the dispute became a crisis.

As the crisis deepened, the British prime minister, Neville Chamberlain, sought a peaceful settlement acceptable to both Hitler and the Czech government. The dispute was finally "settled" in September, 1938 by giving in to virtually all of Hitler's demands, including the reannexation of the Sudetenland by Germany. The Czechs were given no choice but to accept. Chamberlain believed that the concessions he made were the price that had to be paid to achieve "Peace for our time." Many people, Winston Churchill among them, thought that Czechoslovakia had been sold out to appease Hitler and that the ease with which Hitler bluffed his way into the Sudetenland would only whet his appetite for more territory.

Turning his attention farther east, Hitler astonished the world by signing a nonaggression treaty with the Soviet Union. This agreement eliminated the threat of Soviet opposition should Germany make territorial demands on Poland. On September 1, 1939, one week after Hitler and Stalin had signed their nonaggression pact, Germany invaded Poland. Less than three weeks later, in accordance with the secret terms of the agreement between Hitler and Stalin, Soviet forces moved into the eastern part of Poland. Crushed between the two military giants, Poland ceased to exist as an independent state.

Living under the domination of an invader can never be the same as being independent, governed by your own people, free to speak and do as you please. The Czechs, the Poles, the Danes, the Norwegians, the Dutch, the Belgians, the French, the Yugoslavs, the Greeks, the Finns, and a great many others found occupation by the Nazis to be odious, and, ultimately, intolerable. First there was the shock of defeat, which left the people dazed, stunned, and exhausted. Then, by the time this initial period was over, the conquerors had already introduced strict radio and newspaper censorship. They banned such youth organizations as the YMCA and the Boy Scouts and replaced them with the Hitler Youth. Then they established production quotas for materials to be sent to Germany. Slowly, they attempted to "Nazify" the occupied countries by forcing the teaching of Nazi ideas in schools and introducing Nazi methods into government.

As Germany needed more materiel for the war effort, the occupation authorities seized whatever they could find. They forced miners and factory workers to work longer hours and sent the products of their labors off to Germany. They kept the occupied peoples on starvation rations and sent the food off as well. As Germany's manpower needs increased, the occupation authorities called for volunteer labor. When people would not volunteer, they conscripted and deported them to work in Germany, often in slave labor conditions.

When the conquered people of Europe saw what was happening, they refused to stand by quietly. In some instances this meant engaging in such active resistance as blowing up power stations, oil dumps, railroads, and factories; producing and distributing underground newspapers; helping and hiding men and women who had been called up for service in Germany; destroying records; or forging identification papers and ration cards. In other instances it involved passive resistance carried out by individuals when the opportunity arose: refusing to teach or preach Nazi ideas in schools and churches, and giving anti-Nazi counseling to students and parishioners, or working slowly and "carelessly" in order to reduce production.

The whole object of resistance, whether carried out actively by organized groups or passively by individuals, was to do anything possible to hinder Germany's success. No more than two percent of the population of any occupied country was ever actively engaged in underground activities. But a very large number of people did resist passively, and this had a cumulative effect. Their single acts of resistance may not have been very significant in themselves, but the total effect of a great many of these small acts was devastating to the Germans.

It is hard to imagine, without having actually experienced it, what life must have been like under German occupation. Stefan Korbonski fought against the Germans when they invaded Poland, and then continued to fight as a member of the underground all during the occupation. Because so many of the resistance leaders senior to him were either killed or captured, he became the last chief of the Polish wartime underground. For him, the ideal of a truly free and independent Poland has never ceased to exist.

Korbonski was imprisoned by the NKVD shortly after VE-Day. Following his release he was elected to the first post-war Polish Parliament, but because he was an outspoken anti-communist he was forced to escape to Sweden in 1947. From there he and his wife made their way to England and then to the United States. They now make their home in Washington, D. C., where Korbonski is politically active in Polish anti-communist affairs.

Stefan Korbonski:

On November 11, 1918, Poland regained her independence for the first time in more than one hundred years. Until then Poland had been divided into three parts. One part, in which I was born, was ruled by Russia, the second by Germany, the third by Austria. Poles lived in each of these territories under different laws, under different pressures, and under different influences.

I think that the best situation was in the Austrian part of Poland because Austria gave us some liberties. In fact, Poles enjoyed some autonomy. The worst political suppression was in the Russian-ruled part of Poland. And there was economic as well as political suppression in the western part ruled by Germany because, over there, they wanted to Germanize the Poles and at the same time exploit them economically. When we regained our independence these three parts of Poland were finally united.

But we didn't have any established frontiers, so we immediately had to fight to establish and protect them. We had to fight in the east against the Russian Bolsheviks, in the southwest against the Ukrainians, and in the west against the Germans in Silesia.

But how, you may ask, could we fight, since we didn't have an army? First of all, our fathers had managed to organize a kind of underground military organization during the First World War. That was the nucleus of our army. Then, thousands of soldiers returned to their homeland from the Austrian, Russian, and German armies, and they immediately joined. As a result we had a well-trained and experienced fighting army which was organized overnight.

There was an unbelievable outburst of patriotic feeling. People were ready to do anything for their country, even sacrifice their lives. Ironically, some foreigners expressed the opinion that "The Poles know how to die for their Fatherland, but they don't know how to live for it." I ran away from high school without my mother's knowledge, volunteered into the army, and in two weeks I was already fighting the Ukrainians. We were defending a city which was in Polish territory, but in a district where the Polish and Ukrainian populations were mixed. The Ukrainians claimed that the city belonged to them. We were of a different opinion. As a result, fighting started. We were victorious, but it didn't give us any special pleasure because it was a fratricidal kind of war—Ukrainians and Poles are both of Slavic descent and our languages are similar. We were simply guided by the principle that we had to defend all Polish territory.

During this time the authorities appealed to the population to give what they could to help support our new independence. The people gave to the treasury everything they could—gold, watches, heirlooms, diamonds—and on this basis along with American financial aid our system was established.

Reconstruction in all fields followed. Everywhere schools, roads, and public facilities were being built. This period of reconstruction was a time of great national vitality. After having been divided into three parts and ruled by foreign countries for all those years, it was natural for Poles to experience an upsurge of national feeling on regaining independence. The people were overjoyed and this helped them to endure some of the shortages and difficulties that were inevitable under the circumstances.

By profession I am a lawyer, and I know best what was done in my field. We had been governed by three different sets of laws: Austrian, German, and Russian. After independence the best brains in our legal profession started working on the development of our own Polish Law. They accumulated modern legal knowledge and added this into the old systems. The result was that they brought about a very good and modern code of law. I was a legal advisor to some insurance companies in Warsaw and almost daily I had some case before the Warsaw courts. That's why I know that the new Polish legal system worked so well.

After gaining independence in 1918, we started out with a democratic system of government, but it didn't endure. The people at the top were true patriots, mostly people who had served during the First World War in the Polish Legions. As patriots and as good Poles they were impeccable. However, at the same time, they became impatient with our new democracy; they couldn't tolerate all the squabbles in Parliament and changes of government. So, in 1926, they executed an armed coup d'etat and from then on a semidictatorial regime began to rule in Poland. You might call it a paternal dictatorship. It was not so bad, but many of us were dissatisfied with this situation and tried to change the system into a true democracy.

I was a politically active member of the Polish Peasant Party. We opposed the regime and carried out our opposition by organizing peasants into the ranks of the party. Gradually I advanced up the rank and file, and before the outbreak of World War II I was chairman of the Polish Peasant Party in the Bialystock District, approximately 150 miles from Warsaw. We campaigned and voted against the government at the elections right up to the outbreak of the war.

Once we organized something which was unusual, I think. We created a precedent, namely a peasant strike. We instructed peasants, members of our party as well as the broad masses of Polish peasantry, not to bring any food into the cities for a period of one week. They stopped delivering food. It was something very impressive. We didn't want to create any hunger situation in our towns—that was not our intention—but rather to demonstrate our strength to the government. As far as that goes, the strike was a success, but it didn't change the situation.

In 1938–39 we gradually came to the conclusion that war with Hitler was inevitable. So we slackened our opposition activity a little because, faced with the prospect of war with Germany, we didn't want to do anything against the government that would hinder our preparations to resist and fight. But up to the outbreak of the war there were two camps in Poland. One was a very broad spectrum of democratic parties, with the National Democratic Party on the right. The other, to the left, was the Polish Socialist Party. Finally, the true Polish Peasant Party was in the middle. We were all united in our opposition against the semitotalitarian government.

I was a reserve officer and when the government declared mobilization I went immediately, without saying a word. All the opposition parties decided to support the government. We didn't make an official statement but it was clear that everybody, in the event of war with Hitler, would have to unite and follow the government. On this point we were unanimous. It was very interesting that all political parties were in full agreement that we would have to resist Hitler and his demands.

Well, the war was terrible. Terrible. The Germans attacked us from three sides—from the south, west and north. You have to remember the map of Europe at that time. In the north, they attacked from East Prussia to cut the so-called Polish Corridor that linked us with the port city of Gdansk (Danzig, in German) and the Baltic. They attacked us from Germany in the west. They attacked us from Slovakia in the south. Militarily speaking we were in a hopeless situation, but we fought. We fought! And the best testimony to our behavior at the time was given by Hitler himself. After the Polish Campaign he delivered a speech to the Reichstag in which he said that "The Polish soldiers as well as the younger officer corps were excellent; brave and courageous. They fought gallantly. But the top command was not worth anything. The whole organization," he said with such contempt, "was typically Polish."

But there was something in what he said. Our air force, which was small and had many obsolete planes, was destroyed very quickly. From then on we didn't have any defense against the German bombers. In two days everything was settled. Finally the supreme command lost contact with the field commanders. In other words, you could observe a typical Polish symptom: individual units fighting gallantly without any contact with the high command up to the very end.

One example of what happened was a unit that had been

ordered to retreat but found themselves encircled. They broke through, but two days later the Germans counterattacked. The resulting battle was an absolute inferno. The Polish troops were exhausted and half of them had been killed or wounded. About 4:00 A.M. on the last day of the battle the remaining Poles assaulted the enemy positions. The Germans resisted at first, then gave in. Suddenly enemy tanks appeared on the right flank and opened fire at about 100 yards. Our antitank rifles and two antitank guns opened up. Fourteen German tanks were knocked out. More German forces approached, this time from the rear. The handful of soldiers still able to fight made one more desperate attempt to break through. It wasn't successful. The men did not surrender, but destroyed their guns and attempted to escape in order to fight as guerillas.

We were completely overwhelmed by the million-and-a-half men they sent against us with **Panzer** tanks, motorized infantry, Stukas and the rest. Most of **our planes** were destroyed on the ground before they could take off. In the so-called Corridor we counterattacked against their tanks with cavalry. You can imagine the result.

Within a week most of our army was either smashed or caught in a pincer movement around Warsaw. The bombing and shelling of Warsaw was terrible. A cloud of smoke and dust hung over the city, there were thousands of burned out buildings, there was no electricity and no running water. Warsaw held out under siege for nearly a month and finally capitulated on September 29. But on the 17th, the Soviet Russians had already invaded us from the east. The German advance had been so fast that the Russians had to jump in before there was nothing left of Poland for them to take.

Finally, the separated army units capitulated one by one and Marshal Rydz-Smigly, who was commander in chief and head of the government, escaped to Rumania where he was interned— that is, deprived of his freedom of movement—with what was left of his government. Of course, that regime had fallen when we lost the war, and in no way governed Poland.

One professional Polish Army officer by the name of Dobrineski decided not to capitulate. He continued fighting and mobilized around himself people who simply couldn't admit that they must capitulate. His was a group of people ready to take every risk, but first of all prepared to die. And they continued fighting. But finally, in winter, they were surrounded by German troops and Dobrineski was killed. Later he waś buried by the German Army in a Polish Army uniform with full honors. In the meantime his people, those who were not killed in the battle, spread all over Poland and started an underground movement. Fighting on Polish territory never stopped. Dobrineski had picked it up and then the remainder of his people joined. Other guerilla units were organized as well. The woods were full of underground guerilla units and eventually many of these were commanded by people trained in England and parachuted in to lead them. It was an uninterrupted struggle.

What type of reprisals were taken by the Germans against villages that delivered food to these underground units? They were burned to the ground, all the people burned alive. In one case approximately five hundred people lost their lives in this way. As a rule, the Germans surrounded a village and started shooting and burning and would not allow anybody to escape. So children, women, the old people, everyone in the village would be killed. Even so, underground organizations were being born everywhere—in villages, towns, cities. It was an absolutely spontaneous movement.

When Warsaw capitulated, most of the army was marched off to prisoner-of-war camps, but some of the officers stayed behind to organize the first central underground organization. One of these officers spoke fluent German, and so, using a car with an "official" flag on it and pretending to be from the administration in Warsaw—please remember that Germans respect flags and uniforms—he undertook a trip all over Poland. And wherever he went he coordinated the local underground and subordinated it to the central organization in Warsaw. And so our underground army was born.

This professional soldier was a very intelligent man, which is not always the rule among career military people. He came to the conclusion that the underground had to be organized in a way that had nothing in common with the prewar government that had lost the war. The Rydz-Smigly government had become very unpopular with the Polish people almost overnight. Not because the war was lost, but because it was lost in six weeks. We had hoped to resist six months, not six weeks. We would have done better if the government had been properly prepared. The military disaster that had overtaken us was the responsibility of, and reflected the bankruptcy of, the prewar regime. So it was decided that the activities of the underground would be directed by the formal opposition parties that had opposed the prewar government and had proved their loyalty to democratic ideals. So all these opposition parties—the National Democratic Party, the Polish Peasant Party, and the Polish Socialist Party—agreed to form a supreme council of the underground movement. It was a combined organization encompassing both military and political responsibility.

I had been captured by the Russians in the fighting after they invaded us, but I managed to escape from a train which was transporting prisoners of war to Russia, and I came immediately to Warsaw. When I got back the first thing I did was to go to the top leader of the Polish Peasant Party, Matthew Rataj, who was also the former speaker of Parliament. I respected him tremendously and he liked me very much. I came to him. We embraced and he almost wept when he saw me; his son-in-law had disappeared without any trace and he was very saddened at that time. I told him that I intended to go abroad and join the Free Polish Forces being organized by General Sikorski in France.

At that time thousands of young Poles were crossing the Hungarian frontier and proceeding on to France. The Hungarians were allies of Hitler, but they are our traditional friends—we exchanged kings quite often and never fought each other—so when the Hungarian generals saw young men crossing the frontier, they turned their backs, and when our people got to Budapest they were helped to get to France.

I said, "Mr. Speaker, I'm young enough to fight. Besides, I am an infantry officer, they need me, and so I want to go to France."

"No, Stefan," he said "You must stay here." I asked why and he said, "The underground has just been born. And you will be my deputy on the Supreme Council."

I said, "Well, I'm not qualified to be your deputy."

He replied, "Listen, let's forget about party hierarchy. I know you well. You're a fighting man and now we have to have fighting men, not politicians."

We had many talks about the structure of the organization and agreed about the people who should be invited to join. In selecting these people, Rataj completely disregarded their importance in the party hierarchy; the only criteria he applied had to do with their suitability for underground activities. Rataj insisted that the underground movement be free of all factional bickerings.

In the early days of the occupation most of us remained in our prewar homes and believed that if we were quiet and appeared to behave normally the Germans would respond in kind. We were, in the beginning, quite careless and naive in our conspiratorial efforts, though I remember being somewhat concerned that the dozens of people coming and going from the Rataj apartment would put him and his family at some risk. We did hear vague rumors about mass murders and persecution of the Jews, but in the early months of the occupation no one envisioned such horrors as collective responsibility, imprisonment without charges, or genocide.

Then on November 9, 1939, I was taken hostage by the Gestapo along with a number of other men. At first I thought it had to do with the underground, but I soon learned that we were to be held responsible for public order in Warsaw on our Independence Day, November 11. We were told that, should any riots occur, we would be shot. However, the city remained calm and they released us.

A few days later I was shocked to learn that Rataj had been arrested. The Gestapo took him in the early morning without even giving him time to put on an overcoat. Rataj had given my name to the underground leaders as the one who should assume his functions and carry on the work as his deputy. That is how I suddenly found myself as a young man in the highest echelon of the underground movement.

We managed to establish contact with our Free Polish Government which, before the defeat of France, was headquartered in Paris, and later moved to London. Our underground political organization became the social basis for a purely military organization which was subordinate to the Government. The young people active in the political parties would gradually enter the ranks of the underground army. Our first job was to unify all the separate underground organizations in the provinces and have them make contact with the local military centers.

In the last months of 1939 and early 1940, Gestapo activity increased and a number of people were arrested who had been politically active before the war. As a result, we became increasingly careful about our conspiratorial activities and started using pseudonyms which we changed frequently. We also began living in hideouts, frequently changing their location, and avoided going to the residences where we were officially registered.

As the months and years went by, the habit of hurrying along the streets and discreetly glancing around to make sure I was not being shadowed became so deeply imbedded in my being that it was simply a mechanical function. Constant practice sharpened my senses and my instincts to such an extent that they automatically registered everything that was happening around me. I was able to recognize a stranger in the street if I happened to run into him twice in one day. If someone followed me for any distance, I had a sort of "radar" that would sense it. In such cases I would stop in front of a shop window, or turn into a side street, or jump onto a moving train, or enter a building with exits on two streets. It became standard procedure, when going to an underground meeting, to board a train going the opposite direction to my destination, and to change to a train going the right way only when I was completely satisfied that no one was following me.

At dawn on February 20, 1940—I was still living where we were legally registered—I was awakened by a banging on the door and the sound of German voices. The Gestapo asked for me by name and in a few minutes I found myself sharing a truck with a number of frightened men. In all, more than a hundred of us were taken to Pawiak Prison. We were a mixed assortment of office clerks, shopkeepers, lawyers, doctors, and merchants who all happened to live in the same part of Warsaw. As it turned out, the German Governor of Czechoslovakia had come to Warsaw for a visit and the Gestapo happened to round up people from my neighborhood to be held as hostages until his departure. It was an annoying and hopeless feeling to be held hostage, but after about two weeks we were released. I returned home dirty and unshaven and immediately moved to an apartment where I lived, unregistered and under a false name, for quite some time.

One morning, in September, 1940, the milkwoman told us that the entire neighborhood had been surrounded by the Germans. My wife had been working all night on some documents for the underground and we had to decide instantly whether to destroy them or to hide them. Since it was possible that the German action had nothing to do with us, we hid everything. In a few minutes two men entered, and without asking my name took me with them. The entire neighborhood was bustling with activity as heavy trucks arrived empty and quickly drove off loaded with men. Packed like sardines, we were driven to an assembly area where more than a thousand men were standing, not knowing what to expect. We were taken into a huge hall where officials took down personal details about each of us. Then we were made to lie down on the floor. There was strict discipline and no one was allowed to stand up. SS men marched up and down with whips in their hands which they used frequently. At the sides of the hall other SS men had machine guns trained on us.

We lay there for two days, trying to guess what was going on. There were about 1500 of us and the majority thought that we were to be deported to Germany as forced labor. We were given some bread but nothing to drink. On the evening of the second day a group of SS officers entered and called out the names of men who were ordered to stand to one side. My name was called and I walked out of the crowd. About 300 of us were let go "because of the intervention of our employers." Before we were released we were told, "It is necessary to know how to keep silent about certain matters if one does not wish to go to a place from which there is no return. You must hold your tongues. Now you can go." All those who remained, more than a thousand, were deported that same night to Auschwitz. Most of them never returned.

By the middle of 1940, roundups and arrests had become routine, if such things can ever become routine. Reports were passing through the country about the camps and about torture in the prisons and about mass execution in the woods. Motorized squads were driving around Warsaw carrying out searches and arrests almost at random. Before the curfew, masses of people changed locations for the night. After curfew the footsteps of the patrols could be heard in the streets. Everyone felt safer spending the night away from the address where they were registered. But since no one knew where or why the searches would be made, fear and anxiety made sleep impossible. By the end of the year, terror and hunger dominated the city.

But by now the underground began to strike back and carry out the first acts of retaliation. My own activities underwent a change at about this time. In April, 1941, I became a representative at the high command of the military branch of the underground. It was also in April that I undertook to establish secret radio contact with our government in London, the lack of which was an acute problem in the underground movement.

I made contact with a young shortwave amateur who agreed to build a transmitter and receiver for us. He was only seventeen, but in technical matters he was my teacher. I was amazed to learn later that he had only two years of elementary school education and had gained his immense knowledge of radio entirely by his own efforts. Through an underground courier I established a wavelength, call signs, and transmission times with London. But our first efforts were unsuccessful and it took us several months to develop a transmitter with sufficient power to get our signal through.

The problems of building radio equipment and operating a clandestine station in an occupied country were enormous. It was difficult to obtain necessary tubes, valves, and other parts and to find safe places to hide the equipment and do the work. We frequently had to move the transmitters, transformers, and tools from hideout to hideout. The Germans had listening posts which monitored every 5–10 meter band for twenty-four hours a day. If they heard a station that was unknown to them, they would use mobile radio interceptors with directional aerials and other measuring instruments to locate the source of the transmission precisely. Of course, if the Germans found a station, it meant immediate liquidation. The only protection was to change the call signs, wave lengths, and the hours and location of operation frequently. We also used lookouts and runners who were able to notify a located station in time for the operators to close down, hide the equipment, and escape.

On August 2, 1941, we finally established successful radio contact with London. For the next four years we transmitted and received messages on an almost daily basis. We established a secret workshop where we continued to build transmitters in order to have some in reserve. We were given our own codes so that we could transmit without using the international code which the German listening posts could understand. During the occupation we recruited a number of dedicated telegraphers and at times had as many as three stations in operation, each with their own hideouts and codes, and each unaware that the other stations existed. We did this so that if the Germans broke one station, they would not endanger the others.

My wife and I spent much of our time drafting and deciphering messages and getting them to and from the appropriate people. We also functioned as lookouts. As there were endless searches and close calls, we often found ourselves moving equipment from one hideout to another. As the occupation wore on, our radio activities became an ever more deadly game of hide-and-seek. The Germans developed more and more sophisticated methods of tracking us down, and we became better at hiding and covering our tracks.

One of the women who worked with us got a job as a ticket seller in a theatre box office. She had to sit there all day long, so I set the box office up as a clearing station for messages. This worked out well because there was a great deal of coming and going all day long and no one took any notice of the people who stopped there. So under the bright lights of the theatre marquee our agents delivered or collected messages under the guise of buying theatre tickets.

Things did not always work out this well. There were some slipups. The Germans would sometimes find our hideouts and get our transmitters. Sometimes they caught our telegraphers and couriers. Whenever this happened we had to warn all the captured persons' contacts and freeze all the hideouts they knew about. If the captured person knew where you were living, it meant that you had to move. We could never be sure that our people would be able to resist the Gestapo's methods of getting information.

One of our couriers was taking a transmitter from one location to another when she disappeared. It was obvious that she had been caught with the transmitter, clear proof that she was engaged in radio work. I knew her to be a tough girl who would rather be tortured to death than turn us in. But we could not take a chance, so we evacuated the workshop and transmission hideouts which she knew about.

Several weeks later I received a scribbled note that had been smuggled out of Pawiak Prison. It said that she had been searched when getting off a tram. She claimed that she didn't know the contents of the parcel she was carrying, and was to turn it over to a man she didn't know who would exchange passwords with her. She wrote that she had told the Gestapo nothing and would tell them nothing even though they were beating her. She closed by telling us not to fear, but to go on working in the old hideouts and not to worry about her. I remember crying as I read the note. We trusted her so completely that we returned to the locations we had evacuated. Some weeks later we learned that she had been transferred to the concentration camp at Majdanek. The Gestapo never did get her to talk.

While all these things were going on we managed to build a powerful voice transmitter in order to broadcast an underground message from inside Poland to the Free Polish Forces and other audiences in the free world. The first time we tried it the Germans jammed our transmission from nearby and we had to close up and run. On another try the atmospheric conditions were bad. After several attempts we finally succeeded. But the voice transmitter was about ten times more powerful than the ones we used to send telegraphic messages. This made it much easier for the Germans to locate the source of the transmission. Also, the transformers needed for the extra power were very heavy and difficult for us to move from place to place. For these reasons we decided to give up voice broadcasting as too risky.

However, not long after our abortive effort at voice transmission, we got word that a secret underground radio station was broadcasting daily in the Polish language at 8:00 A.M. and 7:00 P.M. We were astounded and could not figure out how or where an anti-German station could be transmitting from inside occupied Poland. I sent a message to London praising the technical quality of the station and asking if they knew anything about it.

The mystery was solved by a "Top Secret" message from London. The station was located in an Allied country but was seeking to create the impression that it was broadcasting from occupied Poland. This would lead the Free World to place greater trust in the reports it broadcast and it would confuse and harass the Germans. The message stressed that we were the *only* people inside occupied Poland who had been entrusted with the secret of the underground station, and this only because the plan would fall through unless our own shortwave transmitters were able to provide the most up-to-the-minute information on the situation in Poland. Only by having detailed knowledge of daily events inside Poland would people believe it was an underground station.

We began to send messages during the day about events that would be broadcast in the evening with expanded commentary. The Germans published a Polish language paper that came on the streets in the early afternoon. It was filled with German propaganda, but there was always some item of interest, especially since one of the objectives of the broadcasts was to discredit this propaganda. The problem was that getting the paper in the early afternoon was too late for same-day comment, because we needed several hours to encode our transmissions and time was needed in London to decode them. Through an underground contact we were able to get galley proofs every day five hours before the paper went on sale. We would scan the galleys, select our material, code the message, and add a single word of instruction: "Ridicule."

We would also find out in advance what the underground papers were printing in their next issue, and when the issue would be out. Thus we were able to select important stories and tell London on what day to use them. On the appropriate day the broadcaster would say, "According to today's underground newspaper . . ." By listening to the BBC we learned that news items broadcast by our "underground" station were being picked up by the radio and press of the entire Free World.

But even more important than the value of these broadcasts to the outside world was their value inside Poland. Early in the occupation the Germans confiscated all radio receivers. They ordered all Poles to bring their receivers to designated places and turn them in. They announced that whoever didn't obey this order would be shot—that was always their most popular form of punishment. But a great many people, guided by instinct, I think, decided not to give up their radio apparatuses, but instead to keep them in hiding. And so a great cross-section of people—common people, peasants, workers, intellectuals—displayed an unbelievable inventiveness as to how best to hide these radios and how to listen to foreign broadcasts. Eventually many people were executed because the Germans did manage to find some of these radios. But that didn't seem to matter. Thousands of people inside Poland willingly endangered their lives in order to listen to these broadcasts.

At the same time as our various radio activities were going on, I was, as a member of the Home Army General Staff, given responsibility for matters of civil resistance. This meant active and passive resistance by the whole Polish nation to the Germans in all aspects of our national life, in all parts of the country, and by every available means. We issued instructions for all segments of the population—farmers, factory workers, civil servants, doctors and lawyers, women, and young people. The basic rules were to offer resistance in every possible way, to remain intransigent, to undermine and sabotage all decrees and laws likely to harm the Polish nation, to have nothing to do with the Germans, and to obey the underground authorities.

For example, doctors were instructed to issue false health certificates if it would help a Pole to avoid doing forced labor for the Germans. Judges were told not to refer cases from Polish to German courts. Citizens were advised to boycott cinemas, and lotteries, and newspapers run by the occupation authorities. The Polish Blue Police were warned not to participate in the roundup of citizens for deportation to Germany as forced labor. Methods were established for sabotaging compulsory deliveries of grain, meat, and other products to Germany. These instructions were distributed through the underground press and through all the underground organizations and eventually by means of our "underground" broadcasts. The great majority of Polish citizens observed them to the letter.

We also established underground courts of justice which were empowered to pass sentence on traitors, spies, and *agents provocateurs*. There were three possible verdicts: not guilty, remission of the case to the proper court after the war, and the death penalty. As proof of the care with which sentences were passed, 90 percent of the cases—all those in which there was even the slightest question—were postponed until after the war. The remaining 10 percent involved about 200 executions in the whole country during the course of the war. Sentences were carried out by teams of men, who, if circumstances permitted, first read the sentence to the condemned. This always began: "In the name of the Polish Republic . . ." Typical of those executed were Blue Police officers who cooperated too willingly with German courts in sentencing Poles to death, Polish officials who were too zealous in pursuing their countrymen for deportation to Germany as forced labor, Gestapo agents, and informers.

There were, of course, hearing procedures for lesser offenses which local leaders of the civil resistance were authorized to carry out. When censure did not act as a deterrent, haircutting was applied to women who consorted with Germans and, in the villages, men who attended German festivals or who misappropriated Polish property were sometimes flogged. Such cases were extremely rare, as were the punishments.

As time went on, the Directorate of Civil Resistance took on a definite form. We established departments to deal with justice and with radio information as I've already described, and we also had departments of sabotage and diversion, armaments, registration of German crimes, and a few other specialized functions. The people who made up the Directorate became a very close-knit group. We met regularly in a variety of places. One was a commercial laundry where we carried on our work amidst the humidity and steam. On other occasions we met in the peaceful calm of an ancient monastery. We were constantly on our guard because the underground's intelligence department reported that the Gestapo was relentlessly pursuing the Directorate. Of course, the Germans read every word in the underground press and since this made clear to them what our areas of responsibility were, they considered us a particularly dangerous enemy.

I knew the Gestapo was searching for me. I had intentionally not checked out of my prewar apartment, and the Germans, being deliberate and unimaginative, would initiate every new search with a visit to the address where I was officially registered. Every time they came, the janitor would send me word through a chain of contacts. Whenever it seemed that they were closing in, my wife and I would vacate the apartment we were staying in and move in with friends or find a new hideout. We had many close calls and when you consider how many friends and co-workers were caught, it is miraculous that we managed to avoid capture.

The Germans used Poland as a source of agricultural and other products to be shipped to Germany. As the occupation wore on we became increasingly effective at sabotaging the delivery of these resources. We used the slogan, "As little, as late, and as bad as possible." It was impractical to impose a total boycott on the delivery of meat, grain, and other farm products, because such a policy would have brought terrible reprisals and the villagers would have had to pay with their lives.

Instead, a great many novel methods of sabotage were devised: railway warehouses and freight cars were soaked with petrol, trains were held up and livestock let loose or grain spilled, officials were bribed to issue receipts for delivery of the same grain a number of times, receipts were forged, and cattle were concealed. But the most ingenious method of sabotaging delivery quotas was the burning of all the quota documents. The documents that served as the basis for fixing delivery quotas were kept in village offices. At the Directorate of Civil Resistance we realized that destruction of these documents would result in total confusion and disorganization, and that it would take the Germans months to reconstruct the quotas. We established a detailed plan for the burning of these records in simultaneous attacks throughout the country, so that we would have the element of surprise and the Germans would have no time to post guards at the village offices. This plan was largely successful. We also burned down lumber mills in order to prevent the destruction of our forests.

I believe that the successful sabotage of delivery quotas, though less spectacular than armed combat with the enemy, was a major Polish contribution to the war against Germany. Though the importance of this effort has never been fully recognized, I believe its value was equivalent to several divisions fighting at the front.

In times of war, conditions in the villages tend to be better than in the cities because it is particularly difficult for city dwellers to supplement their food supplies. The occupation authorities fixed our rations so that they were not enough to live on, but just enough to prevent us from dying. We calculated that in March, 1942, the nutritional value of rationed foods in Warsaw was only about 550 calories per day. By the following month it had been reduced to less than 500 calories. By October, 1943, the monthly ration for children under 14 was only 11 pounds of bread and 14 ounces of all other rationed foods. The difference between our normal requirements and the amount provided by the rations was filled by smugglers who brought enormous amounts of food from the country into the city by the most ingenious means. We encouraged this traffic and it kept us alive. Its scope can be understood by the fact that the Germans themselves estimated more than 2,000 illegal bakeries operating in the vicinity of Warsaw.

Peasant women and street vendors smuggled food into the city in carts and railway carriages. They had food sewn into their skirts and blouses. Never have I seen such oversized busts as in Poland at this time. Dead pigs were even transported in railway compartments dressed up as old women, with shawls covering their snouts. It got to the point where even the Germans recognized that their economic plan for Poland was altogether make-believe. Whatever their official balance sheet may have shown, the unofficial black market turnover was several times higher. Official prices and wages were all a fiction, and legal commercial transactions only served as a cover for enormous unofficial commerce. In addition to the political underground, the Germans had to contend with an economic underground that inflicted irreparable damage on their war economy.

While the amount of food available to us was very limited during the occupation, the consumption of alcohol went way up. The people drank to forget their worries and overcome their feelings of hopelessness and fear. Members of the underground movement, who lived with constant danger and tension and needed relaxation from time to time, were particularly susceptible to the relief supplied by liquor. Throughout Poland there were thousands of illegal stills filling the tremendous local demand both in the villages and the cities. As the occupation continued, the spread of alcoholism became such a problem that we in the underground decided to deal with it. We issued instructions restricting liquor consumption by members of the underground because a number of security breaches and slipups had occurred as a result of people talking when drunk. When it became obvious that our appeals and instructions were not solving the problem, we used underground units of the Home Army to destroy the illegal distilleries. The results of this action were remarkable; about 2,000 illegal stills were liquidated.

One of the main concerns of the Civil Resistance branch of the underground was to find ways to prevent the deportation of Poles to work in Germany. Our underground radio station and the BBC broadcast instructions on how to boycott labor callups, and efforts to avoid conscription into compulsory labor units took on the character of a mass movement. One day the occupation authorities put up a huge billboard showing workers preparing to go to Germany with the message, "Come with us to Germany." The very first night the sign was up someone climbed to the top of it and altered the message to read, "Don't come with us to Germany."

We sabotaged the compulsory labor program in the same way as we had dealt with the agricultural quotas: that is, by burning down the labor exchanges and destroying the card index files used by the Germans for compulsory recruitment. We weren't as successful with the labor exchanges as we had been with the village offices, but we did manage to put about twenty of them out of action, although not the big one in Warsaw. Even so, people went into hiding, carried false papers, joined guerilla bands in the forests, and resorted to all manner of subterfuge, or simply failed to respond to summonses in order to avoid being called up.

However, we could not prevent people from working in factories taken over by the Germans. Since we could not boycott these plants, we introduced all sorts of petty sabotage instead. We saw to it that output was reduced by working slowly and by damaging machinery through such negligence as inadequate lubrication and waste of raw materials. We saw to it that general confusion and disorganization were introduced wherever and whenever possible.

During all this time I lived a double life, working with a strange assortment of people and situations. On the one hand I moved among the top leaders of the underground in my role as head of Civil Resistance, while on the other hand I daily descended to conspiratorial depths in order to personally direct radio liaison, to meet telegraphists, lookouts, couriers, and the owners of the hideouts we used. The civil resistance work gave me greater satisfaction, but the radio work was far more exciting. The people in radio work ranged from street urchins to aristocratic young women to all sorts of ordinary citizens. In time this diverse group became like one big family—working, quarreling, living, and frequently giving their lives together.

The atmosphere at the radio stations was always exciting. I was not a technician and the magic of being able to communicate, through a small box and a piece of wire, with a city a thousand miles away always held me spellbound. I spent a great deal of time at the stations not only because I liked being there, but because the operators didn't like to be alone in the room and my presence cheered them up. The transmission of messages was a long and tedious job and the telegraphists often had to repeat all or part of a message two or three times. Meanwhile, they could hear the mobile interceptors trying to pinpoint our location through the crackling in their earphones. The work was very hard and required great concentration. We always had to worry whether the transmitters were operating properly, whether atmospheric conditions were tolerable, and whether the lookouts were on the job and would be able to give us the alarm in time. In addition, I had to be careful that the stations didn't operate for too many hours at a time.

But radio work gave us a unique opportunity to know what was going on. We were transmitting and receiving messages for all units of the underground all over the country except for the military—they had their own radio links with London. There were couriers traveling back and forth to our government-in-exile, but our radio transmissions were the fastest means of contact, so we handled all priority messages. We also sent out to the world the first word about some of the Nazis' most terrible crimes. When the Germans forced about half a million Warsaw Jews into a walled ghetto and sealed them off, we radioed the news to London. In July, 1942, when they began to liquidate the ghetto by loading about seven thousand people every day into freight cars and sending them off to Majdanek and other extermination camps, we were again the first to send this news to London.

We began to bombard London with daily messages about what was going on in the ghetto and to my astonishment the BBC ignored the dispatches completely and made no use of them. It was not until a month later that the news was broadcast to the world. I later learned that neither our government-in-exile nor the British believed our reports—they thought we were exaggerating for the sake of propaganda! Only after the information was confirmed by other sources was it made public. While the liquidation of the Jews was proceeding, we inundated London with telegrams giving the facts. We reported that Jews from the Balkans, Hungary, Holland and other countries were also being transported to Poland and told of what was happening to them. We requested that Jews in these countries be warned to avoid deportation because it meant certain death. These warnings were, in fact, broadcast by the BBC.

On April 19, 1943, an uprising broke out in the ghetto and the whole of Warsaw was electrified, stunned, and helpless as news spread that the Polish and Jewish flags had been raised over the ghetto walls. One of our transmitters was operating in a house whose roof gave us a view of the fire and smoke and artillery firing inside the ghetto. It was a frightful scene, a blazing inferno, in which a thousand or so starving and poorly equipped Jewish combatants fought offensively at first, then defensively, and finally as guerilla bands against many thousands of well-conditioned and well-equipped German troops. To everyone's astonishment, the ghetto rising went on for nearly a month. During this time we continued to send daily reports to London which were broadcast all over the world. There was little else we could do. The Jews were cut off inside the ghetto and we did not have the resources to come to their aid.

One day in May, 1943, the young man who built our radio equipment was killed. An SS man had seen him running and, thinking something suspicious was going on, called out for him to halt. Instead of stopping, our man pulled out two pistols and fired, and in the shoot-out that followed he was killed. As soon as we got word of this disaster we hurriedly made plans to evacuate all of the radios, tools, and spare parts in our radio workshop. But by the time we got near the place the Gestapo and civilian agents were already loading all of our equipment onto a truck. In a matter of a few hours we had lost the young radio technician who built and repaired our equipment with an infallible instinct, and had also lost all the transmitters being repaired, all our equipment, three hundred spare tubes and other parts, a recording machine and all our instruments.

It was a terrible blow. We had lost everything except the transmitters we were using, which were kept in the hideouts from which they were operated, and a small amount of equipment hidden elsewhere. We were quickly able to recruit another technician and managed to maintain uninterrupted contact with London. The new technician was a gentleman well past his 60's, a well-educated engineer to whom my wife and I became quite close. He treated us in an almost fatherly way and used to tell us, "Be very cautious, you must live until Poland is free again." Through this man we were able to recruit new telegraphists and to establish a new workshop.

Meanwhile in July, 1943, the Directorate of Underground Struggle (DUS) was formed and I was appointed as its only civilian member. This body was responsible for the most important military decisions of the underground. Its work led to the derailment of troop and munitions trains, the blowing up of railway bridges, and similar military actions. The DUS constantly concerned itself with adapting underground tactics to changes in the international situation and circumstances at home. It often had to make decisions with far-reaching implications.

From the very outset of the occupation the Germans inflicted bestialities on the Polish people, and by way of reprisal, the underground inflicted losses on the Germans. In an effort to intimidate the underground the Germans increased their terror tactics, to which we replied with more reprisals. In time a vicious circle of reprisal and counter-reprisal was created that cost the lives of thousands of people. We were constantly preoccupied with this problem and kept asking ourselves if the reprisal policy made any sense. When we suspended our reprisal activities for a time in the hope that the Germans would respond with more humane policies, the results were entirely negative. They systematically pursued their destruction of Poland and we had no alternative but to return to the policy of "an eye for an eye."

It must be remembered that when the underground leadership considered the aims and organization of the country at the very beginning of the occupation, it was unanimously decided to declare a life-and-death struggle against the Germans. No one suggested waiting passively for the end of the war, or adopting a policy of caution, or of coming to terms with the Germans. In retrospect, I'm not altogether sure we were right. Perhaps we should at least have considered the various alternatives. But at the time we were all of the opinion that the struggle against Hitler had to be pursued underground without letup. We started with this policy and we followed it faithfully throughout the long years of occupation. And the years were long indeed.

Then in July, 1944, rumors began going around Warsaw that the Russians had launched a major offensive, that the Germans were retreating westward, and that the front would soon reach Warsaw. One sunny July afternoon, while my wife and I were out for a walk, we saw a sight we had dreamed about during all the years of the occupation. Crossing the Poniatowski Bridge over the Vistula was an endless column of weary German soldiers slogging along on foot, on bicycles, and on carts in disorderly retreat. They were dirty and in rags; some without weapons, some without boots. Among them were many wounded. It was an unforgettable scene and we had difficulty containing our joy.

There was no longer any doubt that the front was approaching Warsaw. For some time we had been observing symptoms of disintegration and fear among the German occupation troops. They were going back to Germany with the furniture, pianos, pictures, jewelry, and other things they had stolen. Those who could not run away were selling anything they could.

In the underground there was great excitement. I took part in several meetings of military and civilian leaders. The hour of decision was fast approaching and the discussions showed clearly that a rising was inevitable. In Polish cities to the east of us the underground had gone into action behind the collapsing German front as an aid to the advancing Red Army. An armed rising in Warsaw at the crucial moment was considered indispensable. By then the Home Army in Warsaw numbered forty thousand officers and men and it was unthinkable that after the years of occupation we should stand by passively and not attack the demoralized and retreating Germans. Further, if we allowed the Russians to capture Warsaw unaided, Stalin would be able to claim that the Polish underground, the Home Army, and the government-in-exile were all a fiction. Finally, the Germans were spreading the report that Hitler had ordered Warsaw to be razed to the ground. In any case, there is no way to prevent a volcano from erupting, and during July, 1944, Warsaw was a volcano ready to erupt. The only question that remained was when the rising should take place.

On July 30 the guns on the front could be faintly heard in the distance and the Russians were reported to be less than twenty miles away. German civilians had left the city and only the troops and Gestapo remained. On the 31st the two German-controlled newspapers were not published and the underground inconspicuously took over institutions that were abandoned by the Germans.

The rising was scheduled for August 1. It started at 5:00 P.M., when the city was busy with people returning from work and the movement of Home Army personnel to their assembly points would be undetected in the general bustle. The trams were crowded—people were occupying even the front platform which was reserved "for Germans only." Women in twos and threes were walking along in obvious haste, carrying heavy bags and bundles of arms to the assembly points. Men and boys on bicycle and foot were hurrying in all directions, exchanging meaningful glances as they went. Occasional German patrols proceeded without seeing anything.

Plans had been carefully laid. Each unit had its specific assembly point and military objective. Enough ammunition and provisions were on hand to sustain the rising for about a week, by which time the Russians would be in the city to help us. Firing started a few minutes before 5:00 P.M. The Germans were taken completely by surprise, and on that first evening about three-quarters of the city was seized by the Home Army. The Germans held the key buildings and intersections that they had heavily fortified for defense against the Russians, who were only about ten miles from Warsaw, just east of the Vistula.

At that point I was greatly upset. My wife and I were with one of the radio units in a loft that was surrounded by tall buildings and unsuitable for radio transmission to London. We didn't know what sections of the city were in the hands of the Home Army and we couldn't move until we did. In addition, I had lost contact with the underground government and the Home Army headquarters. We were cut off from all information and I was anxious about the success or failure of the rising and when the Soviet Army would arrive.

We remained cut off for several days in a house crowded with tenants and passersby who were trying to get to their homes when the rising had started. Everyone shared what little food they had. Debris and gunfire made streets impassable and people began to break openings from one cellar to the next. This was the start of an elaborate maze of underground passageways which, when connected with sewers and other subterranean services, ultimately made it possible to go from one end of the city to the other below ground.

At first the Germans reacted defensively to the rising. They holed up in the telephone exchange and other public buildings. But after a few days we heard German tanks moving and firing in the streets. When I finally got in touch with headquarters, I learned that the Russians had halted their offensive on the first day of the rising—they had stopped their attack and the front had gone absolutely dead. Meanwhile the Germans brought two Panzer divisions and an SS division into the city. What's more, the Russian planes that had been flying over Warsaw daily before the rising were nowhere to be seen, and the Germans began to bomb us heavily and without opposition.

It soon became obvious that the Soviet Union had no intention of coming to our aid. They had no interest in supporting a pro-Western underground army. In the most calculating and vicious way, they were allowing the Germans to destroy the fighting capacity of the Home Army for them. The Western Allies were, we understood from our London government, exerting tremendous pressure on Stalin to resume his offensive and to supply us with food and ammunition. We carried on the fight in the hope that relief would come. When, in a meeting with the head of our underground government, I asked what he thought about Soviet help, I remember that he replied, "They are monstrous felons."

We continued to hold large sections of the city, but the Germans shelled and dropped firebombs on us incessantly and a giant cloud of smoke hung over the city for weeks. Since the city was the front, we had the problem of providing aid to the civilian population as well as to the Home Army. Food was the biggest problem. We had captured some German food stores and the population had some individual food supplies, but we had expected the rising to last no more than a week and we simply did not have adequate provisions for a prolonged struggle. Water was the most difficult and immediate problem because the Germans held the municipal waterworks and cut off the supply. We had to locate old and disused wells and dig new ones in the courtyards of houses. People queued for water and many of them were killed by German bombs while waiting. We had taken a number of German prisoners and they were put to work digging wells and also latrines, which were made necessary by the lack of water.

Electricity continued for several weeks due to the heroic efforts of the power station employees, who not only supplied current, but whose facility was a Home Army strongpoint and under constant fire. Eventually the power station ceased to function and the entire riverfront was captured by the Germans. We moved our transmitters to the Polytechnic Institute which had its own power supply. Light for the hospitals and tunnels was supplied through batteries recharged by gasoline engines.

Sanitation was surprisingly good, considering that the weather was very hot, there was no soap and water, we had open latrines, and thousands of dead were buried in shallow graves or left to decompose in the rubble of bombed houses. In the circumstances we were fortunate not to have the outbreak of any serious epidemics. Firefighting was a problem with no water, and each house organized its own fire watch, with everyone pitching in when necessary, even during raids. Later, when it became obvious to everyone that the rising had been left to its fate, people resigned themselves to the destruction and let the fires burn.

As time went on we were all constantly hungry and food

became a major topic of conversation. We spent a great deal of time searching for food, and put whatever we could into our stomachs. People were eating the city's horses and stray dogs and cats and even their own pets. We kept appealing to London for aid and when the RAF tried to supply us by air from Italy, the Russians refused to let their planes land on nearby airfields. So many British planes were lost trying to make it back to their bases that they had to suspend their efforts. On September 18, American Flying Fortresses came over against heavy antiaircraft fire and dropped hundreds of multicolored parachutes with supplies. Unfortunately, most of them landed on the wrong side of the lines. Because the Russians also refused to let the American planes land and refuel on airfields a few minutes from Warsaw, they had to fly a thousand miles back to their bases. This increased losses so much that missions were limited and Western assistance turned out to be more a token of support than anything substantial.

The situation in the city continued to deteriorate as thousands of people began to live underground in stinking vaults and sewers as a result of the continual bombing. We began to get reports of people dying of starvation. At headquarters we had meetings every few days to review the situation. We were all depressed, haggard, and shabby, but calm and full of determination. We spent much of our time discussing the problems of continuing the rising and of Soviet inactivity. If it wasn't already clear to us that the Russians wanted to destroy not only the Home Army, but the city and its population as well, radio messages from our government in London—which informed us that the Allies' intervention with Stalin to get help for Warsaw had been ineffective—drove the point home once and for all.

For a week or so the Soviet air force flew fighter cover over the city and dropped supplies (without parachutes!), as a cynical response to Western pressure. But after the Russians stopped this charade, the Germans resumed their bombing and shelling. Warsaw was burning and civilian discipline had begun to crack. By the third week in September the situation had become hopeless. By wireless, General Bor, the Commander-in-Chief of the Home Army, informed Marshal Rokossovsky of the Red Army that resistance would end if we received no support within 72 hours.

We received no reply at all and on September 29, General Bor agreed to capitulate to the Germans. On October 2, the agreement was signed and firing ceased. All members of the Home Army were taken into captivity as prisoners of war, and all civilians were forced to abandon the city.

I was offered a chance to go into captivity as a POW, as it was likely that the Germans would be after me. I declined and, with my radio associates, slipped out of the city in order to continue our underground work. But before leaving we performed a short ceremony. Four of us lifted a modest wooden coffin to our shoulders and, accompanied by several mourners who walked with us in a funeral procession, we made for a nearby cemetery. There we lowered the coffin into a prepared grave and carefully covered it with earth. In this way we buried our remaining transmitters and other radio equipment. Some time later, after Soviet troops had finally "liberated" the city, we "exhumed" the transmitters and again made use of them.

We were among the last to leave Warsaw. The city was in a condition difficult to imagine. Except for German sentries, not a living soul was to be seen. The rising, planned for a week, had lasted sixty-three days. Two hundred thousand people had been killed. Desolation and destruction were everywhere; broken tram cables and smashed tram cars, cratered streets, uprooted lampposts, barricades and rubble, and the remains of bombed and burned-out houses. Out of this dead landscape we eventually emerged into a living world in which houses were intact, shops were open, and people were working in the fields. Outside of Warsaw we quickly resumed a relatively normal life. The people were well dressed and the food was plentiful. We soon reestablished contact with the underground, got our hands on a transmitter, and resumed contact with London.

Meanwhile the Germans were looting the city and sending thousands of wagonloads of furniture, pictures, and clothing back into Germany along with museum and library collections, and factory and laboratory equipment. When the looting of any section was completed, the Germans systematically set it afire. In sacking and destroying the city they acted in accordance with carefully prepared plans.

Finally, in January 1945, the Soviet guns opened up again and kept on firing. Their offensive had begun again. Long columns of German foot soldiers and horse-drawn wagons began to stream westward, attacked repeatedly by Soviet fighters. The Germans began retreating rapidly but without panic. When the last of the German vehicles had passed, there was a relative lull. We heard artillery fire in the distance. Then we saw some tanks advancing across a field and the Russians were there. Within a matter of minutes the German occupation ended and the Soviet occupation began.

3

DUNKIRK:
1940

John Fowler

I remember on the march down, from way back inland, all the animals were being driven with us. It was very much like a forest fire, this German Panzer attack. So animals, human beings, and the lot were all being driven toward the sea. I remember seeing dead animals lying around, the same as one saw men. The thing I remember about the horses was that they raced past us, up and down. And quite a number of men were injured, and some were killed, by simply getting a horse's hoof through their skull.

—Sergeant John Fowler

Dunkirk: 1940

Britain and France had a treaty obligation to come to Poland's aid should her western frontiers be attacked. Three days after Hitler invaded Poland on September 3, 1939, these powers did declare war on Germany. But they sent no material aid, and the Poles were quickly overrun.

The day after the British declared war they began sending military units into France to supplement the forces of the French Army. But for six months there was a curious period of inactivity on the western front. Instead of launching an attack on Germany, the Allies waited passively and prepared defensive positions. The Germans refrained from aggressive actions as well. During these six months of quiet, which came to be called the "Phony War," there was even some talk that an armistice might be reached without active hostilities.

It helps to understand what was happening if you remember that some years before, from 1914 to 1918, the French, English, and Germans had been engaged in what Ernest Hemingway called "the most colossal, murderous, mismanaged butchery that has ever taken place on earth." The First World War claimed an astronomical number of casualties—in all, more than thirty million men were reported killed, wounded and missing. Individual battles cost hundreds of thousands, if not millions, of lives.

Both the Allied generals and Hitler had experienced the carnage of this war, in which the front lines were made up of elaborate systems of opposing trenches which were endlessly assaulted by one side or the other. But they learned different lessons from their experiences. The French concluded that they could avoid heavy casualties by building impregnable fortifications and concentrating massive firepower within them. Hitler, on the other hand, believed that mobile firepower, in the form of planes and fast-moving tanks, would enable his forces to punch through—or maneuver around—any static defenses.

The French favored a static, defensive war in which they could "wait out" the enemy. As a consequence they built the Maginot Line, a vast complex of fixed fortifications that stretched from the Swiss border to the Ardennes Forest on the border with Belgium. Hitler believed that time was his enemy; that Germany lacked the resources for a long war and needed a quick and decisive victory. He therefore concentrated German efforts on the development of air power, the *Luftwaffe*, and mechanized *Panzer* divisions.

On March 30, 1940, Winston Churchill reported on the situation in Europe: "All is quiet on the Western Front. So far nothing has happened. But more than a million German soldiers, including all their armored divisions, are drawn up ready to attack at a few hours' notice." Indeed, Hitler's appetite was whetted by the dramatic success of the Blitzkrieg in Poland and he was ready to move against Western Europe. On April 9, German forces invaded Denmark and Norway. Denmark was overrun in one day. Norway, despite stiff resistance, fell in a matter of weeks. The "Phony War," with its waiting and uncertainty, was finally over.

A month later, on May 10, the German army invaded Holland and Belgium. Using parachutists and glider-borne troops in addition to heavy tanks supported by dive-bombers, they occupied most key transport and defense positions and had virtually destroyed the Dutch Air Force and Army by the end of the first day.

In response to the German attack the British Expeditionary Force, which was dug into defensive positions on the Belgian-French border, was ordered to move forward along with French troops to new positions in Belgium. But as soon as they moved they were cut off from the main French armies to the south by a powerful mechanized force. The German offensive under Field Marshal Gerd von Rundstedt was not following the plan that the French High Command had anticipated. Instead of sending their main force down the flat terrain from the north through Holland and Belgium, the Germans brought their armor through the rough and wooded terrain of the Ardennes. Because the French thought the Ardennes would be impassable to mechanized units, this was the weakest part of their line. It was thinly defended by poorly trained troops. Once through the forest, the German Panzer units struck due west toward the English Channel, advancing at a speed which amazed the French, sometimes forty miles a day against opposition. They used dive-bombers to support the advance of the Panzers because their artillery could not keep up.

The French High Command was badly shaken by its failure to stop the German advance. It was disorganized and out of touch with the situation in the field. What many had considered to be the finest army in Europe was now, for all practical purposes, a flock of sheep in the process of being devoured by wolves. DeGaulle wrote later that the French General Staff lacked hope and the will to win: "A sort of moral inhibition made them doubtful of everything and especially of themselves." The Germans continued to widen the wedge, trapping the Allied forces in the north and making it impossible for them to reestablish contact with the main French army in the south.

The situation continued to deteriorate. Many French units became disorganized and ineffective. Hundreds of thousands of refugees clogged the roads. There were wild rumors and uncertainty about where the Germans were. It was only a matter of time before the Allied army—500,000 French, 400,000 Belgians, and 200,000 British trapped against the sea—would have to surrender or face liquidation.

But there was to be another outcome. On May 26 Lord Gort, commander of the British Expeditionary Force, began to move his troops into a perimeter around Dunkirk. The Royal Navy had been making preparations for an evacuation—with the hope of lifting perhaps 50,000, or at most 100,000 men. No one expected the Allied perimeter to hold for more than a few days.

If the German armor had pressed its attack, it would have wiped out or forced the surrender of the entire Allied army. However, in one of the most controversial decisions of the war—and for reasons never made clear—Von Rundstedt ordered his armored units to halt, which they did for three days. This delay, coupled with stiff rearguard resistance and remarkable work by the RAF and Royal Navy, allowed 366,000 men, 224,000 of them British, to be evacuated to England.

On June 4—the last day of Dunkirk—Churchill, now Prime Minister, told the House of Commons: "We must be very careful not to assign to this deliverance the attributes of a victory. Wars are not won by evacuation. . . . Our thankfulness at the escape of our armies . . . must not blind us to the fact that what happened in France and Belgium is a colossal military disaster."

Sergeant John Fowler was one of the men evacuated from the beaches of Dunkirk. His story is representative of hundreds of thousands of other stories, for every person who lived through this moment of history had similar experiences.

After the war he studied law and now is a solicitor in London.

Sergeant John Fowler:

You know, you're bound to wonder if you're going to get away. Time was getting a bit short. We had fought a rearguard action all the way down from Louvain, so we didn't know what the situation was on the beach. We thought we were going to stay through, and either be killed or captured—if we thought at all.

It was a Friday, during the evening, when a company commander's conference was called. We were told that we were leaving the following day. We were, in fact, leaving soon that night and were to march down to the beach.

We formed up as a battalion, in companies, platoons, and so on.

We split up either side of the road—the usual thing—single file. And we marched from Furnes down to La Panne, a little village on the beach. This was very grim. It seemed that it was the only road open to us, and the Germans knew that we would use it as a route, and they plastered it. The shelling was very heavy, but it always seemed to be ahead of us. And I thought—this I can remember very clearly—I though we were walking straight into an inferno. I got very cross, very angry, because I was frightened, I suppose. But the road twisted and turned a great deal, and always seemed to twist away from where we thought the shells were bursting. I wasn't hurt, and, as far as I can remember, I didn't see anyone hurt. But to me it always looked as if we were walking straight into it.

The muzzle of my rifle got caught in a bit of wire that was hanging down. You know what it's like—wherever there's been shelling, telegraph wires are hanging around on the road. I got caught in it, and couldn't get out. And the more I tried to get out, the more I got tangled up. It was, in fact, around my neck when I'd finished, and I was utterly panic-stricken: swearing, cursing everybody because the blokes were just marching by, naturally. It was tramp, tramp, tramp, and I was being left behind. My great fear was to be in one spot for more than two seconds. Because of the law of averages I thought this was going to be the spot that'll get the next shell. A company sergeant-major got me out of that. Very calm and collected, he came up and unwound me. And that's my main recollection of that road.

We arrived on the beach, I would think about two in the morning, and there were officers calling out, "This way, Number 2 Company! This way, the Grenadiers!" and so on—the usual sort of assembly-point noises. Very shortly after that, I heard someone call out that the planes were coming over, we must keep still. The sand was very wet, it was a bright night, and if you moved, your footprints made phosphorescent shimmers which were as good as flares to the pilots. We lay flat on the ground.

The next thing I remember is the horses. How many there were, I don't know. I remember on the march down, from way back inland, all the animals were being driven with us. It was very much like a forest fire, this German Panzer attack. Animals, human beings, and the lot were all being driven forward to the sea. I remember seeing dead animals lying around, the same as men. The thing I remember about the horses was that they raced past us, up and down. And quite a number of men were injured, and some were killed, by simply getting a horse's hoof through their skull. There were pigs and sheep and various other things down there. Chickens too. It was a chaotic setup on the beach.

We arrived on the beach as a battalion, perfectly orderly. We went back off the beach, to the other side of the dunes, to rest—to hole up where we would be less likely to get a bit of shrapnel, and get some sleep, wait till light, and then weigh up the situation and see what we could do. We snuggled down into the sand—that's about the only way you can describe it—and we went to sleep. I don't know for how long, very short. And I think a bit dozy—things kept waking us up.

I called the roll at first light. There were two or three of my chaps missing. I remember one of the chaps telling me that he thought one of them had been killed. Two others had gone off, I think he said. They'd gone for water or they'd gone scrounging around somewhere.

Now, the scene early in the morning—this would be Saturday. Dunkirk, as I remember, finished on Sunday, to all intents and purposes. That Saturday morning I remember getting a bit of time to look at the scene purely from the point of view of appreciating the drama of it. I was frightened, but for a moment or two, I was not too frightened to stand and watch this scene. It was fantastic! It was slightly misty. The ships were lined up—I don't know how far—200–300 yards out in a great long line level with the beach. They were going into Dunkirk. The men were lined up in great wadges level with the seashore and were going into Dunkirk as well. And they were meeting there and loading up. The ships were being heavily attacked by aircraft—tracer shells and all the rest of it. There were blowups—we saw several ships go up there. This was a fabulous scene in the early morning.

As it got lighter, Dunkirk itself looked to me to be a complete hell. I had not been issued any specific orders because, one assumes, the officers expected us to keep together, and we would be ordered here, there, and everywhere as we went along. But my own sense told me that one had to march into Dunkirk to get on a ship. On the other hand, there were a great many queues already going out into the water, blokes up waist-high. And I was rather inclined to join one of these queues.

Now, I'll tell you why: I'm a very strong swimmer. Dunkirk looked most uninviting. The job, it seemed to me, was to get away and get to England. I was responsible for, at that point, about half a dozen men. So we went down to the beach, and we tagged onto a queue.

The queue was a very long one and a bit zig-zaggy. They were passing stretchers over our heads with wounded people on, to go out to the boats. And, I remember, the German planes shot up the queues, which was a nasty business. You were pretty helpless when you were up to your chest in water, and all you could do was duck under the water. Well, we got away with that. As far as I know, all my chaps got away with it.

The next thing that happened was I heard the crack of a gun, and a bullet zipped into the water beside me. Sure enough, there was one of our officers who had actually fired his revolver at me—I'm quite sure with no intent to hit me, but it shook me. It was because I had jumped queue. He told me in no uncertain terms that I had jumped it and I was to get my men the hell back out and join at the proper place.

I took my men up to the dunes to have another think. "Well," I said, "Can you all swim?" Not one of them could swim. A little while later one of them saw a boat out there, floating around, and I said, "Right. Well, I'll go and get it." It was only a hundred yards or so out.

I stripped down, literally stripped naked. I kept my tin hat on because this was a great comfort psychologically when things are flying about. And I left my clothes with the corporal, Corporal Henderson, and told him to wait there until I got back with the boat.

I swam out for this boat. When I got to it there were a couple of soldiers in it, and there were also two dead bodies in it, which they were busy heaving out. They were obviously going to take it somewhere else. One of them was all for letting me get in. The other one wasn't, and the moment I mentioned that I'd got some men on the beach, that was the end of it. There was no question of them coming back with me to the beach to pick my men up. So I abandoned this boat because I felt that I was in full view of the blokes sitting back on the beach, and I didn't want to arrive back in

England and have a couple of my chaps level a charge of having deserted them or something. I didn't think this out very clearly, but that's why I went back to the beach, because of the responsibility of three stripes.

When I got out of the water, I didn't know where I was. I couldn't see anybody I knew or recognize anything. But I did realize that the tide had probably carried me down. So I began to walk back, and eventually, about a half-mile up the beach I came across Henderson, sitting there with my clothes, rather like a terrier. Everybody else had gone. He said they'd chased up into the dunes because the Germans had strafed the beach. And he carefully said that he also had gone, but he'd come back.

Well, that left the two of us, and I decided not to go and look for the men. It was pretty hopeless business. The beach was very crowded, and they knew where we were. We sat there for some time deciding what to do. I was at that point all for walking into Dunkirk because I couldn't leave Henderson. And I said, "Come on, we'll march into Dunkirk," and he said, "Will you swim out with me?" Well, eventually I made an agreement with him that if he took all his clothes off to make it easier for me to carry him, I would swim with him.

You see, I was loaded up with a good many things. I'd got a pack full of stuff that we'd lifted. I'm sorry to say it, but there it was. We were billeted to one point in a cellar above which was a fur store and a jewelry store, and somebody had said, "What we don't have, the Germans will." This is a reprehensible thing, but there it was. And I loaded my pack with the best bracelets and wristwatches I could find. I also had a twelve-pelt silver fox fur cape wrapped up in my gas kit. I wasn't going to drop this lot, if I could avoid it. Henderson, I made him take all his kit off. Well, I'm afraid we threw away our rifles. This was a dreadful thing, of course, but since I had no ammunition, I really didn't see any point in perhaps being drowned by the weight of a couple of rifles. We were very short of ammunition the whole way through that lot, so we dumped all this, and Henderson (quite naked) and I set off, and I probably half drowned him on the way out, ducking him here and there. But he was alive and safe and sound when we were picked up by a longboat.

I call it a longboat—it was a very big boat, the sort of thing that the Navy has. There were very big, strong oars. There was a brigadier in charge of this, a big white-haired chap. After they'd hauled in Henderson, he said to me, "You'll have to drop your kit, sergeant." So reluctantly I undid my belt and let the whole thing slip off, and I got into the boat.

We went toward a destroyer that I think was called the *Ivanhoe*. And as we pulled toward the destroyer, I was very frightened by the planes. I didn't like this business of being dive-bombed just sitting in a boat. There wasn't much one could do, but the one thing I managed to do was change places with a bloke and start rowing. Then we were stopped by a loud hail from the destroyer. The chap said, "I'm on the mud. I'm churning up to get off. Wait until we're clear." Something like that. So the brigadier ordered us to stop rowing.

Then what happened was that some fool on the tiller allowed the boat to drift near the destroyer, which was in fact churning up like mad. And the very next thing I remember is the boat we were in smashing against the side of the destroyer. And my oar, to which I was hanging on rather grimly, caught in the side. And I was pulled up, sort of catapulted, a few feet—I don't know how far—but, anyway, literally heaved up out of my seat, and I grabbed a grid on the side of the destroyer, which acted as a ladder. I was aboard like a jackrabbit, staggered across the deck, and the next thing I heard was a great deal of shrieking and shouting. And I turned 'round and there were several sailors, leaning over the side over which I'd just climbed, looking down. They'd got a rope overboard, and I went to look over. And what I saw—Corporal Henderson hanging onto this rope with about six blokes clinging 'round his neck. And I saw them sink and they went down to the propellers. Then, as I was soaking, I took off my clothes, and a sailor gave me a blanket and a pack of cigarettes, and he said I could get some tea in the galley if I wanted it.

Soon after, the ship was hit. She got a bomb straight down her funnel, which went out of the bottom of the ship and burst and didn't kill anyone, or didn't do much damage, except to the ship. They kept the *Ivanhoe* afloat by bringing two ships alongside, one on either side, and they got the men off. This I don't know about for certain because by that time I had gone over the side. I was stark naked, without even a tin hat, and I swam madly away from the ship. I remember thinking that one might get caught in a whirlpool or something, and I was furiously pedaling to get away. Then I collected my senses a bit and had a look 'round, and of course I was surrounded by ships. The nearest was a trawler, which I swam to, and a very kind old gentleman, Scotsman, asked me if I was tired. Because he'd got rather too many aboard, and he didn't want to take any more, and there was a much bigger one, he said, over there. And he pointed to this ship and I swam to it—I quite felt I could swim to England that day very easily.

I swam to this minesweeper, it was the *Speedwell*, and was taken aboard and herded down below, where we were absolutely packed—literally like sardines. We were limb to limb, and some could hardly move or breathe. The ship started moving and swaying around. Bombs and shells, I suppose, were going off outside in the sea, and every time one did, it felt as if we'd been hit. In fact, the ship was weaving, zig-zagging, and a noise went off somewhere close by, just at the point where she zig-zagged. It felt at last as if we'd been hit. This was a terrible position to be in. If we were going to be killed, it was about the worst way you could be, jammed in the bottom of a ship. Next someone asked for volunteers to go up and man the small arms that they'd got set up on the decks: Bren guns, Lewis guns, that sort of thing. They had them all mounted. Anybody that had brought a gun aboard, they'd mounted them upstairs for the aircraft. I leapt at this. I went up, acted as sort of a number two on a Bren gun for a little while, much to the amusement of everybody, because as I say, I was stark naked. A sailor, I remember, came up and said, "Haven't you got any clothes?" And that was really the first time I was conscious of being naked, and he gave me a pair of slacks and a sweater, in which I eventually arrived at Dover.

The ship had been working her way 'round into Dunkirk harbor. That was why all the row was going on. We thought that we had been on the way to England. It was a terrible disappointment to everybody. Anyway, we lay in the harbor taking aboard a lot more men. There are two things I remember particularly about the harbor, standing up on the deck. One was seeing three men unload boxes, and then a bomb burst—it may have been a shell—killing them all, or anyway, knocking them out. And one of the boxes burst and a lot of lavatory paper rolls came falling out of it. The other thing was a beautiful little pleasure craft—a yacht—with three boys in white cricket shirts and flannels, punting away. I shouldn't think they could have taken more than four people.

I did see a lot of other things—things like bodies floating around, looking rather weird with their hair floating like weed on the sea. And seeing ships go up, too. I saw a ship which was there one second and the next second it wasn't there. This, this I shall always remember.

We finally got to Dover, and then much to my surprise and considerable discomfort, my battalion, as many as were on that boat, marched off the ship in full fighting kit and in good order, while I hid behind one of the ventilators, peeping 'round the corner, horribly embarrassed in a blue sweater and a pair of gray flannels. And I never dared to join them, for that reason. I was terribly ashamed of myself, seeing all these people lined up, you know. Eventually I got on a train and—that's it.

4

THE BATTLE OF BRITAIN: 1940-1941

Reggie Dexter

The water now seemed much colder. I looked down at my hands, and not seeing them made me realize that I'd gone blind. So I was going to die. It came to me like that—"I'm going to die"—and, oddly enough, I wasn't afraid.

—Reggie Dexter

The Battle of Britain: 1940–41

After the fall of France, Winston Churchill braced his countrymen for the ordeal to come by telling them, "The whole fury and might of the enemy must very soon be turned on us. Hitler knows that he will have to break us in this island or lose the war. . . . Let us therefore brace ourselves to do our duty. And so bear ourselves that if the British Empire and its Commonwealth were to last for a thousand years, men will still say, 'this was their finest hour.' "

France's defeat focused the war on a single issue—whether Britain would be willing and able to continue the fight or whether she would accept a settlement. Hitler favored a negotiated peace because it would permit him to save his military strength for the planned invasion of Russia. But the British would have no part of any negotiations with the Nazis.

With a peace settlement out of the question, Hitler had to make a tactical decision whether to blockade and starve the British or to bomb them into submission from his newly acquired air bases in France, Belgium, and Holland. He decided that the best way to accomplish his aims was to destroy the Royal Air Force so as to clear the way for an invasion. On July 16 he issued a directive, codenamed "Operation Sea Lion," to prepare for, and, if necessary, carry out an invasion of England. The directive stated that the RAF must first be reduced to insignificance.

Hermann Goering, head of the Luftwaffe, boasted that he could force the RAF to its knees in a matter of weeks. He believed that the Luftwaffe's effectiveness would pave the way for an invasion by sea, and very likely eliminate the need for it. But the British knew that if they could withstand the German air attacks, Hitler would have to abandon his invasion plans. These were the stakes in early July on the eve of the Battle of Britain. At the time, the Germans had a front-line strength of 3,000 aircraft, while the RAF's was 1,200.

In the first phase of the battle the Luftwaffe tried to establish air supremacy over the south of England. By the end of the month the RAF had lost 150 planes, but the Luftwaffe had lost 300. Because the British were short of planes and shorter still of pilots, each man had to fly many sorties in a day.

Though outnumbered in planes and pilots, the British had a sophisticated early warning system based on a chain of coastal radar stations, as well as a network of aircraft observation posts. Pilots were able to wait on the ground for precise instructions where and when to intercept the enemy. This permitted them to stay airborne and fight longer because they did not have to waste fuel searching for the enemy. Further, British intelligence had broken the German military code. This gave the RAF exact knowledge of the Luftwaffe's strategy, which was to draw as many British planes into battle as possible. By sending up relatively small fighter formations to get in among the massed German aircraft, the RAF was able to keep the balance of losses in its favor and thereby avoid the erosion of their fighter force. Small formations of fighters also had the advantage of maneuverability over the larger German formations.

In early August the Luftwaffe began to concentrate its attacks on the RAF's fighter bases and radar stations, expecting to cripple the fighters on the ground or to provoke them into a major air battle. This phase of the battle, which lasted into September, caused heavy damage on the ground. German losses were approaching 1,000 planes while Britain lost 550, but RAF fighter losses were beginning to exceed production and pilots were being lost at a rate about twice as fast as new ones were being trained.

The pilot whose story follows, Reggie Dexter, was one of the many RAF fliers shot down over the English Channel who were picked up by air-sea rescue and brought back to fight another day. He is one of those people who has come as close to dying as possible, and still survive.

Now he is a London business executive involved in international trade and finance.

Reggie Dexter:

September 3 dawned dark and overcast, with a slight breeze ruffling the water of the estuary. Hornchurch wore its usual morning pallor of yellow fog, making visibility practically impossible. We came out onto the tarmac about eight o'clock. All our machine tools, oil, and general equipment had been left on the far side of the aerodrome.

I was seriously worried, as after a recent bombing ordeal my plane had been fitted out with a brand-new hood. This hood unfortunately wouldn't open, and with a depleted ground staff and no tools, I began to fear it never would. But miraculously, Uncle George, our squadron leader, produced a lorry and three men who quickly returned with a large file and some lubricating oil. Thereupon a corporal and I set upon the hood in furious haste, taking it turn by turn to file and oil, oil and file, until at last the hood began to move, but agonizingly slowly. It was still sticking firmly halfway along the groove.

By ten o'clock, when the mist had cleared and the sun was blazing out of a clear sky, down the loudspeaker came the voice of the Controller: "603 Squadron take off from control base. You will receive further orders in the air. 603 Squadron take off as quickly as you can, please."

As I pressed the starter and the engine roared into life, the corporal stepped back and crossed his fingers significantly. I felt the usual sick feeling in the pit of my stomach as though I were about to row a race, and then I was too busy getting into position to feel anything. Uncle George, in the leading section, took off in a cloud of dust. Brian Corby looked across and put up his thumb. I nodded and opened up to take off.

I was flying Number 3 in brown section with Stapleton on the right. The third section consisted of only two machines so that our squadron strength was only eight. The sun was brilliant and made it quite difficult to see the next plane when turning. I was peering anxiously ahead, for the Controller had given us warning of at least fifty enemy fighters approaching very high.

When we did first sight them nobody shouted, as I think everyone saw them at the same moment. They must have been 500 to 1,000 feet above us coming straight on like a huge swarm of locusts. I remember cursing and automatically going into line astern. The next moment we were in among them and it was each man for himself. As soon as they saw us they spread out and dived, and the next ten minutes was a blur of twisting machines and tracer bullets. One Messerschmitt went down in a sheet of flames on my right, and a Spitfire hurtled past in a half-roll.

I was weaving and turning in a desperate attempt to gain height with the machine practically hanging on the propeller. Then just below me and to my left I saw what I had been praying for: a Messerschmitt climbing away from the sun. I closed in to 200 yards and from slightly to one side gave him a two-second burst. I ripped off his wing and black smoke poured from the engine, but he didn't go down. Like a fool I didn't break away, but put in another three-second burst. Red flames shot upward and he spiraled out of sight.

At that moment I felt a terrific explosion which knocked the control stick from my hand and the whole machine quivered like a stricken animal. In a second the cockpit was a mass of flames. I reached up to open the hood, it wouldn't move. I tore off my straps and managed to force it back. But this took time, and when I got back into the seat and reached for the stick in an effort to turn the plane onto its back, the heat was so intense that I could feel myself going. I remember thinking, "Well, this is it," and putting both my hands up to my eyes. Then I passed out. I regained consciousness free of the machine and falling rapidly. I pulled the ripcord on my parachute and checked my descent with a jerk. Looking down I saw that my left trouser leg was burned off, that I was going to fall into the sea, and that the English coast was deplorably far away. About twenty feet above the water I attempted to undo my parachute. I failed and flopped into the sea with it billowing around me.

The water was not cold and I was pleasantly surprised to find that my life jacket kept me afloat. I looked at my watch. It was not there. Then for the first time I noticed how burned my hands were. Down to the wrist the skin was dead white and hung in shreds. I felt faintly sick from the smell of burnt flesh. By closing one eye I could see my lips jutting out like Michelin tires. The side with my parachute harness was particularly painful, so I guessed that my right hip was burned. I made a further attempt to undo the harness but owing to the pain in my hands, soon gave up. Instead I lay back and reviewed my position.

I was a long way from land, my hands were burned, and so, judging from the pain from the sun, was my face. It was unlikely that anyone on shore had seen me come down, and even more unlikely that a ship would come by. I could float for possibly four hours in my life jacket. I began to feel that I was perhaps premature in considering myself lucky to have escaped from the machine.

After about half an hour, my teeth started chattering, and to quiet them I kept up a regular tuneless chant, varying it from time to time with calls for help. It was futile yelling for help, alone in the North Sea with a solitary seagull for company, but it gave me a certain melancholy satisfaction. I had once written a short story in which the hero, falling from a liner, had done just this. The story was rejected.

The water now seemed much colder. I looked down at my hands, and not seeing them made me realize that I'd gone blind. So I was going to die. It came to me like that—"I'm going to die"—and, oddly enough, I wasn't afraid.

It has often been said that a dying man relives his whole life in one rapid kaleidoscope. I merely thought rather gloomily of the squadron returning, of my mother at home, and of the few people who would miss me. Outside my family I could count those on the fingers of one hand. This realization came as a surprise to me. The manner of my approaching demise appalled and horrified me, but the actual vision of death left me unmoved, and I thought that only for my own curiosity and my own satisfaction, in a few minutes, or a few hours, I was to discover the answer to the question civilization had never solved.

I decided it should be in a few minutes. I had no qualms about hurrying things along a bit and, reaching up, I managed to unscrew the valve of my life jacket. The air escaped in a rush, and my head went under water. It is said by people all but dead from the sea, that drowning is a pleasant death. I didn't find it so. I swallowed a large quantity of water before my head came up again. I tried again, and I couldn't get my face under. I was so enmeshed in my parachute that I couldn't move. For the next ten minutes I tore my hands to ribbons on the spring-release catch; it was stuck fast. I lay back exhausted, and then I started to laugh. I was totally hysterical. My grand gesture of suicide being so oddly thwarted struck me as grotesque.

Goethe once wrote, as a young man, that no one, unless he had lived a full life and realized himself completely, had the right to take his own life. Providence seemed determined that I should not incur the great man's displeasure. What did gratify me enormously was to find that I indulged in no frantic abasements or prayers to the Almighty. It is an old jibe by God-fearing Christians that the irreligious always change their tune when they're about to die. I was pleased to be able to prove them wrong. I was neither relieved nor angry. I was past caring.

Faced with an indeterminate period of waiting, I began to feel depressingly lonely and sought for some means to take my mind off my plight. Knowing that I must soon become delirious, I attempted to hasten the process by encouraging my mind to wander vaguely and aimlessly. And I experienced a certain peace. Then I forced myself to think of something concrete and found that I was only still too lucid. I went on doing this with varying success until I was picked up.

Watchers on the coast had seen me come down and for three hours they'd been searching for me. They were just giving up and turning back for land when, ironically enough, one of them saw my parachute. I remember hearing someone shout, as if in a dream. It seemed so far away and quite unconnected with me. Then willing arms were dragging me over the side, my parachute was taken off, and with such ease. A brandy flask was pushed between my lips and a voice said, "Okay, it's one of ours and still kicking." And, after three and a half hours in the water, I was safe.

While in the water I had been numb and felt very little pain. Now that I was beginning to thaw out, the agony was such that I could have cried out. The stretcher carriers made me as comfortable as possible, put up some sort of a screen keep the sun from my face, and phoned through for a doctor. After what seemed an eternity, we reached the shore. I was put into an ambulance and driven rapidly to the hospital. Through all this I was quite conscious but unable to see. When I arrived at the hospital, they cut off my uniform and I gave the requisite information to the nurse about my next of kin. Then, to my infinite relief, I felt a hypodermic syringe being pushed into my arm.

5

THE LONDON BLITZ: 1940-1941

Nancy Spencer, Gillian Gordon

Little dark-red flames were going on along the brick walls. Piles of houses all collapsed were on fire. Warehouses like blazing cathedrals standing up and then falling down. Bricks going up, bombs coming down, the most terrific muddle of fire, and everything reflected in the water. Then in the basin, which was like a sheet of flame because it reflected the entire blaze of the fire, I saw two steamers completely on fire except for their black funnels.

—Nancy Spencer

It simply astounded me without really shocking me at the time, I remember, to see lots of bodies sitting there with crossed arms but no heads above them. And then I saw somebody creeping around in a vague, sort of dreamlike way, and this man came up and he felt around. He felt my hand, which was lying lax—I really was feeling most odd—and I finally realized later that what he'd done was take a ring off my finger.

—Gillian Gordon

The London Blitz: September, 1940–June, 1941

Through July and August the Luftwaffe continued to attack the RAF's fighter bases. In turn, British pilots continued to shoot down two German planes for every one they lost. Planes were fairly evenly matched: while the British aircraft were more maneuverable and better armed, those of the Luftwaffe were faster. The difference in performance between the two forces was the greater fighting spirit of the RAF pilots—they were fighting for the survival of their homeland. It was of these men that Churchill said, "Never in the field of human conflict was so much owed by so many to so few."

But British resources were wearing thin. They were running out of planes and their pilots were dead tired. In late August the Luftwaffe was sending a thousand planes a day against Fighter Command. The RAF began to lose more planes than the Germans. Then, with the scales beginning to tip in Hitler's direction, Reich Marshal Goering made a major mistake. In retaliation for the RAF's bomber raids on Berlin, which began on August 25, he ordered the Luftwaffe to switch its attacks to London. The city got its first taste of the Blitz on September 7, when a thousand planes came over on a daylight raid. Had the Luftwaffe kept up its missions against Fighter Command in the south of England for another week or two, they probably would have finished off what was left of the RAF's fighter force. Instead the pressure was relieved—but at a terrible price.

Night after night hundreds of thousands of people slept in the deep tunnels of the subway system while leaping flames lit whole areas—sometimes many square miles—as bright as day. Night and day for eight months the Luftwaffe raided London with high explosives and incendiary bombs. The city was being reduced to piles of rubble. The bombs fell indiscriminately on docks, homes, rail terminals, churches, and on warehouses and factories. There were a great many civilian casualties, tens of thousands killed and many more wounded.

But not everybody was underground. In the midst of the bombs, the smoke, the flames, the rubble, and the chaos, life in London went on. The firemen, the police, the air raid wardens, the Home Guard, the soldiers, and the ambulance drivers kept working in the open. People kept doing what had to be done.

Nancy Spencer was one of these people. She was a "conductor," a sort of first-aid volunteer, in an ambulance. One must "multiply" her story of a particular trip on a particular night by nearly two hundred times, because the people of London and the rescue services went through essentially the same experiences each time there was a raid.

The war demonstrated that people can adapt themselves to even the most unnatural situations. As the Blitz went on, people became accustomed to it and began to go on about their business. Despite the bombing and rationing, restaurants remained open, as did pubs and cafés. On an evening out with a soldier on leave, Gillian Gordon was in the wrong place at the wrong time, a cafe that was bombed shortly after she arrived there. Her story follows Nancy Spencer's. When interviewed a few years ago both were housewives living in England.

Nancy Spencer:

At 9:15 the call came through. They wanted one ambulance to go to 69 Oriental Road. I was very lucky because I had a driver who was in the last war, so he was very experienced. I was only the conductress. We went off, and we weren't allowed any lights at all. The streets were absolutely pitch black, except when they got the full glare of the fire. On we went, and I kept urging my driver to go faster. He said there was no hurry, we'd get there just as soon in the end. And sure enough, two ambulances that raced past us got themselves ditched in the pavement. We passed them.

We went on for a mile or two, and then after a bit we came to a sort of formation of ambulances—buses, all sorts of vans and things in a collection—and we took our place and waited. After a bit I asked an officer if this was Oriental Road. "Good gracious," he said, "No, this is Group 69. Oriental Road's in Silvertown."

So we tried to get our ambulance started up. It didn't start and we had to get four men to push us off. We went on a bit, and then I met a man and I said, "Is this right for Silvertown?" And he said, "Oh, no, that's about ten miles further on. It's no good going there; it's entirely ablaze from end to end."

We went on, and now we found we were completely alone. There wasn't a soul in any street. One minute we were going down a pitch-black street, and the next minute we were going down in the full glare of the fire. We went on and on, and eventually we came to the swing bridge into Victoria Docks. And from then on the whole thing was absolutely one blazing fire. I've never seen anything like it—from eye to eye right across the sky there was nothing but blazing things—with everything going up. Little dark-red flames were going up along the brick walls. Piles of houses all collapsed were on fire. Warehouses like blazing cathedrals standing up and then falling down. Bricks going up, bombs coming down, the most terrific muddle of fire, and everything reflected in the water. Then in the basin, which was like a sheet of flame because it reflected the entire blaze of the fire, I saw two steamers completely on fire except for their black funnels, which were absolutely jet-black against everything else.

Well, by now we were in a complete jam. There was nothing but firefighting apparatus, ambulances, hosepipes—the whole thing a complete and utter traffic jam—and we just had to take our place in the rather narrow road and wait. Well, we waited there for about ten minutes or so. Then my driver got rather fed up and he edged our way along. Just as we were getting near the top, to see what was holding everything up, a warehouse crashed right across the road. We had blazing stuff right across our roof, and it was impossible to go on. Well, then we were truly jammed. It was very uncomfortable because about four feet away there was a blazing patch of flame and a large pile of tar barrels just waiting to catch fire. My driver said to me, "Do you see what I see?" And I said, "Yes, I do." He said, "Well, it'll be a hell of a job to get out of here." However, we did manage to turn, with people helping us and firemen pushing.

We went back along our tracks. The other ambulances all

shouted to us, "You can't get through!" And we said, "Don't we know it, we can't get through. But we know another way." And they said, "Wait for us!" And I said, "We can't wait for you because we can't stop here. We're jamming the road."

So we went on, and it was an absolute mercy that no bomb hit the swing bridge, because if it had, we should all have been absolutely trapped. However, it didn't, and we edged along. On every side roofs fell in with the most terrific explosions. Gas mains blew up. There were constant bangs of bombs and antiaircraft guns. But it was quite impossible to feel frightened, because it was all on such an enormous scale. Every few minutes one of those blazing piles shot like a fountain into the sky. It reminded me very much of an eighteenth-century print of hot geysers in America, because the constant sort of fountains of stuff flittered up and fell down with a crash.

At any rate, we did get over the bridge. We went on for some time, and then we got blocked and couldn't go through, and we had to go back and take another fork. We went on for a bit more, past piles of burning stuff. Then we couldn't get through again.

Well, then my driver had an inspiration, and he left the road completely and cut across a wharf. Now we were in sort of a maze of cinder tracks and truck lines going here and there, and nothing but hosepipes and people fighting the fires. Then we came to what seemed to be a sheet of flame, but my driver said, "Oh, I think this is nothing much. We'll get through this." He put a terrific spurt on, and we got through it, and that was all right. Then we came to a whole group of firemen all wearing masks, fighting against one of the warehouses which was blazing. And I said to him, "Anybody hurt here?" And he said, "No, all dead. Go on." So we went on.

Then we came across a man completely distraught, his face absolutely black with soot. Of course, all our faces were black, but we didn't notice it. He'd lost his wife and his mother, and so we gave him a lift on the way. Where to I'd no idea, but he wanted to come that way, so he came. Then we asked a man, "Is this right for Oriental Raod?" "Oriental Road?" he said. "That's absolutely hopeless. It's ablaze from end to end. You'll never get there."

Well, we did. We went on, and quite shortly we came to a little deserted village, everything quiet except for, of course, the tremendous bomb racket, which went on all the time. It was a little deserted village, with two-story houses. And not a single house had a roof. A lamppost lay right across the road, and there were enormous craters, and in each crater there seemed to be a burning jet, a gas main or something which had blown up. Prams, stoves, and everything were scattered across the road. We had an awful job getting by because the craters were so big and the road was so narrow that half the time we had two wheels on the pavement and two wheels over the crater.

Then we came to another road, and there wasn't a single house standing. There was nothing, nothing at all except holes. And out of several of these holes, people **popp**ed their heads. It was exactly like a Chinese war film. I said, **"Is th**is Oriental Road?" And they shouted, "Ambulance!" And I said, "Yes. Anybody hurt?" And they said, "Over in the shelter, under the arches." And then they said, "Oh, you can't get your ambulance there. There's no possible road. You'll have to leave it."

So we left the ambulance, and I got out with a stretcher and went over to the shelter, and put my head in. I suppose there were about forty people there. I said, "Is anybody hurt?" And they . . . nobody answered. So I went up to one woman and tapped her and said, "Is anybody hurt here?" And she said, "Over there, there's a mother and a two-day-old baby. They've just been dug out. And I think further on there's a boy with a very bad knee. He got dug out. He was buried up to his waist. And I don't know about the others."

So I went over to the mother. She didn't speak. And I wrapped her in a blanket and put her on the stretcher. And I said, "Is there a warden here?" And somebody said, "No, he was killed half an hour ago." So I got a couple of men to help me, and we took her back in the stretcher, put her in the ambulance. And I came back again and collected the boy, with some help, and after that I just filled the ambulance with as many people as I could cram in, about fifteen or sixteen. Nobody spoke. It was all the most deathly silence, and I got in beside them this time, not beside the driver, and drew the curtains to shut out the ghastly glow and deafen the noise a bit, and we drove off. And it didn't take us, of course, nearly as long to drive back. About halfway back, there was the most tremendous explosion and the whole ambulance left the ground, and I thought this time we've had it, and the man has hit a crater. But he hadn't actually. It was a bomb that was dropped in

Liverpool Street Station, and we were very close then. Anyway, we got them all back to hospital. And we got back to our station, I suppose, about half past one in the morning. And the joke was, when we got back, the station officer said, "Oh I'm frightfully sorry. You had the wrong message altogether. You should have gone to Group 69 and waited, not gone to Oriental Road at all."

Gillian Gordon:

We got to the Café de Paris just after ten. Only a few minutes, I think, before the bomb fell. We hadn't eaten our dinner yet. We decided to dance and went out on the floor. The tune was "Oh, Johnny." And then the bomb fell.

I'll always remember that it was like swimming through cotton wool, if you can imagine such a thing. I didn't lose consciousness. At least I don't think I did. I remember everything that happened. And when I sort of came to, I was sitting on somebody. It turned out to be an officer wearing a kilt. How it happened was your guess as well as mine. And I discovered that my leg was broken—I couldn't stand on it. My back was very wet, and that was blood, I found later. I didn't feel any pain. I didn't feel anything at all, except astonishment.

I looked around. There was a lot of dust, a lot of bodies lying around, still and quiet, and a lot of flares were burning in the darkness. I remember looking up, and in the Café de Paris there was a balcony or gallery that ran round. And it simply astounded me without really shocking me at the time, I remember, to see lots of bodies sitting there with crossed arms but no heads above them. And then I saw somebody creeping around in a vague, sort of dreamlike way, and this man came up and he felt around. He felt my hand, which was lying lax—I really was feeling most odd— and I finally realized later that what he'd done was take a ring off my finger.

Then, a little later on, there came a very large officer, fully dressed with an overcoat, who I found later was Dutch. He probably came in off the street. He picked me up, and he carried me into the kitchen. And he put me down on the hot plate, and he set my leg with a wooden stew spoon, washing it first of all—believe it or not—in champagne, which was the only thing handy. And while he was doing that, a very agitated waiter tried to clean off my face—which obviously was very dirty—with a napkin. And the awful thing about that was, my face was full of little bits of glass, and it was absolutely torture to have him do this. However, he was well-meaning. And while he was doing that, all around me on the floor there were casualties. There were a lot of Canadian nurses there that night and they were working like Trojans—really trying to help. They started to improvise stretchers by using the screens, because the stretchers had run out or something, and I was carted up the rickety stairs and laid out in Leicester Square.

By that time, the second half of the raid had started. In those days, they used to come in two waves. And I remember lying in Leicester Square and just feeling that nothing really mattered. I wasn't in any particular pain—I just felt dead, that was all, I was dying. The planes were coming over and dropping flares, and there was a lot of noise, and people screaming, and ambulances, and just bedlam. Several times they picked me up and tried to put me in an ambulance, but somehow it just never happened, and back I went.

Finally I was put in one, but they put me in the bunk underneath, and somebody above me—I don't know who it was—was bleeding like pigs. It was dripping down—the stretchers in those days were sort of wire mesh—and the blood was dripping down. By that time I was rigid with cold and shock, I suppose. I just couldn't move my head away, and in about three minutes my eyes were stuck. When I did get to the hospital, I'm sure I must have presented quite a sight. Anyway, when I did, they stuck something in my arm, and that was that. It was all over.

6

THE ATLANTIC: 1939-1943

Tom Mastrangello

It was late December, cold as hell, and we had gale winds and blinding snow squalls. Weather like that is especially tough on the gunners because they have to stand watch on the forward and aft gun decks. Waves are breaking over the bow and the wind is driving ice-cold sea water into the faces of the forward gun crew, while the aft deck is bouncing all over the place. You'd see the new guys who really got affected by seasickness walking up to the forward gun deck with buckets because they didn't want to throw up and have it blow back into their faces. So they were throwing up in the buckets.

—Tom Mastrangello

The Atlantic: 1939–1943

In the late 1930's many Americans believed that the United States should not concern itself with European affairs, but should follow a policy of nonintervention into foreign squabbles. Even though President Roosevelt did not share this view and believed that America could not remain isolated from events abroad, isolationist pressure was such that when Britain, France, and Germany went to war in September, 1939, he issued a proclamation of American neutrality. At the same time he went on to say, "But I cannot ask that every American remain neutral in thought as well. Even a neutral has a right to take account of facts. Even a neutral cannot be asked to close his mind or close his conscience."

When Japan joined with Germany and Italy in September, 1940, in an Axis coalition that spanned the continents of Europe and Asia, Roosevelt believed it to be a threat to American security. For this reason he favored aiding all those states that opposed the

Axis. He believed that ". . . there is far less chance of the United States getting into war, if we do all we can now to support the nations defending themselves against attack by the Axis, than if we acquiesce in their defeat . . . and wait our turn to be the object of attack later on."

The debate continued for some time, with such well-known Americans as labor leader John L. Lewis arguing that economic aid would inevitably lead to military involvement. Charles A. Lindbergh, famous for making the first nonstop trans-Atlantic flight and an active supporter of a right-wing isolationist group called "America First," took the position that the Atlantic and Pacific Oceans provided a natural buffer that secured the United States from the threat of attack.

However, the situation in Europe was grim. British losses as a result of the evacuation from France, from German bombing, and from U-boat attacks on her merchant ships, led to serious shortages of food, fuel, and military supplies. England's hopes for survival, let alone for winning the war, depended on economic and military aid. Desperate for help, Churchill asked President Roosevelt in February, 1941, to "Put your confidence in us . . . Give us the tools and we will finish the job." Roosevelt's response was to provide aid in every way possible short of actually declaring war. In 1941 alone, in addition to food, fuel, and other supplies, the United States sent to Britain 2,800 planes, 1,000 tanks, and 13,000 trucks.

Aid soon took an even more direct form. In July, 1941, American Marines were sent to Iceland to garrison an important base for the protection of convoys. Their presence freed British troops for duty elsewhere. In September, Germany reacted to this by having one of her submarines attack an American destroyer, USS *Greer*. As a result, Roosevelt announced that American ships would "shoot on sight" all German and Italian warships interfering with American shipping. In this way, the U.S. Navy became a combatant in the war a few months before the rest of the country.

Being an island nation, Britain is even more dependent on her merchant shipping than are most other countries. For this reason the German Navy made a special effort to close Britain's maritime lifeline. The Allies did everything they could to keep it open. The result was the Battle of the Atlantic.

The British had 2,500 merchant ships at sea on any given day and each of these ships was vulnerable to submarine attack. Hitler believed that his U-boats could so disrupt British shipping that they would accomplish what the Blitz had failed to do—force Britain into submission by starving her of food and supplies. To defend against submarines, merchant ships sailed in large convoys protected by a naval escort. The convoys were made up of roughly ten columns of ships across, with a line of five or six ships in each column. This formation reduced the target which the flank of the convoy offered to submarines. Escort vessels moved back and forth around the outer perimeter of the convoy, screening the merchant ships.

As the war progressed it became evident that convoys were not only effective for defensive reasons, but for offensive purposes as well. They attracted submarines like bees to honey, and once there were enough escorts—especially escort carriers with radar-equipped planes—they became lethal to submarines. The development of effective sonar made it possible for surface ships to seek out and destroy submerged U-boats.

During the course of the war Germany built nearly 1,200 submarines and lost more than 700 of them in action. 32,000 German sailors were drowned. U-boats accounted for the sinking of 2,800 Allied merchant ships, 150 warships, and the loss of tens of thousands of Allied seamen. Even though merchant seamen were civilians, their casualty rate was higher than that in any of the armed services. These men went back to sea again and again simply because they believed in what they were doing.

Tom Mastrangello was a U.S. Navy signalman assigned first to a destroyer on escort duty and later to a merchant ship. He spent nearly four years on convoy duty. After the war he became an accountant and is now the treasurer of an industrial corporation in New Jersey.

Tom Mastrangello:

I spent most of my time in the Navy on convoy duty, going back and forth from New York and Halifax to England, and later to the Mediterranean. I enlisted in June, 1941, just after graduating from high school, about six months before Pearl Harbor. First I served on a destroyer and then as part of the Navy armed guard on several merchant ships.

I remember that during my senior year, 1940–41, the war news was pretty much all bad. We still weren't in, but it seemed that we were getting closer and closer to coming in. England was going it alone and taking a hell of a beating. We all figured it was only a matter of time before the United States would join the fight. It was a very patriotic time. Very few people who were classified 4-F could live it down. Most of the guys who couldn't get into the armed forces because they were 4-F joined the merchant marine because the physical requirements were less rigorous. Of course, there were one or two guys who cheered all the way down the block at being 4-F, but they were a very small percentage. Everybody I knew wanted to go in and considered it a stigma not to. We had a class of twenty-one boys in high school and everyone went into the service, someplace, except for one guy. He went into the seminary and became a priest, but he'd always had a vocation, so it wasn't a matter of avoiding the service.

I could have made 4-F if I'd wanted to. I'd had polio when I was three and as a result one foot is quite a bit smaller than the other. In fact, I wear one shoe size 10 and one size 6. When the guys aboard ship found out about my foot they called it the "million dollar wound." That's a wound that would get you shipped home but wouldn't permanently disable you. The guys would say, "If that was me, tomorrow I would start limping so bad, and in about three days I wouldn't be able to move that leg. I'd tell them that the polio had come back! How the hell would they know?"

I went to a small parochial high school in Jersey City where they taught chemistry but no physics. We all wanted to become Navy pilots and we knew that we had to have physics to get into the Naval Air Corps program. A science teacher agreed to teach us a special physics class at eight o'clock in the morning. Eight or nine of us signed up. The course was free—the guy was just teaching it out of patriotic feeling.

We all went to take the examination in May of our senior year, 1941. In the morning we took the written exam—math, physics, all kinds of stuff—then we sat around and they came out with a list of names and dismissed the people who'd failed. The rest of us were still sitting there waiting for the physical, which they usually did in alphabetical order. But they came out and said, "Who's Mastrangello?" Somebody had read my preliminary physical report and noticed that I'd had polio at age three. I'd had to put that down or I'd have been lying, but I hadn't put down that one foot was shorter than the other. Let them find that out for themselves. They said, "Mastrangello, you come first."

When I went into the examination room the doctor asked me about the polio and I said that I'd had it, but that it didn't bother me any. I used to stand with my legs apart so that people wouldn't notice my feet. The doctor asked, "Where'd you have polio, right leg or left?" As he looked he said, "This foot's smaller," and on examining the foot he noticed that I'd had a bone removed; he knew the operation.

He said, "This is gonna hurt. Do you know how much it costs to educate a pilot? $25,000. And we just can't take a risk on a cripple." The SOB called me a cripple! He'd probably been in the service all of four weeks and was pissed off about being in at all. What sensitivity the guy had! So I went home devastated. I was seventeen and had made up my mind to go into the Navy as a pilot, but they didn't want me. The Navy pilots seemed more glamorous than the Army's and their uniforms looked nicer, and anyway I figured that if the Navy wouldn't take me for pilot training, the Army wouldn't either.

I was stuck and was feeling kind of low. My mother said to me, "Will you stop feeling sorry for yourself! Do something about it! If they won't take you as a pilot, go up and enlist in the Navy. Fight them and make them take you." So I went to enlist, and as I went through the physical they found everything again, but the doctor made no comment. I finally got down to the last reviewing board and the doctor said, "Mastrangello, I see that you've had polio."

I said, "That doesn't bother me. I play basketball, I play football, I play baseball, I can run as fast as anybody else, and I can do anything that anyone else can do in this world."

He said, "OK, do five deep-knee bends." I did them. "OK, do five push-ups." I did the push-ups. "Now stand only on that one leg and do what I tell you." I did a whole bunch of stuff, everything he told me to do, and he said, "You're damn right you can do anything anyone else can." He was reviewing my case, expecting to turn me down, but he let me in.

I think it would have ruined my life if he hadn't. You'd have had a hell of a time if you were left out of the war, especially afterwards—with everyone coming home with their stories and going off to college on the G.I. Bill of Rights. I think I would have been marked. You're always compensating when you've had polio anyhow, that's probably why I played sports so hard. Years later my mother told me she was shocked but pleased that the Navy took me. She thought that they'd turn me down.

Anyway, they took me and sent me to boot camp and after that to signal school where I got my rating as a signalman. You learn to communicate with other ships by means of flags, signal lights, and semaphore. A signalman's station is on the bridge or out on the wing of the bridge where he sends and reads coded messages by means of flag hoists, receives and sends blinker light messages directly from ship to ship, and receives and sends semaphore messages by means of hand flags. There are other things that a signalman does at varous times, but these give a pretty good idea of the job. When I finished signal school I was assigned to a destroyer doing escort duty in the North Atlantic.

Early in 1941 we started shipping an enormous amount of food and fuel and war material to Britain as part of a program called Lend-Lease. The Germans considered any Allied or neutral merchant ship bound for Britain with supplies to be fair game and were sinking an awful lot of these ships. They sent their U-boats out in "wolf packs," groups of ten or twenty submarines stationed on the main shipping lanes and in radio contact with each other. When one of them spotted a convoy he would radio the others to join him and they would shadow it by day and attack by night. Even before we were officially at war, the Navy began to escort merchant ships partway across because the British were short of escorts. They couldn't afford to send the ones they had all the way across. We worked with the Canadians, escorting convoys to a mid-ocean meeting point south of Iceland where the British took over, and then we picked up ships going westbound. The wolf packs were so lethal that if we hadn't done this escort work, most of our aid would never have made it all the way across.

Convoys were the main defense against submarines. The idea was to take a large number of merchant ships, usually anywhere from 30 to 60, and arrange them into maybe 8 to 12 columns wide, with each column having five or six ships in a line, front to back. This formation presented the smallest possible target to the submarine, as a great many inner ships were protected by a relatively small number of outer ones. Naval escorts, mostly destroyers and destroyer escorts, moved back and forth and around the outer perimeter of the convoy, screening the merchant ships and looking and listening for submarines. In addition blimps and, later, planes protected covoys as far out as they could go at either end of the trip.

Destroyers really had the toughest duty in the convoy because they needed to be everywhere at once and never got a chance to take it easy. This was especially true early in the war when we were short of escorts. Destroyers sort of went across the ocean sideways. If you were in front of the convoy you kept zigzagging from side to side, trying to pick up sonar bleeps in order to find out if there were any U-boats and, if so, where. If you were on the side of a convoy you also kept going back and forth trying to pick up bleeps. In certain parts of the ocean where attacks were likely, we were often sending commands by flag hoist to tell the merchant ships to shut off their engines. Immediately the whole convoy would shut their engines off so that in the quiet we could pick up better sonar.

When we picked up a bleep we would go dashing through the convoy or alongside it at flank speed throwing depth charges. If we made a contact we might spend hours tracking it and running depth-charge patterns, or we might stay with the convoy to protect it even though we knew there was a U-boat around. As the war progressed our antisubmarine techniques improved and convoys were used as bait to attract U-boats. Carrier-based planes then killed them working together with surface ships. But in early 1942 convoys were still on the defensive. The idea was to get the ships through, rather than to kill subs.

We weren't always successful, and one of our main jobs was to pick up survivors after a ship was hit. Sometimes, on a bad convoy, we would finish up with a hundred or so survivors. They would be all over the ship, wandering around with nowhere to go, in the forecastle, the galley, on the deck, anyplace they could find. They would be wrapped in blankets, or in borrowed clothes, or in their own oily rags. Some would be cheerful—glad to have been rescued—others would be frightened or sick or wounded.

If your ship was hit, the chances of surviving weren't all that good. Especially in the North Atlantic in winter. Everybody knew that. Don't go into the water, don't even worry about it. If you're hit you're not going to make it anyhow, once the ship goes down. How long can you last in the water? Nobody had any rafts. If you got hit really good on a tanker everything on the ship would be blown up. The only way to get off was to jump off. When we were in school they taught us how to swim when oily water was on fire. You swim under the water, stick your hands up to the surface to push the oil and fire away, make a little hole, poke your head up and take a breath. That's all very nice to practice in swimming classes, but you know you're not going to be able to do that in a big fire. It always amazed me that guys joined the Navy who couldn't swim, but a lot couldn't. Take a guy from Kansas or Nebraska who'd spent his summers on a farm. He'd have to go a long distance even to find a decent pond so naturally he'd have no need to swim. Everybody was supposed to learn and I guess it saved some lives because we occasionally picked up survivors who'd made it out of burning tankers even in the freezing water.

I don't remember too many details about destroyer duty in the winter of 1942 other than that foul weather was the rule rather than the exception. It was terribly cold and windy and the seas were rough, and when the wind wasn't blowing there was plenty of wet fog. We were under terrific pressure and tired most of the time. I do remember that the destroyer was extremely uncomfortable. It rolled and pitched constantly, even in a calm sea (which we seldom had), and it was cramped and crowded. In heavy weather it rolled and pitched so much that it was often impossible to sleep or do other normal things, like cooking. Sometimes we lived on Spam and other cold rations eaten directly out of the can. We occasionally got rests in Iceland or Newfoundland or Halifax, but these didn't last long and I remember that the weather was always bad.

It was very difficult for the old merchant marine officers to be in a convoy. Out at sea, in peacetime, they stayed great distances away from each other so that there was no chance of an accident. Their entire peacetime training and experience told them to keep their distance, and when they formed convoys during World War II the constant message coming from the commodore was, "Close up. Close up. Close up." The old captains were almost in a panic because everybody was so close. They'd never traveled that way before in their lives. They were always dropping back just a little bit or ranging ahead a bit, until they'd get the signal, "Ship number such and such, take station and keep station." It was amazing to see the same ships day after day, always in the same relative position.

When we got close to England the orders which told each ship where to go were usually opened or dispatched. The amusing part was that after the message was given, all you could see was blinker lights going between every ship in the convoy, asking back and forth, "Where are you going?" It seemed that the people who were going to Scotland had the most to worry about, because normally if you went to Scotland, you probably would continue on the run to Russia which was very dangerous. Bringing supplies to Murmansk was really disastrous duty because you were vulnerable to constant air and sea attacks from the German bases in Denmark and Norway. The Germans could take cracks at you all along the route. The guys knew the statistics on ships getting through. A very small percentage made it. You might start out with forty ships and only fifteen would make it. If you got hit and had to go in the icy water, you were dead almost instantly. I always considered myself lucky that I never had to go on the Murmansk run.

Right after we got into the war the U-boats began to have a field day all along our Atlantic Coast. They would hang around the coastal shipping lanes submerged all day, surface at night, and knock hell out of our merchant shipping. It always amazed me that we were so unprepared for this. Here we were, escorting convoys all the way across the Atlantic, but unable to protect our own coast. We just didn't have enough escort ships and it made no sense to send convoys up and down the coast without escorts. So unarmed freighters went out on their own and took their chances, which weren't all that good. During 1942 there must have been 200 or 300 ships sunk along the Atlantic Coast, many of them in sight of land and with spectators watching from shore. We weren't even getting out of harbor because the U-boats patrolled the approaches to New York, Chesapeake Bay, the Caribbean and the Gulf of Mexico.

What the Navy finally did was to put an armed guard on the merchant ships to man five-inch or three-inch guns which were mounted fore and aft. Machine guns were also mounted on the bridge. Merchant vessels had their regular merchant marine crews but they also carried a 16- or 17-man armed guard provided by the Navy. This was usually made up of a 13-man gun crew, two signalmen, a radioman and an officer. Eventually every merchant ship had an armed guard. I guess they needed experienced signalmen for the armed guard, because I was transferred into it.

I was assigned to the Brooklyn Armed Guard Center as my home base. It was in a converted car barn where they used to keep buses. They put destroyer bunks four-high in the barn, all over the place. A trolley line ran right through the base, in one gate and out the other. It was really strange having trolleys full of passengers running through the place.

Crews were always forming up to go. You'd go down to a muster and they'd call out names and say, "You guys are leaving tomorrow morning. Be ready at 0600 hours." It was such a transient place that if you knew that a crew was moving out at six in the morning, you woke up at six in order to protect your possessions. Everybody had fast hands when they were walking out the door. On some naval ships they had a theory that if one guy stole from you and you stole from another guy, by the time you got back everybody would have their own clothes again. There was a lot of stealing going on—"midnight small stores," they called it. On the merchant ships I never heard anybody complain about stealing.

My first armed guard duty was aboard a brand new T-2 class tanker which we picked up in the shipyard at Chester, Pennsylvania. The ship was called the *Tullahoma*, like Tulsa, Oklahoma. When they ask you "What ship?" on a signal light and you say "*Tullahoma*," nobody knows what the hell you're sending. Out of Chester we did a shakedown cruise to Baytown, Texas, to see how the ship was operating. The merchant marine people did all kinds of tests with the engines and deck gear. We fired the guns to see if they worked by attaching a rope to the trigger mechanism and getting everybody off the gun deck in case there was something wrong with the gun and it blew up. When we got to Baytown we took on a load of gasoline and oil and came back to New York. Within two or three days they had loaded big crates of airplane parts and planes all over the tanker's deck and built all kinds of catwalks over the crates. If you wanted to walk from one end of the ship to the other, you walked on a catwalk right on top of the deck cargo.

So, loaded with oil in our tanks and crates on our decks, we formed a convoy out of New York and headed out into the North Atlantic. We were a newly formed armed guard crew and about half of the men had never been to sea before. I remember feeling sorry for the new guys because we hit some really rotten weather. It was late December, cold as hell, and we had gale winds and blinding snow squalls. Weather like that is especially tough on the gunners because they have to stand watch on the forward and aft gun decks. Waves are breaking over the bow and the wind is driving ice-cold sea water into the faces of the forward gun crew, while the aft gun deck is bouncing all over the place. You'd see the new guys who really got affected by seasickness walking up to the forward gun deck with buckets because they didn't want to throw up and have it blow back into their faces. So they were throwing up in the buckets. Now if we got into really rough seas they might move the gunners from the forward gun deck. But meanwhile these new guys are sick and throwing up and cold and terrified that they're going to be swept overboard.

I stood watch on the bridge, which was higher up. My theory was that the higher up you were on the ship the better off you'd feel because supposedly you wouldn't get as much of the pitch. I don't know if this theory is right or wrong, but I never got sick. Of course, merchant ships are bigger and much more stable than destroyers and destroyer escorts, especially when loaded with cargo; but on a tanker the bridge is on the fantail, not amidships, so you get quite a lot of motion.

To me, the cold was worse than the motion. When you went on watch you'd put on your long johns, your dungarees, your heavy black Navy sweater and then a fur-lined pair of pants like overalls. Over these you would put on a fur-lined jacket and a fur-lined peaked cap with the earflaps down. Then you'd put on a hooded windbreaker. Finally you'd put on a pair of wool gloves and over these a pair of rubber gloves. When you finally went on watch you looked like a little kid whose mother had bundled him up against the cold. You could hardly walk, you just sort of waddled out onto the deck. I stood watch on the wing of the bridge where our signal light and the 20mm machine guns were mounted. I spent most of my four-hour watches on that trip trying to hide behind something to get away from the wind, which was blowing like hell.

The *Tullahoma* ran at twenty-two knots, which is very fast. So fast that she was running in a convoy of troop ships. Troop ships were converted passenger liners. Not the big ones—the *Queen Mary* and *Queen Elizabeth* and other luxury liners ran by themselves—but much faster than most cargo ships. Their speed made convoy unnecessary. Fast convoys were much safer than slow ones because they could run much faster than the U-boats. The tankers were put on the corners or on the rear of this particular convoy so that if they got hit they wouldn't blow up the rest of the convoy. The troop ships were more important than the tankers, so they put them on the inside where they had more protection.

We had two signalmen and a radioman. We normally stood two four-hour watches and didn't keep communications watch at night because the merchant marine also had radiomen on board who stood night watches. But since we were running with a very fast convoy they kept up communication by walkie-talkie at night, so we had to keep a walkie-talkie watch at night. We never transmitted signals, we only received them. The only one who ever opened up on the walkie-talkie was the commodore, the naval officer in charge of the convoy. He made all the decisions about what the convoy would and wouldn't do. He would signal us whether or not to take certain actions, or if he wanted us to change course or positions. If he wanted the ships to do some kind of maneuvering, he would give a quick maneuvering message. But somebody had to monitor these messages all night long. You would sit on the floor in a corner of the wheel house waiting for somebody to talk on this little radio. We were warm, but there are no chairs in the wheelhouse and you had to keep out of the way of the merchant marines who were running the ship. You could go out of your head with boredom. You'd just sit there and all you would hear was little noises and finally somebody might relay a message. Maybe you'd be there for four hours and nobody would say anything.

One night we saw a startling thing: a light on the horizon that was bright as hell. We were blacked out in the middle of the Atlantic. If you went outside you stepped through a cloth and then pulled it shut so that no light would show through. Only after this blackout curtain was drawn would you open the door. Conditions were really critical and it was important that no light appear on deck. So we saw this light on the horizon coming toward us and wondered what the hell is this. It was a hospital ship coming back with wounded and running with full lights and floodlit illumination of the red crosses painted all over her. It lit up our convoy and silhouetted us against the glow. It scared the hell out of us. They went scurrying past us, running by themselves, brightly lit all the way across.

When we got to England we unloaded the cargo very fast, in eight hours. Then they put us into a cove and kept us hidden. You couldn't really see us from the sea in this little cove. We stayed there for about a week but we couldn't go ashore: we had to keep standing watch. There was nowhere to go anyway, and they wanted to get us out of there as fast as possible.

Coming back the convoy ran into a terrific North Atlantic storm with gale-force winds and mountainous seas. I've never seen ships disappear so quickly before. You're running in a convoy of forty ships and within fifteen minutes you look around and everyone's gone in a different direction and you feel like you're all by yourself. This separation wasn't intentional—the sea did it when it got too rough. Our tanks were empty and there was no cargo on board so we were running high in the water, but we were taking water right over the whole deck, from stem to stern. A destroyer came up alongside and stayed with us and we ran into a few other ships. Eventually the whole convoy regrouped and made it home safe.

By that time no one was seasick anymore, even in the heaviest weather. But you didn't necessarily feel like eating a whole lot. You would feel like eating until you walked into the mess hall. As soon as you actually smelled the food you'd walk back out again, you just couldn't do it. And of course, the guys who were in really good shape, the veterans who had gotten over the seasickness, would always try to get you to eat something: "Why don't you have some bacon?" The last thing you wanted in the world was some greasy bacon. The guys would put it under your nose and you'd almost throw up on the spot.

In the spring of '44, it was before D-day, they decided that they weren't going to use the walkie-talkies on the fast convoys anymore, or that the tankers weren't going to run in the fast convoys. In any case, they took the signalmen off the *Tullahoma* and I was assigned to the armed guard on the *Benjamin Brewster*. We made three trips back and forth on that ship before we were assigned late in the war to what they called shuttle duty—back and forth from Oran in North Africa to Naples. It took us a couple of days each way. We were stuck doing this for two or three months. By that time the Mediterranean was owned by the United States Air Force and there wasn't much action. We used to lay on the hatch in the evening, smoke a cigar or a pipe and watch the stars come out. Just lay on your back and watch the night come. All of a sudden, the stars were there.

The *Benjamin Brewster* was very slow. It was a Liberty Ship, one of the cargo ships that were built during the war by Kaiser Shipbuilding. They built them very fast—one would come off the line just about every day. Out of the water they looked like bathtubs. They carried a tremendous amount of cargo, but they were very slow. And the longer they were in the water the slower they got because of barnacles. At best they could do twelve knots and after a while they were mostly doing six or eight knots. It took us sixteen days from New York to Casablanca on the *Benjamin Brewster* and only six days to England on the *Tullahoma*.

The strangest message I ever sent was from the *Benjamin Brewster* when we were in Naples. When the Germans left Naples they scuttled anything that was in the harbor in order to make the port unusable. Ships were sunk and capsized all over the place. Our Army Engineers came in and just used the scuttled ships as platforms; they built docks right on top of them. When you came into port you pulled up to a scuttled ship and it was a ready-built dock. But, of course, it cut down on the total amount of dock space available so ships that weren't loading and unloading were nested bow-in to save space.

A bunch of British destroyers were nested in this way, and we were going out of the harbor and all of a sudden one of these destroyers backs out right across our path. Now, right up forward in the bow of a liberty ship is the ammunition locker where all your shells and 20mm magazines are stored. If you ram something with your bow there's likely to be quite an explosion. I was on the bridge and could see what was happening.

Our captain shouted, "Full astern!" and pointed the engine telegraph full astern. We were running rather slowly but the damn thing just shook as it slowed down. The destroyer kept coming and coming and it looked like we were sure to ram it. I don't know how close we got to it, but it looked like we were almost at it—only a few feet away—when we started moving back again. It kept coming and pulled all the way across our path when all of a sudden the signal light comes on and a British signalman sends over, "Sorry." That's all he said—"Sorry." So I went to the captain and said, "The British destroyer reports 'Sorry.'" The captain says, "Tell the British destroyer, 'Kiss my ass.'" I said, "What, sir?" He says, "Tell them, 'Kiss my ass.'" So I opened the light and sent the message, "Kiss my ass." We made our way out of harbor without further reply from the British.

For the most part being a signalman is pretty straight work. You do a little chit-chatting with other guys on the light but it's mostly business. Occasionally somebody says, "I think I have a buddy on that ship over there, check for me." You'd call on the signal light, "You got a guy by the name of so-and-so over there? Tell him so-and-so is over here."

I suppose my toughest job was trying to send a message to a plane by signal light. Once we were traveling alone and had a sixteen-year-old mess boy who was very sick—we later found out that he had spinal meningitis. We had no medical help on board and we couldn't open up on the radio. At the time we were off the Florida coast and Navy pilots were buzzing us all day long. Whenever you got buzzed by a Navy plane you had to put up the code of the day on the flag hoist.

When this guy came over I got on the light and tried to communicate that we had sick personnel on board. It's very difficult to signal an airplane that's flying around. I was almost hysterical because I couldn't communicate with this guy, but I finally got the message across and they opened the radio up to us. They told us to come close inshore and they sent a cutter to meet us. I remember we got in pretty close because the water turned from blue to green.

The accommodations were very good aboard the merchant ships. Every week the steward's department would give us two sheets, a pillow case, a spread, and books of matches. They'd do our laundry once a week. The Navy issues you a hammock, two blankets, and a mattress but I never slept in the hammock after boot camp. The food on the merchant ship was fantastic. You were served by a mess boy. In the morning you ordered scrambled eggs, or whatever else you wanted. At night you had a choice of meats and vegetables. Then, at about eight o'clock at night, an enormous platter of coldcuts was put in the refrigerator for guys going on duty. There were always gallons of coffee waiting when you went on and off watch. All in all, living conditions were better on the merchant ships than on Navy ships. We weren't as crowded; laundry and other services were provided, and the food was better.

We were on a convoy coming back to the States when VE-Day happened. After they announced it the convoy got a little loose. The commodore wasn't on top of it and the ships were not closing up as they should. There was an English ship directly behind us, one of the Fort ships. We used to call them that because they were named for Fort this and Fort that. All of a sudden, boom! and the Fort ship is hit. It's daytime and everybody takes off like a bird, going full steam and forming up close again with the destroyers darting back and forth looking for the sub and running back to the ship that's hit. They never found the sub.

This happened just a day or two after VE-Day; the German High Command had already ordered the subs to turn themselves in. This guy was probably on his way to turn himself in and was just nasty enough to say, "I may as well get rid of my torpedoes, what the hell, I'll get me one more." It's kind of strange to think about living through four years of war and then catching it after the danger's supposed to be over. I wasn't afraid, but it sure made me wonder about a lot of things.

I think that fear or the absence of fear is really dependent on age. When you're younger you mostly want to get in on the action. You figure that if anything happens to you, your family and maybe a few other people will miss you, but you're not thinking, "What is my kid going to do? What is my wife going to do?" The single men didn't have these questions preying on their minds. It's pretty clean in the Navy. If you're going to get it, you're going to get it quick. It was all anticipation but it was never realized. A nineteen-year-old kid trapped at Bastogne or in the Battle of Midway with planes crashing on the deck and fires all over the place might have a different attitude. If you're in a real mess the feelings of fear might be different. Anyway I never particularly felt any fear—I think I was too young to feel it—but I've seen guys who were in their 30s and had families, they were practically paralyzed by it. You only feel fear if someone at home is going to suffer. I especially remember one night when we were in the Mediterranean. Our holds were full of ammunition and there was a radio broadcast from Germany—I don't think it was Axis Sally, but someone like that—that said, "Benjamin Brewster, we know where you are and we know you have ammunition on board, and we're coming over tonight."

After the broadcast, of course, we went on general quarters. I got exhilarated every time we went on general quarters; it was exciting to me, like an adventure. But I was in a gun bucket with an older guy who was almost breaking down. He was sweating and trembling and wondering why the hell we were sitting there and when the Germans would come over and what would happen to us. Eventually some planes were spotted, but our Air Force had pretty good control of the Mediterranean by then and they didn't get anywhere near us.

I spent nearly four years on sea duty and was never torpedoed, though I saw many ships that were, and I was never on a ship that sank a U-boat, though I spent plenty of time searching and depthcharging them. I suppose my time in the Navy was uneventful compared to what happened to other guys, but I don't think of it that way.

One of the great experiences in the Navy was meeting guys from all over the country. It was my first association with guys from the South, and at first they scared me. They were mostly hillbillies, rough and ready guys who were young and uneducated. They were different from me and I couldn't get a peg on them. They had a boisterous type of humor. When I got to know them better I realized that they weren't going to do you any harm, they just had this wild manner of having fun.

I also got to know guys who were 30 or 33 years old who had enlisted in the Navy. Now you're 17 and your buddy Jim is 30, and you have a hell of a time calling him Jim, because up to then you'd called anyone that age "Mister." All of a sudden now he's your messmate and your drinking buddy. You begin to find out about people and about life because you're thrown into a situation with people from all over, with different ideas and ideals. Your own beliefs and ideals are being challenged.

You also realized that age doesn't necessarily make somebody smart. You find out how really dumb some people are. It was a great shock coming out of Jersey City—which was then 85 percent Catholic, and where we lived a very ghetto-type life with the Church at the center—to find out that guys did things that you'd been brought up to believe were so horrible. It was an even bigger shock to find out that you liked these guys anyway. The Navy was a great education for me. I wasn't bored. It was more fun than anything else, and it sure was better than standing on street corners.

7

PEARL HARBOR:
December 7, 1941

Charles Merdinger

As we got toward the top of the thing, I could smell fresh air for the first time in all those hours. And that was the greatest blessing. I had never felt anything so wonderful as that breath of fresh air. But when we got out on the ship's deck and looked around, it seemed as if there were just dead bodies everywhere. We got out and looked all over the harbor, and you've never seen anything like it. . . . Just ships on fire everywhere you looked.

—Captain Charles Merdinger, U.S.N.

Pearl Harbor: December 7, 1941

"Hello NBC . . . Hello NBC . . . this is WKCU in Honolulu, Hawaii. I am speaking from the roof of the Advertiser Publishing Company building. We have witnessed this morning a distant view of a battle off Pearl Harbor. . . ."

This eyewitness report was the first news that most Americans heard about Pearl Harbor. Although the actual attack was a complete surprise, the outbreak of war with Japan was not unexpected. Since Japan is an island nation with relatively few natural resources, she depends on overseas sources for raw materials and foreign markets where she can sell her manufactured goods. In the days before World War II, the overseas sources and markets she wanted—Indochina, Malaya, Burma; and the East Indies—were all possessions of the European colonial powers.

When Commodore Matthew Perry signed a treaty in 1854 opening trade between Japan and the United States, he set in motion one of the most remarkable transformations in modern history. When Perry arrived in Japan, he found a conservatively governed feudal society that had chosen to shut itself off from contact with the outside world. But the Japanese found themselves to be adept students of technology and foreign commerce and, by the early 1900's, they had achieved a level of economic and military development that enabled them to win the Russo-Japanese war decisively.

Japan studied and learned from the West in order to compete with it, but was selective in the lessons it brought home. The result was a curious blend of industrial and military technology adapted to fit into a rich and ancient cultural tradition. An important part of that tradition was the samurai warrior, and it was a group of young modern-day samurai that provided the leadership and the energy that eventually led to Japan's economic and political rise. These men were nationalists and militarists, and they felt themselves ready to stand toe-to-toe in competition with the West. They constituted a "war" faction within the government and, in opposition to the more moderate "peace" faction then in power, they precipitated the expansion of Japanese interests in Manchuria into an undeclared war with China.

At the time there were 74 million Japanese packed into the home islands, an area smaller than the size of California. It had long been a dream of the war faction to create a Japanese Empire that would extend from Manchuria and China all the way to Southeast Asia and the Dutch East Indies. Under the guise of an "Asia for the Asians" policy, the Japanese appealed to the anticolonial aspirations of Asian nationalists by developing a political and economic program called the "Greater East Asian Co-Prosperity Sphere." The militarists had developed, in theory, at least, a very definite plan to achieve their goals. It required the destruction of the U.S. Navy's Pacific Fleet, followed by the rapid seizure of Thailand, Burma, Malaya, Singapore, the Philippines, and the Dutch East Indies before the United States could oppose these moves.

The moderates strongly opposed this plan, but they were

unable to prevent its being carried out. President Roosevelt also opposed Japan's military adventure in China, which had been going on since 1937. In order to pressure the Japanese into withdrawing from China, Roosevelt froze all Japanese assets in the United States in July 1940. He followed this by imposing an embargo on the shipment of all vital materials to Japan. These moves infuriated the war faction, who felt that they had sufficient provocation to implement their military plan. The moderates, in turn, insisted that efforts be made to negotiate a settlement.

By late 1941 the negotiations in Washington were deadlocked and going nowhere. The moderate Japanese government was forced to resign and was replaced by a new one dominated by the militarists. France and Holland had been overrun by Germany and Britain was fighting for her life. The militarists knew that the rich far eastern territories, which they wanted for Japan, could not be successfully defended by the European powers who controlled them. It was time to strike.

The attack on Pearl Harbor had been carefully planned to the last detail. Six carriers with a protective screen of warships and submarines were ready to strike. It remained only to set a firm date for the action. This was done on December 2. The fact that the attack was carried out with complete surprise has always rankled Americans because it didn't seem morally right or sporting to "sneak up" on an opponent. However the element of surprise is an accepted and even admired aspect of Bushido, Japan's feudal code of honor.

In retrospect it is possible to wonder why the Navy and the Air Force were caught flat-footed, why radar contacts weren't followed up, why an explicit warning was not sent sooner from Washington. The fact is that the attack on Pearl Harbor was a spectacular success for the Japanese. It lasted only a few hours, but set United States naval power back two years. Eighteen warships were lost or damaged. Six battleships—the Arizona, California, Nevada, Oklahoma, Tennessee, and West Virginia—were sunk or beyond repair. 350 aircraft were destroyed, and over 3,000 men were killed. The naval base in Hawaii, once the symbol of American strength, was reduced to a sea of flames.

Charles J. Merdinger was a young officer aboard the USS

Arizona when the attack occurred. It was a Sunday morning, and peacetime Honolulu was lazily beginning to enjoy a day of rest.

Captain Charles Merdinger, U.S.N.

The first thing that I was aware of was the alarm clanging. This wasn't unusual because we were always being subjected to "man overboard" drill, or fire drill or something else at odd times on the *Arizona*. So I thought it was a drill when I first heard the alarm. It was Sunday morning and I was sleeping in. I was intending to go to church about a half hour later so this was going to be my late day for sleeping in, and it was almost eight o'clock.

I heard the alarm and decided to get into my clothes early. I had just put on one sock and was putting on the second when, all of a sudden, I heard a boom! and a rat-tat-tat—and all of a sudden the whole place seemed to erupt, and a fellow ran outside my room and said, "It's the real thing! It's the Japs!" So I put on my slippers and my dungarees and my officer's hat, and I went to my battle station about five decks below the main deck. That was the last I ever saw of my room, because just then a bomb landed and we started to sink, and I went right down with the ship since, as I say, I was five decks below the main deck.

We knew we were sunk, and we knew we were under water pressure because the plates were beginning to go on top of us and water was beginning to drip from the overhead. So we knew we were flooded above. In essence, we were in a big air bubble. But then the water started coming in through the door by which we entered. And it was really coming in. The gaskets were giving way, and now it was swirling around our ankles. I called out to the executive officer and told him it was impossible for us to hold this more than a few minutes longer, and we requested permission to secure and someone said "Yes, go ahead!"

So I gave the word and everybody took off his phones and wrapped them up the way they always do and put them on the wall in the normal places—we always put them away. This with the water rushing past everybody's feet. And yet they were so well trained that they did it exactly the way they'd done it a hundred times before. They put those phones right back in the regular slot.

As we got toward the top of the thing, I could smell fresh air for the first time in all those hours. And that was the greatest blessing. I had never felt anything so wonderful as that breath of fresh air. But when we got out on the ship's deck and looked around, it seemed as if there were just dead bodies everywhere. We got out and looked all over the harbor, and you've never seen anything like it. Just ships on fire everywhere you looked.

Our own ship was on fire, and smoke was coming out from every conceivable place. Although these were metal ships, we had built up several inches of paint on them, and the paint just burned for days. This was true all over the harbor. But the thing that remains with me to this day is the smell of diesel oil. It was all over the place—all over the water. As you know, a number of people had to swim through burning oil to get to safety. To this day, when I smell it I can still recall Pearl Harbor. The amazing thing about it all is that while the ship had been completely lost below the waterline, here above the waterline the guns were being manned. As a matter of fact, we continued on the ship through that night. All the wounded and dead were taken off, and we simply manned the guns. We were just another gun platform.

Unfortunately, that was the night that the Enterprise planes came in. I'll never forget that either. Somehow we knew that they were friendly, and yet somewhere in the harbor somebody started shooting at them, and the next thing you knew, everybody was firing, even our own ship. There was a kind of horrible beauty to this cone of fire that was coming up and shooting down our planes, and we did get a couple of planes. I recall our gunnery officer telling people, "Don't shoot! Stop shooting! They're friendly planes!" But there was a madness that seized everybody, and they just fired away.

I'd gone to my battle station in my slippers and they were soaked. They had sort of rotted off me so I put them someplace. And I hung up my dungarees to dry, and somebody walked off with those. So I ended up starting the war with just my hat.

8

CORREGIDOR: 1941-1942

Irving Strobing

My love to Pa, Joe, Sue, Mack,
Carrie, George and Paul. Also
to all family and friends.
God bless 'em all.

—Irving Strobing

Corregidor: 1941–1942

According to plan, the Japanese followed up Pearl Harbor with simultaneous attacks on Hong Kong, Malaya and the Philippines. It was expected that American and Filipino forces would defend the Philippines tenaciously and prevent Japanese occupation of the main islands. However, fighting there got off to a bad start when more than one hundred planes—half of the Air Force in the Philippines—were destroyed on the ground at Clark Field just ten hours after Pearl Harbor. It has never been explained why, in spite of advance warning, the planes were caught on the ground bunched together wingtip to wingtip.

Shortly after the bombing, a powerful Japanese force landed on the island of Luzon. There, 50,000 land troops, 6,000 of them Americans, were under the command of General Douglas MacArthur. Because his troops were greatly outnumbered by the invading Japanese, MacArthur decided that it would be futile to fragment his force in an attempt to defend the many Philippine Islands.

Instead, he concentrated his strength by withdrawing to the Peninsula of Bataan and the island fortress of Corregidor, both in Manila Bay, to await reinforcements. He did not fully appreciate that after the losses they took at Pearl Harbor, the Navy was not in a position to send aid. On December 29, the Japanese launched a major offensive; by January 2, 1942, Manila had fallen; and on February 22, President Roosevelt ordered MacArthur to leave the Philippines for Australia for security reasons. On March 11, the General and his family left Corregidor by PT boat and, promising to return, he turned his besieged command over to General Jonathan Wainwright.

Japan extended its control over the Pacific at an astonishing rate. Guam and Wake Island were captured before Christmas, Hong Kong fell on Christmas Day, and Singapore surrendered on February 15, 1942. Even Australia, which had been thought safe from attack, was bombed in February. The Allies fought and lost a naval engagement in the Java Sea in late February, and by March 9, the Dutch East Indies (present day Indonesia) were in Japanese hands.

General Wainwright's troops held out on the Bataan Peninsula until early April. By then their rations had been exhausted and they were eating dogs, mules, monkeys, and snakes. On April 8, Wainwright ordered the 37,000 troops still on the Peninsula to abandon it. Those who could, made for Corregidor; others escaped to fight as guerillas; still others surrendered. Corregidor held out for another month. But on May 6, battered from constant bombing and shelling, Corregidor surrendered. The Philippines were now in Japanese hands.

On May 5, 1942, a final message was sent from Corregidor. It was transmitted by a Signal Corps wireless operator named Irving Strobing. There is no record of what became of him.

Irving Strobing:

They are not near yet. We are waiting for God only knows what. How about a chocolate soda?

Not many—not near yet. Lots of heavy fighting going on. We've only got about one hour twenty minutes before we may have to give up—by noon. We don't know yet.

They are throwing men and shells at us, and we may not be able to stand it. They have been shelling us faster than you can count. We've got about 55 minutes, and I feel sick at my stomach. I am really low down. They are around now smashing rifles. They bring in the wounded every minute. It is a horrible sight. We will be waiting for you guys to help. This is the only thing, I guess, that can be done. General Wainwright is a right guy, and we are willing to go on for him. But shells were dropping all night, faster than hell. Damage terrific—too much for guys to take. Enemy heavy cross-shelling and bombing. They have got us all around and from sky.

Just made broadcast to Manila to arrange meeting for surrender, talk made by General Beebe. I can't say much, can't think at all. I can hardly think. Say, I have 60 pesos you can have for this weekend. The white flag is up. Everyone is bawling like a baby. They're piling dead, wounded soldiers in our tunnel. I'm vomiting. Arms weak from pounding key. Long hours, no rest, short rations, tired. I know now how a mouse feels caught in a trap, waiting for guys to come along, finish it up. Got a treat: canned pineapple. Opening it with Signal Corps knife.

My name Irving Strobing. Get this to my mother: Mrs. Minnie Strobing, 605 Darby Street, Brooklyn, New York. They are got get along O.K. Get in touch with them soon as possible. Message: My love to Pa, Joe, Sue, Mac, Carrie, George, and Paul. Also to all family and friends. God bless 'em all. Hope they be there when I come home. Tell Joe wherever he is, give 'em hell for us. I love you all. God bless and keep you. Love. Sign my name and tell my mother how you heard from me. Stand by . . .

9

JAPANESE-AMERICAN INTERNMENT: 1942-1945

James Kazato, Roy Yano

When a person cannot have privacy, that is really bad.

—James Kazato

Even now, years after the war is over, we still have certain unsolved questions in our minds about the Constitution—how is it possible to have American citizens in concentration camps?

—Roy Yano

Japanese-American Internment: 1942—45

The Japanese first started coming to the United States in large numbers in the 1890's. Because they were willing to work long hours for low pay, American workers and farmers felt their jobs and their earning levels threatened. They resented the Japanese and opposed their presence.

Hostility reached such a level that, by 1905, the labor movement in San Francisco formed the Asiatic Exclusion League to keep all Orientals from entering the United States. Three years later. pressure from the League and similar organizations influenced the federal government to enter into a "gentlemen's agreement" with Japan not to issue passports to laborers (except for those who were formerly resident in the U.S.). Although this greatly reduced the number of Japanese entering the United States, those already here continued to suffer both personal and institutional discrimination.

The Alien Land Act, passed by the California state legislature in 1913, forbade Japanese to own any land in that state (although the Japanese got around this by buying land in the name of their American-born children). Another act barred aliens from obtaining commercial fishing licenses. To these measures were added the discriminatory provisions of the United States naturalization laws.

It was in this atmosphere that first-generation Japanese-Americans, called "Issei," raised their American-born children, called "Nisei," to accept the United States as their new country and to adopt its ways. But the United States didn't accept them. Animosity toward Japanese-Americans was quickly rekindled by the flames of Pearl Harbor.

On the night of December 7, 1941, the FBI and police picked up six hundred Issei community leaders, organization heads, and people who worked for Japanese trade organizations. They were all jailed until they could be sent to internment camps where most of them remained for the duration of the war.

On February 19, 1942, President Roosevelt signed Executive Order #9066 which called for the removal of all persons of Japanese ancestry from the West Coast and their relocation in internment camps. The ostensible reason for this was to protect the West Coast from spies and saboteurs.

As a result of this order, thousands of Japanese-American families were forced to give up their homes, their farms, and their businesses, often at substantial economic loss. They were transported to hastily constructed relocation centers and internment camps in desolate parts of Arizona, California, Colorado, Idaho, Utah, and Wyoming. They lived behind barbed wire, under the surveillance of armed guards, for more than three years. Nearly 120,000 people were sent to live in these camps. Sixty percent of them were American citizens.

Despite the discrimination they suffered before and during the war, most Japanese-Americans displayed unfailing loyalty to the United States. There was not a single incident of sabotage. On the contrary, Nisei with particular language skills were recruited for military intelligence work. On the day the army announced that they would accept Nisei volunteers, more than 1,200 signed up.

Before the war was over nearly 18,000 had joined the Army. No Nisei ever deserted. In Italy the famed 442nd Infantry, made up entirely of Nisei, lost three times its original strength, and was awarded 3,000 Purple Hearts with 500 oak leaf clusters, 810 Bronze Stars, 342 Silver Stars, 47 Distinguished Service Crosses, and 17 Legion of Merit awards. Bill Mauldin wrote of the 442nd that "no combat unit in the Army could exceed them in loyalty, hard work, courage, and sacrifice . . . their casualty rates were appalling." Yet, when a Nisei who had lost a leg in Italy visited San Francisco during the war, he was beaten.

It was not until after the war, when people's attitudes had begun to change, that the Alien Land Act was declared unconstitutional and the law preventing Orientals from becoming naturalized citizens was removed. But these official acts of conciliation could not erase the experience of internment from the memories of those who had lived through it.

James Kazato, who had come to the United States in 1919, was one of the first 600 Japanese-Americans taken into custody. He was held in a detention camp for enemy aliens. Roy Yano came here with his parents in 1917. He was sent to what the government euphemistically called a "relocation center." To the people who were forced to live in them, these relocation centers were America's concentration camps.

James Kazato:

When the war broke out, all of us were really shocked. But what shocked us—what shocked me most—was that all of us, regardless of whether we had American citizenship or not, were put into concentration camp. If they had taken just the noncitizens, then it would have been all right. But I say to myself, why do they have to take all the American citizens? Because I knew that those born in the country, regardless of color, were American citizens. At that time Japan and Germany and the Italians were allies. Now I say to myself, well, if they are to take Japanese people, why not the Italians and Germans, too? That was my big question.

We were given very short notice. The government gave us just about ten days to pack and leave. I didn't have American citizenship. I wasn't given that chance—to be naturalized. So, as far as I'm concerned it was all right. But for my wife—she was an American citizen, and so are both my daughters, who were born here in San Francisco.

The government did not guarantee whether we could come back or not. They didn't promise us anything. So I told my wife, perhaps the good thing would be to sell our furniture and with that buy a bit of food and medicine and things like that. Since our younger daughter was only four months old and the older one was four years old, and we didn't know if there was doctors or hospitals in the camp, we took in as much medicine and baby food as possible.

Of course, I did have a number of nice friends. They came and gave us moral support, you might say. But at the same time there were a group of vultures who came in knowing that we had to leave. They came to buy our furniture in a way that was almost giving it away. They try to buy off your furniture for 50 cents or a dollar, something like that. We had this brand-new mangle. Now we had two children, and I thought it would be nice if my wife can use that mangle for her ironing work. So we bought this brand-new mangle about a month before this. It was still new, we used it only a few times. And this man said he'd give us ten dollars. I said—by that time I got kind of mad—I said," I would rather give it to someone who would just say thank you. Why should I give you for ten dollars?" So he said, "Well, I give you fifty dollars." By that time I was so mad, I said, "Get out!" I told him I'd sooner give it away free to anyone who would appreciate it and say thank you. But I don't want his dirty money. So I just kick him out.

We were sent to Topaz, Utah. That is about 200 miles directly south of Salt Lake City. I think there were close to 9,000 people in the camp, mostly from San Francisco. The living conditions were quite different from our home. Topaz was one mile square and within that there were 42 blocks. Each block consisted of barracks. Each barracks had about six rooms. And each family lived in one single room. Of course, if a party had a large family, actually he was given a larger room. Whereas a single man or a couple with no children were given a much smaller room. There were four of us.

My room was, I would say, 12 by 12 feet. Well, of course, there were just beds there, a small table, and a small bench—that was about it.

Now out of each twelve barracks, one was for dining and one was set aside for the shower rooms. So we had to eat out every time. We go to dining room where we had to line up. That's where we had our breakfast, lunch, and dinner.

When we first went to the camp, these barracks were built in such a hurry that there was no paved road or anything like that. It was just full of dust. It was built in the desert—every time we walked, all that powder would fly up, and from top to bottom we were covered with that white powder. And inside our room, too—no matter how many times you dust off, in a half hour the inside was full of dust. Eventually they watered the places, and later on they put a little oil on the dust so it wasn't too bad—say, maybe about a year or two later.

All the work was done by Japanese people who volunteered. Those who worked were paid. Like myself—I wanted to do something else other than barbering. But since I was a barber, most of my friends from San Francisco asked me that I should keep on as a barber. So I did, together with other barbers from other places. We were given $12 a month, but using our tools and all that, we thought that wasn't enough, so we asked for a little raise. So we got $16. I think those professional people, like doctors, were given $18. Naturally, with what little money we were given in those days, I bought whatever I can for the children. We were able to get out of the camp—not all of us. A few people represented the blocks, and they were asked to go and buy a few things.

The first thing we did in the camp, we built our churches. The Buddhist people got together and built their Buddhist church, and the Christian people built their own church. The older Nisei, who were out of college or high school, started teaching the children, and we set up schools.

Pretty soon the young people started playing baseball, and this and that, and it was just like outside. Older high school children had baseball games with outside teams. Like Caucasian people—we invited them to have a game with us.

To me the worst thing I experienced in the camp was that we didn't have privacy. For instance, each barracks had six families. And each was given one room, whether large or small. The barracks was built in such a way that there was a wide-open ceiling. So what happens is, when someone at the end would light up, the whole barracks would light up. And people with teenagers—what would happen in one room with a father and a mother and these children in the same room? If it's an overnight trip or something, it's all right. But we stayed there three and a half years.

When a person cannot have privacy, that is really bad. For myself, my children were young— it didn't matter too much. But I felt sorry for the people with teenage children. I remember when we got into the camp that a lot of bread and vegetables were carted in with cardboard boxes and things like that. You ought to see those people go after those cardboard boxes. We used them to make partitions, so as to make a little privacy. A lot of us had to adjust, but living under those conditions didn't do too good for the young people.

The mood of the Japanese changed considerably in those times. They adjusted themselves, knowing that they won't be able to get out. Of course, we were told that if we would like to get out voluntarily to outside of the camp, we were able to—other than to the Pacific Coast or Atlantic Coast. I don't know about the other people but, as far as I'm concerned, my children were still small and I thought staying in the camp was better for me simply because of the rumors. So, naturally, I wanted my family to stay because we knew that being in the camp we would be safe.

When the war was over I was very happy. But still we had to stay in the camp. But later on we were told that we can go back to California. By that time my landlord, an Italian fellow—he was a very nice man—he kept this barber shop for me. During the wartime, all these three and a half years, he pulled the shades down and he just waited for me. And when he heard that we were able to come back to California, I had a letter from him saying, "Well, James, your shop is ready for you to open up, so you gotta come back." And I was really happy about it.

After we came back I would say I was one of the very few

fortunate ones. Here I had my shop already waiting for me, and I was one of the very first ones to come back. I opened up and there were hardly any Japanese barbers then, so it kept me awfully busy.

Roy Yano:

When the war broke out in 1941 I was in Texas. It happened all of a sudden. I remember I heard the news on the radio and was totally surprised. I didn't expect anything like it to happen between Japan and America. The FBI picked me up that same night and put me in jail.

I didn't know why, and they explained to me that I was an enemy alien. At that time Japanese people who were born in Japan were ineligible to become United States citizens. So when the war started we were enemy aliens.

They didn't apologize for picking me up and putting me in jail. They explained that since the war had started between the two countries it was their duty to put us in jail. We didn't argue. There were some Italians and Germans in the same jail. First we stayed in a city jail in Texas, then they sent us to a military establishment in San Antonio. Conditions weren't so bad because we didn't stay there too long. Then they established some kind of concentration camps for enemy aliens, not only Japanese, but Italians and Germans as well. So they sent us to Lordsburg, New Mexico, where there was a detention camp. At that time I was not married yet, I was single.

I had friends who came from Japan and worked for the Japanese Consulate or the foreign trade information office. They had to go back because they were sent from Japan especially for the job. I worked for the foreign trade office too, but I had a choice to stay here or go back because I had the status of permanent resident of the United States. I chose to stay here.

As an ineligible alien I was a Japanese subject. So when the war came, naturally I was considered an enemy alien and was sent to a regular concentration camp. We were sent to the camp in New Mexico in Army transport vehicles. When I was picked up, some of my American friends telephoned me, and others gave me notes of sympathy and so on, but not many of them came to help me because there wasn't much they could do. My car and all the personal property in my apartment were confiscated by the government and stored in a government warehouse.

At the camp in New Mexico we had about five thousand Japanese people from all over the United States—Hawaii, Alaska, Texas, New York—but mostly from the Pacific Coast. And we lived in barracks under the control of the U. S. Army. There wasn't much furniture in the barracks. We had a bed, a couple of chairs and tables to write letters, and a mess hall where we could cook our own breakfast, lunch, and dinner.

The food was not bad. But the majority of people craved for rice instead of meat. We asked for rice and we got it, but they cut down the meat.

Concentration camp life was very much like the relocation camps for Japanese-Americans evacuated from the Pacific Coast. The only difference is that the camp I was in was not for Americans. No American citizens were in the camp, only Japanese subjects. We were not prisoners of war. But prisoners of war rules and regulations were applied for daily living. The camp was run in accordance with the Geneva Convention Regulations for detainees.

There was a daily routine. We woke up in the morning at six o'clock. We had breakfast between six-thirty and seven. Before lunch we were supposed to clean the compound, and later on we volunteered for some type of work around the camp, cleaning and other things. Later on we were given a certain section of land on which to grow our own vegetables, so we had time to spend raising vegetables which we used in our kitchen. Provisions were supplied by the Army. We had a kitchen for every section of between seventy-five and a hundred people and regular rations were delivered every day.

We didn't know what was going to happen next, so the general feeling in the camp was anxiety and insecurity. The morale was very high because we knew that we were well protected from anything that might have happened out there. The camp was way out in the desert and nobody came to bother us. We didn't have any reason to be afraid that anything would happen to us. But we didn't know what was going to happen tomorrow or the next day.

We were mostly men separated from their families. So the first concern was what the family was doing back home. Back in San Francisco, Los Angeles, or Hawaii, or even Alaska.

There was much breaking up of families. When a man with a family was apprehended and sent to camp like that, he couldn't carry on business and he didn't know what to do. So there was much anxiety and worrying, and every day there was writing home and asking them how they're getting along.

Some people experienced a bitter resentment when they were picked up by the FBI. They didn't know why they were being apprehended, so they argued back and forth and had a very bitter experience. They had a very bitter feeling against the United States. As for myself, I thought of the United States as my second home and I lived according to the belief that I would spend the rest of my life here. I thought of the war just as a temporary thing. I was in a camp for Japanese aliens who were suspected of loyalty to Japan because they were officers of Japanese organizations in the Japanese communities.

But there was another type of camp in the United States at the same time. These were camps for the detention of all Japanese-American people whether American citizens of Japanese ancestry, or Japanese subjects. All Japanese-American people living on the Pacific Coast were evacuated to relocation camps. That was done against their constitutional rights as American citizens.

Even now, years after the war is over, we still have certain unsolved questions in our minds about the Constitution—how was it possible to have American citizens in concentration camps? I sometimes wonder why we didn't protest this at the time. But we couldn't have done that because people were put in the camps by executive order of the President and we didn't have any way of protesting or demonstrating. All around the camp was a barbed-wire fence, and every hundred yards there was a watchtower with American soldiers with loaded guns and sometimes machine guns, so we didn't have any chance for a protest.

When the FBI or American soldiers came to pick us up, the first thought when they knocked at the door is, if I say no, they will just shoot us to death. We knew they were ordered to shoot. Once we were in the camps, I don't think we ever feared for our lives. We knew we would come out of there some day sooner or later, but we didn't know how long. Maybe two years, three years, some day we would come out. That was for sure, we knew that.

There was some propaganda that Japan would win the war, and if Japan won the war, well, we would take over the United States. The Japanese government would come over and we were going to have a big time. That was one rumor, of course. We took it as a joke. But there was such rough talk in the camp. Of course, since the war, this executive order was revoked and declared unconstitutional, so we have had some opportunity to educate the public that such unconstitutional racism hurts not only one group of people but the whole United States. We have certain elements in our society that have hatred against other groups of people because of difference in color or culture or something. When you have such a hatred, it's not healthy. Certainly it's not safe for anybody to live in such a society.

When I came to the United States I was educated in an American school and went to college, so I consider myself an American. In fact, I was naturalized in 1952, so I'm a bona fide American citizen. But long before that I would do anything for the United States, even risk my life.

When I was in the camp I volunteered to help win the war for the United States. I had reasons for that. The first reason was I didn't like the Emperor system—it was not good for the people of Japan. Another thing is I felt loyal to the country I adopted. By that time I was married and had children who were United States citizens so I tried to make them proud by volunteering to do something to win the war. And the United States government took me as a member of the Office of Strategic Services—the OSS. It was a secret service similar to the CIA, established by the executive order of President Roosevelt. I was involved in psychological warfare and was sent to Calcutta, India, for fieldwork. And that's where I was when the war ended. I'm very proud that I did something to win the war for the United States even though at the time I was a Japanese subject. After the war I went to Tokyo as a translater and interpreter for General MacArthur's headquarters.

10

NORTH AFRICA AND ITALY: 1942-1945

Gerard Hacquebard

"I've been 'ere since 1936, I 'ave, and look at the time now, it's 1941!"

With that, the sergeant rolled up his shirtsleeves and looked at one of three watches to make sure it was 1941. I think the watches were purloined; in fact, I know they were, from felled German pilots. I did it myself in later years in the desert—pinched watches. Very naughty. This particular Coldstream sergeant was a bit of a lad in his way. . . . Among other things, he taught us how to wait for a troop train without becoming too impatient. After the first three hours of waiting in the hot Egyptian sun, he taught us to sing what was to become our usual song of waiting: "Waiting, waiting, waiting. Always bloody-well waiting. Waiting, waiting, waiting." If you hear a thousand men singing that in unison and some of them happen to be Welshmen and some happen to be Scots, it can really be quite stirring.

—Gerard Hacquebard

North Africa and Italy: 1942—45

World War II was truly a global war. Not only were the combatants from literally dozens of countries, but what happened in one part of the world had a major impact on the war in other parts of the world. It was for this reason that Hitler signed his nonaggression pact with Stalin. He did not want to fight Russia in the east while he was fighting France and England in the west.

Even though Hitler failed to defeat Britain before moving

against Russia, he knew that the British would not be strong enough to open a second front for quite some time. Since he believed that he could defeat Russia quickly, he began to make the necessary preparations. He pressured Hungary, Rumania, and Slovakia into joining the Tripartite (Axis) pact and then quickly began to concentrate troops near these countries' and Poland's borders with Russia. But his strategy for the impending invasion was disrupted by his Italian allies.

On September 14, 1940, Benito Mussolini's forces in North Africa launched an offensive from the Italian colony of Libya against the British in Egypt. On October 28, Mussolini invaded Greece without telling Hitler of his plan. The Greeks counterattacked within a week, and by mid-November there were no Italians left in Greece. Meanwhile, the British had stopped the Italian drive in Egypt and in December, with a force of only 30,000 men, they counterattacked an Italian army of 210,000. Within two months the British had advanced five hundred miles along the coast and across the desert. They had destroyed an army six times their own size, capturing 400 tanks in the process. But at Benghazi the British advance stopped.

Hitler had to bail Mussolini out in Greece in order to protect his position in the Balkans and secure his southern flank for the coming Russian campaign. He invaded Yugoslavia and Greece on April 6, 1941, in campaigns he hoped would be completed before the coming attack on Russia. Yugoslavia fell in a week. Greece, aided by fifty thousand British and Commonwealth troops sent from North Africa, held on until the end of the month. Had the British been able to pursue their North African offensive instead of diverting men to Greece, they would almost certainly have cleared out the Italians. Instead, the Greek campaign ended with the British getting most of their forces away in a Dunkirk-like evacuation.

Meanwhile, Hitler also had to come to Mussolini's rescue in North Africa. He did this early in 1941 by sending Field Marshal Erwin Rommel "the Desert Fox," and his elite Afrika Korps to aid the demoralized Italians. In less than two months they pushed the Allies eastward from Tripoli all the way back inside Egypt to a point less than one hundred miles from the Suez Canal and the vital port of Alexandria. However, in order to threaten Rommel's flank and disrupt his lines of supply, an Australian division fortified and held the port of Tobruk behind enemy lines. In desert warfare, where mobility and safe supply routes are everything, Tobruk was a painful thorn in Rommel's side.

For more than a year Rommel's Afrika Korps and the British and Commonwealth "Desert Rats" pushed and chased each other across the desert. There were long advances and retreats but no decisive battles. Both armies were plagued by shortages of supplies and, as they advanced, the difficulty of getting what fuel, water, ammunition, and food there was to their units in the field. Because both sides saw the North African campaign as having less strategic importance than the fighting on other fronts, they scrimped on supplying their desert armies.

In June, 1941, much of the Luftwaffe was diverted from the Mediterranean to bases in Europe in preparation for the invasion of Russia, which began on June 22. Air power was essential to both sides in protecting the ships that supplied their armies in North Africa and in attacking those of the enemy. The withdrawal of German planes put Rommel at a disadvantage because supplies being shipped across the Mediterranean could not be adequately protected from attack. The island stronghold of Malta provided the Allies with an air and sea base in the middle of the Mediterranean that was so effective that, early in 1942, Rommel persuaded Hitler to divert a strong air fleet from the Russian front to Sicily in order to bomb Malta. For months the Germans bombed the island several times every day. The base survived, but its effectiveness was reduced. On the other hand, the removal of planes from the Russian front cost Hitler dearly.

By late May, Rommel had enough supplies to launch a major offensive. He broke through the Allied lines and forced them to withdraw all the way to El Alamein. The most successful tactic used by both sides in North Africa was that of outflanking the enemy. The endless expanse of flat, open country was almost like an ocean and provided room for enormous sweeping maneuvers. But at El Alamein, the British knew that they could not be outflanked because their position was bounded on the north by the sea and on the south by a salt marsh at the bottom of a line of canyon-like cliffs. Tanks could neither maneuver in the marsh, nor climb the cliffs. The fifty-mile El Alamein front was the setting for the final head-on confrontation of the war in North Africa.

For months Rommel and the British staged a series of unsuccessful attacks and counterattacks that weakened Rommel's reserve strength at a time when he was having a harder time getting resupplied than the British. Churchill, desperate for a victory at a time when things looked extremely bleak for the Allies, sent Generals Sir Harold Alexander and Bernard Montgomery to North Africa to change the inconclusive sparring into a decisive victory.

By the middle of October, Montgomery felt that his men had been adequately trained and that he had sufficient superiority of manpower and materiel to begin his offensive. But by then the German and Italian troops were dug into very strong positions. Finally, on the night of October 23, under the light of a full moon, a thousand artillery pieces opened fire. Behind the barrage, men from England, Scotland, Australia, New Zealand, India, and South Africa advanced through the minefields and began to overwhelm the enemy positions.

Day and night for ten days the Eighth Army made slow but steady progress. Montgomery took advantage of weakness where he found it, but avoided wasting resources where resistance was stubborn. By November 2, the Allies had driven three corridors through the German defense; Rommel seemed to realize that the battle was lost and made preparations to withdraw. But on the 3rd he received a message from Hitler forbidding retreat. Rommel nevertheless felt retreat necessary. El Alamein cost the Germans four divisions and the Italians five. The latter lost almost 60,000 men and most of their guns and tanks. It was a decisive victory for Montgomery.

On November 4 the British pursuit of Rommel began. It was the Eighth Army's final advance westward over a familiar route. In roughly 80 days they covered nearly 1,400 miles, snapping the whole way at Rommel's rear. The Battle of El Alamein was a major turning point in the war and Churchill was ecstatic at the victory.

On November 8, a few days after Rommel began his retreat, a strong Anglo-American force of more than one hundred thousand men under General Eisenhower landed fourteen hundred miles away in French North Africa. This Allied force, after landing in Morocco and Algeria, pushed eastward into Tunisia while the

Eighth Army drove the Germans westward into Tunisia. The plan was to crush them in a pincer movement between these two forces. But the Germans and Italians reacted quickly to the Allied plan. They occupied Tunisia and drew impressive reserve strength from nearby Sicily. The Germans were not willing to lose Tunisia without a fight. They even sent four hundred planes there from the Russian front. Throughout February and March Rommel mounted a series of counterattacks, among them a rather sharp defeat of the Americans in the Kasserine Pass. These actions slowed the Allies down, but did not stop them. On April 7 the Allied First and the British Eighth Armies linked up.

Rommel was quite ill, and as the Allied armies closed in he handed over his command and returned to Germany. On the 13th of May, 125,000 German troops and almost as many Italians surrendered. Almost three years from the time that Mussolini's armies attacked the British in Egypt, the war in North Africa was over. In all, the Germans and Italians had lost almost one million men killed or captured.

For the Allies the long struggle in the desert was invaluable. It bought them time to build up their strength and it tied up German resources that could have been used elsewhere. It gave Allied servicemen combat experience, and the generals a chance to learn from their failures and work out successful tactics for the invasion of Europe.

Roosevelt wanted to invade northern France, but the Allies were not yet ready for such an undertaking. Churchill wanted the attack to come from the Mediterranean. Both agreed that a 1943 invasion would build Allied momentum and help divert German forces from the Russian front. Finally they decided to invade Sicily. The landings there on July 10, 1943, caught the enemy off guard and were virtually unopposed.

The Sicily invasion had unforeseen consequences. The Italian people had become disillusioned with Mussolini and on July 25, two weeks after the landings, he was removed from office, arrested, and sent to prison. He had left Italy in a bad position to defend itself. A great many Italian soldiers had been killed or captured in North Africa; another 160,000 were killed or captured in Sicily; and nearly a million others were fighting along with the

Germans in Russia and Yugoslavia.

The first task of Mussolini's successor, Marshal Pietro Badoglio, was to make peace with the Allies on the best possible terms. He immediately began secret negotiations to persuade them to invade Italy in the north in order to prevent a long and damaging fight up from the south. The Allies agreed to the Italian surrender, but insisted on invading from the south. On September 3, the surrender of the Italian government was secretly signed.

On the same day, the invasion of Italy began. The Allies did not meet the resistance they expected, and advanced steadily northward. Badoglio had persuaded the Allies to keep Italy's surrender secret for five days, so that his troops could occupy airfields and other strategic positions and thus deny their use to the Germans, who were operating on the assumption that the Italians were still fighting on their side. Badoglio was unable to accomplish this in the time allotted, and asked Eisenhower for an extension of time. But Eisenhower distrusted Badoglio, refused the extension, and announced Italy's capitulation on September 8.

What Badoglio had hoped to avoid now took place. The Germans immediately occupied Rome's airfields and other key strategic positions. It became obvious that the Germans were going to fight to stay in Italy. When the Allies launched a major amphibious assault at Salerno, the Germans were waiting. Resistance was so stiff that the Allies were almost forced to evacuate, but a beachhead was established and they began their advance northward.

German strategy was to make the allies pay dearly for every foot of progress, using the mountainous terrain to defensive advantage. The advance north was split into two main thrusts flanking the Apennine mountain range that runs up the center of Italy: the American Fifth Army under General Mark Clark on the western side and the British Eighth Army under Montgomery on the eastern side of the range. The Allies had hoped to be in Rome by Christmas, but it was to take a great deal longer.

Months and months of tough mountain fighting lay ahead. The Germans used the terrain to establish one defense line after another. The Allied generals decided to attempt an amphibious landing as an alternative to their frontal attack. On January 22 the Allies landed at Anzio, sixty miles behind enemy lines, with the intent of cutting off German supply lines. The landing met with no resistance, but it took some time to consolidate the beachhead and by the time they were ready to move inland the advance met very heavy resistance. The Germans organized a strong counterattack and almost threw the Allies into the sea. By then it was obvious that the intended objective of the Anzio assault—to assist the forces attacking the Gustav Line—had failed. After fighting to break through the line for five months the Allies were finally successful and on May 18, 1944, Monte Cassino was captured.

With the fall of Monte Cassino, the Germans withdrew to positions northwest of Rome. On June 4—two days before the D-Day landings in Normandy—the Allies entered Rome. The fighting in Italy continued as the Germans slowly withdrew to the north, moving from one defensive line to another. By early 1945 the Allies, facing the Germans in the mountains north of Florence, were actually outnumbered because many of their units had been diverted to France. Nonetheless, in April they renewed their attack and pushed the Germans across the Po River and into Austria. By April 30 the German armies in Italy were virtually eliminated as a fighting force.

It took nearly five years and some of the most bitter fighting of the war to drive the Germans out of North Africa and Italy. The men who did this suffered from the heat and lack of water in the desert, and from the cold and too much water in the mountains of Italy. As a member of the famed Grenadier Guards, Gerard Hacquebard fought in both of these campaigns. He was wounded four times, twice in North Africa and twice in Italy, yet he looks back on his experiences with an undamaged sense of humor. He is a real estate developer in New York City.

Gerard Hacquebard:

When I went to see a recruiting sergeant early in the war, he wanted me to apply for the Irish Guards. I said, "No! I want to be one of them!" I pointed to a huge poster on the wall showing a Grenadier Guards drummer. Without further ado, I placed my hand upon the Holy Bible and beseeched the King's shilling* and signed away my life, unbeknownst to me, for the next six years and eight months.

The Grenadier Guards are part of the Royal Family's household brigade of which there are five regiments. They stand guard at Buckingham Palace or wherever the Queen is in residence. The men of the Household Brigade are not only England's finest professional soldiers, but her finest fighting soldiers as well.

So here I am now, at Chelsea Barracks, in the Army, marching up and down the barracks square shouting out, "One, two, three. . . . One, two, three. . . . One, two, three!" After about a year and a half of training at the various Guards depots, I eventually found myself a member of the Sixth Battalion, Grenadier Guards.

Late in 1941 we found ourselves, a thousand men, aboard a troop ship en route to parts unknown. The orders for our destination were to be opened only after we were at sea. But since we were equipped with tropical uniforms and our vehicles were painted the hue of the desert sand, we had a good idea of where we were going. We knew at least that we were not going to the North Pole. We had been issued pith helmets, which even then were somewhat reminiscent of yesteryear in the British Army. We were on the high seas for three weeks as part of a forty-ship convoy. During this trip some of the ships were sunk by submarine torpedoes or aerial bombing in the Bay of Biscay and in the Indian Ocean. Sometimes even our own Royal Air Force would in vain fight off the fighter-bombers that would catch the slow ships at the tail end of the thirty-mile convoy. Happily, the ship we were on, a passenger liner whose name I forget, came through safely and landed us at a place called Durban, South Africa.

We were in Durban for four glorious weeks recuperating from the voyage and from the bombings and the warfare in London and the Spam and margarine and two pieces of bread per day per man,

*A shilling given by a recruiting officer to a recruit. Until 1879 the recruit's acceptance of it constituted a binding enlistment in the British Army. Since then the gesture has been symbolic.

and sausages we sometimes got that we thought were filled with sawdust. After four weeks of eggs on steak, bananas, oranges, strawberries and cream, beautiful girls, and beautiful motorcars to ride about in, we left Durban.

Again our orders were to be opened at sea, but we knew where we were going. We sailed for about two and a half weeks up the East Coast of Africa and the length of the Red Sea, one of the hottest areas in the world. Especially if you are aboard a troop ship. Finally, we arrived at Port Taufiq, Egypt, which is at the southern end of the Suez Canal. There we were met by an advance party of Coldstream and Scots Guards who had been serving garrison duty in Egypt, which was then a protectorate of the British government. They were caught by the war in 1939 just as they were about to go home at the end of their four-year term of duty.

"Where shall I put my kit bag, sergeant?"

"Who do you think you're talking to? Stand to attention when you talk to me! And where 'ave you been?"

"I've been in England, sergeant."

"I know that. You look like a lily-white to me. I've been 'ere since 1936, I 'ave, and look at the time now, it's 1941!"

With that, the sergeant rolled up his shirtsleeves and looked at one of three watches to make sure it was 1941. I think the watches were purloined; in fact, I know they were, from felled German pilots. I did it myself in later years in the desert—pinched watches. Very naughty. This particular Coldstream sergeant was a bit of a lad in his way, but humorous and good fun. Seeing all of these newly arrived soldiers who had been undernourished for a few years in wartime England, he was quite a good fellow and showed us what to do and how to get along.

Among other things, he taught us how to wait for a troop train without becoming too impatient. After the first three hours of waiting in the hot Egyptian sun, he taught us to sing what was to become our usual song of waiting: "Waiting, waiting, waiting. Always bloody-well waiting. Waiting, waiting, waiting." If you hear a thousand men singing that in unison and some of them happen to be Welshmen and some happen to be Scots, it can really be quite stirring. Eventually, there puffed into the station an old steam engine hauling about twelve wooden passenger carriages. This train whisked us away not into the North African desert as we expected, but about a thousand miles to the northwest, where we found ourselves a few days later encamped outside of Damascus, Syria, in a small Arab town.

We were warned while we **were** there to watch our rifles and always to chain them to our tent poles. If we had a "walking out pass" (leave) to travel by truck the forty miles to Damascus, we were advised to remove the bolts from our rifles so that if the Bedouins or the Druses—Arabs from the hills—were to sneak into camp and steal the rifles, they would be useless.

We were sent to Syria because at the time Churchill had a plan to strike through Syria, Turkey, and the Balkans and attack Hitler from what was then known as the "soft underbelly of Europe." That plan was never implemented and a year later we were suddenly sent to the North African desert where we had our first baptism of fire as part of the famed 201st Guards Brigade.

Our brother guardsmen of the 201st had suffered through desert warfare for more than two years as Field Marshal Rommel's Afrika Korps and the British Eighth Army chased each other back and forth across the desert between El Alamein, Sidi Barrani, Tobruk, Derna and Benghazi. The "Desert Fox" would push us one way, then we would push him back, until our supply lines got too long and became vulnerable. Then the Germans would bomb our supply lines and interrupt the flow of our petrol, water, food and ammunition, so that we would have to fall back again, shortening the distance between ourselves and our supplies, and stretching the distance the enemy's would have to travel. Then when Rommel's supply lines were vulnerable we would do the same thing to him. Desert warfare is usually fought as a series of flanking and encircling actions. The idea is to stay highly mobile and keep your fighting force intact, rather than to try to defend a fixed position.

Toward the end of October in 1942, the Eighth Army engaged Rommel's forces at El Alamein in a monumental struggle that lasted nearly two weeks. We had the advantage of supply and the terrain was in our favor, and in the end the Germans and Italians were pretty badly beaten. Rommel started the long retreat west to

Tunisia. It was the beginning of the end for the Germans in North Africa, but the end didn't come quickly.

The Germans and the Italians were tough men. The Italians in particular had the finest and most accurate artillery pieces. Whenever they gave us a stonk (shelling) we knew we were in for it because they could zero in with their guns almost to a pinpoint. That's why I was always well dug down in my trench or foxhole, not four feet, not five feet, but six or seven feet deep into the sand or even stone terrain.

As the Eighth Army chased Rommel west nearly a thousand miles, the Americans and British landed in Morocco and Algeria and were working their way eastward. The Germans were being forced into a pocket in Tunisia. One feature of this pocket was the Mareth Line, a strong defensive position running along a ridge of foothills for about twenty miles westward from the Mediterranean. The Mareth Line was first prepared by the French in the mid1930's. Rommel had taken it over in 1939 and had continued to fortify it during 1940 and '41. Once his Afrika Korps and Panzer Divisions were behind the relative safety of the Mareth Line, it was pretty likely that he would launch an attack from it in an attempt to break out of the pocket.

We were moved into defensive positions on a ridge named El Medenine, south of the Mareth Line. Along with a number of other units, we were ready to repel a major attack. The entire 201st Guards Brigade were on the line: Grenadiers to the left, Scots Guards in the center, Coldstreamers to the right. On our left flank was the famed Gurkha regiment made up of men from the Himalayas who are short of stature and, in accordance with their beliefs, keep their heads shaven. They carry the famed knife which can, in one fell swoop, dislodge a man's head from his shoulders. On our right flank was another colonial regiment, the Sikhs, who, directly opposite to the Gurkhas, wear their hair long. In battle they remove their turbans, and these beautifully groomed men, who are six feet tall or more, let their long black hair fall to their waists. If you are the enemy and you see a Sikh suddenly approaching you from out of the smoke with his hair flowing in the breeze, you know you are at war.

We are now all well dug in, anticipating the German attack. It came at sunup, about 5:30 on the morning of March 6th, 1943. It started with a shelling using maybe five hundred guns and was followed with a frontal attack by three Panzer divisions, one of them—the 21st Panzer Division—directly against our positions. But we were ready. They had to break through the front of the 201st Guards Brigade and that was a tough job.

Several hundred tanks began to advance across a plain below the ridge where we were dug in. Each of our battalions had its own company of armor-piercing, six-pounder antitank guns, six crewmen to each gun. This particular antitank gun was quite new and we were about to give it a testing. Our guns were well hidden and the tanks were only a few hundred yards from them when we opened up. Our antitank men had prepared dummy minefields, and each time a German Tiger tank would pivot on its tracks to avoid the dummy minefield, he would enter what we called a "pukkadink" minefield. "Pukkadink" is an Indian expression for a real minefield. This was the first time that Rommel had used his Tiger tanks with the famous 88 gun mounted on them. We knocked off about twenty of them in the first hour of action, but the Germans kept shelling us and coming on with their tanks.

I was lying behind the ridge in my trench with a fellow guardsman. We each had an attaché case, if you please, with six sticky bombs in it. We had been instructed by our officer how to use them. "Hacquebard, now should a tank come alongside your trench, I want you to leap out and smite the side of the tank with your sticky bomb." This was a cylindrical glass vial, approximately eight inches in diameter, filled with nitroglycerine. In the neck of the vial was a release pin. You had to release the pin, hold the handle down, stick the bottle on the side of the tank and then jump back into your trench or run around behind the tank, hoping not to be shot by the crew in the meantime. As you released the handle of the sticky bomb and stuck it against the tank, some sticky plasticlike substance would enable it to adhere to the tank. The handle would then release a plunger pin which in turn would strike a detonator cap, a small explosive device, which would then cause the nitroglycerine jelly to explode.

Happily, I didn't have to use any of my sticky bombs. I did hear the creaking tracks of the huge 50-ton tanks maybe a hundred yards distant, and I was ready with my attaché case and sticky bombs, but our well-trained antitank gun crews managed to turn the tide for the infantry lying in wait behind them. By about 4:00 o'clock in the afternoon, we were out looking at the tank crews, charred, dead, some of them under their tanks. Just burnt, charred corpses. Of course, we weren't looking for corpses, we were looking for any American chocolate and cigarettes that the Germans had in their tanks that they might have stolen from American troops they had been fighting further north in Tunisia.

Anyway, that day we destroyed some fifty tanks and turned the tide. Despite the fearsome stonk the Germans gave us, they could not quite get their shells to lob onto us—most of them landed several hundred yards behind us—and our casualties were very light. That was the last major attack the Germans made on British troops in North Africa.

The day after the battle, General Montgomery came to visit his troops, and of course, in proper Guards fashion, we all had to polish our boots and our brasses. Montgomery came, as he usually did, in an open reconnaissance car. Each company was sitting platoon by platoon, in the sand, listening to occasional stray shells from the enemy. If the sound was right, you knew it was all right to stay put—a humming sound like "mmmmm, mmmmm" you knew wasn't for you, but if you heard a whistling sound like "sssss, sssss," that was the time to scatter back into your foxholes. Montgomery talked to each platoon personally, "I want to compliment you men upon the job you did in holding the line. We've turned the Boche back into his lair, the Mareth Line. However, I've brought you Guardsmen back into the line, to show the little boys the way." He meant that, of course, in the right spirit. The Guards regiment's average height is about six foot two and the average height of a Britisher is, I believe, around five foot seven. But don't decry that: good stuff comes in little parcels.

There was some humor attached to Montgomery's visit to us. Each man was allotted half a pound of flour for his rations plus, as a bonus, an extra half-pint of water per man. What do you do with a half a pound of flour and an extra half-pint of water? Well, soldiers being somewhat ingenious, especially in the middle of a vast desert, we found a way of putting the flour and extra water ration to good use. We had a very good sergeant who was also a cook, and a good one. We removed a couple of sideplates from the engines of our Bren gun carriers. We washed off the sideplates and they became a table for kneading the flour and water into a mass of dough. Rummaging about our kit bags, one or two men sheepishly and somewhat reluctantly came up with a couple of cans of Libby's evaporated milk. Another fellow had some sugar. Another fellow took a Bren gun, fired at a palm tree, and quickly brought down a couple of branches loaded with dates which were rather ripe. So they wouldn't be covered with sand when landing on the desert floor, we had several tarpaulins spread out to catch the branches. We quickly cleaned the dates, removed the stones, and kneaded the dates into the dough which was by this time piled about a foot high and approximately a foot long. The sergeant then asked which man who owned an undershirt had worn said undershirt for say, only a week or two. Most of us had worn our undershirts for about a month, having been in the line that long. Up came a fellow who said, "I have an undershirt, sergeant, in my kit bag. In fact I haven't worn it at all." Wonderful! We tied off the neck and sleeves, in went the roly poly duff—a popular English dish somewhat similar to a suet pudding—and we placed the whole mess in a ground oven we had fashioned. Using branches from the date tree doused with petrol for fuel, after about forty-five minutes of cooking out came our bayonets, out came the roly poly duff and we rationed off pieces for each man. It was quite delectable and very appetizing, and our officers, too, partook of the roly poly date pudding. These are some of the ways you can survive under tenuous conditions.

When we were bivouacked outside of Alexandria, under the hot Egyptian sun, we would upon occasion be issued eggs. These eggs in the Middle East are the smallest eggs you'd ever wish to see. They're no larger than pigeon eggs. If you were given four or five eggs you had no way to keep them fresh under a sun that's beating down maybe 90 to 100 degrees. Well, you simply don't keep them; instead you use your billy can, a metal can for cooking in and eating out of. If you put your eggs in the can and left it in the sunshine for about half an hour, the eggs would very quickly fry. On occasion, just for the fun of it, we would place three or four eggs on the side of one of our vehicles which had been sitting in the sun for hours. Within five minutes you'd be scraping the eggs off the vehicle, fried and ready for eating with some hardtack (large biscuits about four inches square and about a quarter of an inch thick). Occasionally, if the biscuits were not kept properly airtight, they would become encumbered with weevils. Then, before you ate your biscuit, you would tap it on a hard surface to shake the weevils out and then break it open to make sure there weren't any weevils that were still hiding inside.

During Montgomery's visit he informed us that there was to be a "sticky do" ahead. A "sticky do" implies a coming ferocious battle. Our job was to break through the Mareth Line. The Mareth Line was held along a ridge of foothills about three hundred feet high, and with a gradual slope. The approaches to the line had been seeded with what were estimated to be several hundred thousand mines. If you walk on one, off goes your leg. If a tank hits one, off go the tracks.

For a few days after Montgomery's visit we were busy cleaning our weapons, getting our gear in order, anticipating the coming day of the attack. It was a sort of idling away the time from March 6 until March 16. During those ten days we whiled away the time writing letters home and playing cards. In fact, some of the fellows being illiterate, I would write letters for them, in exchange for which they would clean my rifle. We had one or two gypsy fellows who couldn't read or write, but they could play cards and win all the money.

There we were, awaiting word to advance. Actually we knew that we were waiting for Monty's moon. Montgomery always attacked under moonlight, so we watched the phases of the moon day to day, from a half moon, three-quarter moon, finally to a full moon. During those ten days, there was a two-day desert sandstorm when all firing and shelling halted from the enemy's side and also from our side. If you fired your artillery or rifles during a sandstorm, the breeches would stick and the rifling in the barrel would seize up.

During a sandstorm, all you do is sit tight, lie still, cover your face and your head, and wish it were over. You cannot see ten feet beyond you, especially when it really blows. That is why camels are endowed with two pairs of eyelids. This provides extra protection from the storms, a sort of double indemnity for their eyes. The only consolation about a sandstorm, and we had come through quite a number, was the fact that all action would stop and you had a slight respite from the fear of shells roaming around the skies—shells which you never saw, but only heard.

March 16 arrived and word went around that we were to attack the Mareth Line at dusk. Our objective was to clear the high ground known as "the Horseshoe," over which the main coastal road passed, and from which the Germans had excellent artillery observation. Reconnaissance reported that "the Horseshoe" was lightly held. On the strength of the intelligence reports only two Guards battalions—my unit, the 6th Grenadiers, and the 3rd Coldstream—were to carry out the attack.

All superfluous gear, such as kit bags and great packs (which usually carried an overcoat and extra pair of boots), were left behind in our positions. All we carried were our ammunition pouches, water bottles and small arms. In those days infantrymen carried the Bren gun, the famous small machine gun that came out of Czechoslovakia in the mid-thirties. In addition, each battalion had thirty-six Bren gun carriers, small tracked vehicles which the Germans termed "coffins on tracks." This proved a very apt description. The Bren gun carriers were loaded with small arms ammunition, mortar bombs and mortars along with their crews of two and three men.

Montgomery had prepared his artillery half a mile behind our lines. He had seven hundred pieces of artillery ready for the attack. We were informed by our officers that smoke would be shot first, to lay a smokescreen down in front of our lines. Toward eight o'clock in the evening the sky behind us became ablaze with flashes of light from our guns. If you can picture and hear seven hundred guns, maybe each a hundred feet apart, all firing at once, it's something to recall. I didn't see them, I just heard them and saw their flashes against the sky. Smoke-emitting canisters were being laid in front of us. We were then told by our officers to leave our trenches and advance behind our own shells, which were forming a creeping barge. That is, the artillery men would fire their shells a hundred yards in front of us, sweeping any possible enemy outposts, then lift their range another hundred yards, and so on.

As we moved forward, an officer known as "Cigi" Rowan, because he was an incessant smoker (we always liked to give officers nicknames), said, "Hacquebard, don't stoop, don't stoop."

"No, sir. No, sir," I said, straightening up, much against my will. I was stooping slightly from the waist hoping the shells would go over my head as they went whistling by.

Eventually, we were nearing the enemy position, maybe a hundred yards away, when they opened up with a wicked barrage of mortar fire. I think they must have covered every square yard of the ground in front of us. A mortar looks just like an iron pipe, four feet long and maybe four or five inches in diameter. The mortar team drops a small shell into the pipe and, as it falls, the weight of the shell being dropped against a detonator pin automatically fires it. The shell has three fins to guide it into a high arcing trajectory—practically a straight up-and-down lob. They are fearsome, because mortar men can achieve pinpoint accuracy. The Germans had what we termed the "Chicago piano," six groups of nine mortars each, all electrically fired at exactly the same instant. That came to fifty-four mortar shells at a shot, all in the air at the same time and falling among the advancing troops.

They also greeted us with machine guns that fired six hundred rounds per minute. So we were swept by an enfilade of thousands and thousands of bullets, all traveling at waist or knee or shoulder level. In addition to the mortar and machine gun fire, the Germans had artillery behind their lines which began to open up on us, so we had to contend with that too. We also knew that there were thousands and thousands of mines laid, and every step you took you prayed a little that you wouldn't walk on a mine and lose your limbs, your foot, or your life. Sadly, many men did walk into minefields and that was their end. In this particular attack, the first wave was led by my battalion, and it quickly became obvious to us that "the Horseshoe" was far from lightly held. As it turned out, three battalions of the crack 90th Light Division's Panzer Grenadiers were dug into the commanding ground of "the Horseshoe" and had heavily mined the approaches to their positions with both antipersonnel and antitank mines.

As we continued to work our way forward there was, in addition to heavy fire from both sides, a lot of shouting, hullabalLooing, and screaming during this holocaust. But I was, in my own mind, protected and felt that I would come through. Then our artillery pieces stopped firing, which meant that we were engaged in the enemy's lines.

All I carried was a Bren gun and half a dozen magazines in my pouches. I found myself shooting at the enemy, who was close up and clearly visible in the trenches. And the enemy was shooting back. I was lucky. I was shot in the right arm by a young fellow who appeared no more than sixteen years of age, and I fell to the ground.

My friend and officer "Cigi" Rowan was going by at the time in a Bren gun carrier, and he saw me on the ground: "Hacquebard, are you all right?"

"Sir."

"Are you wounded? Where are you wounded?"

"Right arm, sir," I answered.

"All right, take these prisoners back to headquarters."

So with my left arm I picked up my Bren gun and ordered these two Germans to walk in front of me. I was happy to be ordered to take prisoners back to headquarters, and the Germans were no doubt happy to be leaving the battle scene as well. We were near a wadi, or dried riverbed, and as we made our way down the wadi bed perhaps a hundred yards, we kept passing comrades wounded, comrades dead, and comrades dying. Luckily, my arm only had a bullet through the flesh. It was a through-and-through shot that missed the bone. It bled and it hurt and I thought that I was badly wounded, but I found out later that I wasn't really.

Suddenly, there was a burst in front of me, a flash of light. I must have been knocked out for half a minute or so. I came to, lying in the sand of the wadi bed, and thought, "Hacquebard, what has happened?" I saw that the two prisoners were quite dead. Either a mortar shell or an artillery shell had fallen among us, or maybe one of the Germans had stepped upon a mine. What it was I didn't know, nor will I ever know. I know this, that when a man meets his death on the line, he never knows what hit him.

I was fortunate not to have lost my life, but I received wounds in my stomach and thigh. I could move and wanted to move, because if I lay there and waited for an ambulance or a stretcher party; they might never get to me. There was too much going on at the time. Also, our officers had advised us that if you can move after being wounded, you should move. If you can crawl, crawl, if you can limp, limp. We knew why. If you stayed where you were, suffering from your wounds, they would fester within twenty-four hours and maggots would form in them from flies that would impregnate the wounds with eggs. Once your wounds became septic and swollen and filled with maggots, you could be a goner. I crawled, I limped, I crawled. My battle dress was partly blown off me. My boots were filled with blood. I thought my feet were wounded too, but they weren't; it was just the blood draining down my legs into my boots.

Eventually, a Scots Guardsman who was lying back in reserve saw me and called forth, "Halt, who goes there?" Strange in the middle of the battle scene for a man to be calling, "Halt, who goes there?" but that's how the Guards regiments are trained. I immediately responded, "Hacquebard," but my name could sound German, it could sound anything, so I had the sense to also call forth, "Grenadier." Without further ado, he and his comrade got hold of me, bound me to a stretcher, put the stretcher on a jeep, and took me to a field ambulance where I had my wounds dressed in the dead of night and was given an anesthetic. Then I was put in a small shallow trench filled with wounded. There were several dozen of these trenches. I remember Dr. Winters, who first dressed my wounds. He was awarded the Military Cross for bravery in the field. During this battle several hundred men went through his hands in this ambulance, and I recall well that shells were bursting all around the ambulance and that even machine gun bullets were whistling over the trench where I lay wounded. Dr. Winters was eventually shot in his ambulance.

I remember lying in the trench, wounds dressed, feeling sort of tranquil, waiting for an ambulance to take me to a field hospital. But feeling good because I was out of the battle. As a young soldier it was an heroic feeling, that although wounded and out of action and of no further use to my battalion, I had played a part in an historic attack in which we had taken most of our objectives but had suffered heavy casualties.

At roll call the following morning, the 6th Grenadier Guards, a battalion of 984 men, had lost in one night approximately five hundred men killed, wounded, and missing. If I remember correctly, thirty-three officers were lost, and I believe that only three officers were remaining and they too were wounded.

Eventually I was transported by ambulance with five other wounded men, three of whom died en route, to a field hospital where my wounds were more properly administered to. I stayed there for a few days and then, somewhat groggy from loss of blood, was sent to a hospital in Tripoli where I lay for several nights recovering from wounds. I wasn't too happy there because each night the Luftwaffe would fly over Tripoli and bomb the daylights out of us—I have an idea that they did try to miss the hospital, but we came very near to being hit a few times. A few days later, I was put aboard a hospital ship loaded with maybe five hundred wounded men and sent from Tripoli to Alexandria in Egypt. From Alexandria I was taken to the Fifth South African hospital unit in Cairo where, among the flies—every man had a flyswatter at his bed—I recuperated from my wounds for several months under the tender and loving care of the South African nurses. From there I was sent to a convalescent home in Alexandria, a beautiful mansion quite near the Mediterranean, where we used to go for swims during the day.

Eventually I found myself in a reinforcement camp in Palestine, where, though I did not need it, we underwent field training. A few days later sixteen of us, all from the Guards regiment, were given two trucks and told to make our way with all haste back to Tripoli. So we drove our trucks as slowly as possible on the tarmac ribbon of road "up the blue"—we had an expression in the desert, "going up the blue," or "being in the blue," because you had just a vast dome of blue sky touching the horizons north, south, east and west—reminiscing as we went through the various small towns and villages, many of which had been the scenes of former battles: El Alamein, Tobruk, Derna, Benghazi, and thence to Tripoli.

We were on the road for sixteen days, bartering with the Arabs along the route for watermelons and grapes in exchange for salt and tea. We would visit British and American quartermaster's stores begging for supplies. We would go to a quartermaster and tell him we were poor and had no money, and he would say, "All right, here's two pounds of tea, four loaves of bread and five cans of Libby's milk. Now get going." Off we'd go and barter that with the natives. Then we found the next quartermaster's store, where we would be given coffee, sugar, milk, biscuits, and C rations. We never had it so good.

By the time we finally arrived in Tripoli, we were just too late to embark for the invasion of Italy. But we did arrive in time to be shipped to Italy with the quartermaster's stores, a much safer way to go. I learned, upon arriving in Italy, that my battalion had been beefed up to full strength with another five hundred men and had landed with the entire 201st Guards Brigade at a place called Battipaglia, about seven miles south of Salerno. The landing had been harrowing, as the Germans were waiting and had launched vicious counterattacks, but we finally gained a foothold.

I finally caught up with my battalion and, on my first day back, went out on what we called a prisoner patrol. The idea was to pick up an enemy prisoner and bring him back for interrogation in order to learn his regiment and the strength and deployment of his troops. So I am on the outskirts of a village in the dark of night seeking German prisoners. Instead, I am shot in the left leg. Back to the hospital, Hacquebard. Wonderful.

I would make myself useful in the hospitals once I recuperated by helping the nurses to polish the floors, feed the wounded, make the beds, pick up the linens, put the men back in their beds. You became a sort of a nurse's aide and at the same time you got three square meals a day and clean sheets. However, the medical officer would finally catch up and back you would go to your battalion.

When I had recuperated from the shot in my left leg and rejoined the battalion, it had fought its way from Battipaglia up through Santa Maria and across the Volturno River to Capua. I remember that about this time, mid-October, I believe, we were in a delightful village surrounded by orange groves and vineyards. We arrived there at the height of the harvest season, so we'd feed upon oranges and grapes and peaches. We bivouacked out in the vineyards using the grapevines as camouflage for our vehicles. I wasn't overjoyed to see vineyards that had been in place for maybe two hundred years swept up by tank tracks. However, as they say, "War is hell."

I was always amazed at the openness of the western desert which seemed to reach for miles and miles, but in southern Italy we encountered a completely different type of mountainous terrain where one felt closed in a great deal of the time. In fact, we were bogged down for almost a year in this rugged, rocky, mountainous country trying to break through a series of German defensive positions. The strongest of these was the Gustav Line, which was dominated by Monte Cassino.

We had to fight for every inch of ground above the Volturno. Before we got to the Gustav Line we had to battle our way through the Bernhard Line, a system of positions anchored by the heights of Monte Camino, Monte Difensa, Monte Maggiore, and Sammucro. Each of these was 3,500 to 4,500 feet high, and each was able to support the others defensively. These mountains were a jumble of bald slopes, false crests, ledges, and deep gorges. They were extremely steep and, because they dominated the narrow valleys through which we had to advance, the German artillery observers could watch our every move.

The weather was terrible. It was bad in October, abominable in November, and though it seemed impossible, it got even worse in December. There was almost constant cloudiness and incessant rain, there were biting winds and a cold and clammy fog. These conditions made the ground so muddy that the roads became impassable. The problem was that there were very few corridors through the mountainous terrain; the rain and mud made these corridors difficult, if not impossible, to use; and because the Germans were on the heights they could see every move we tried to make and bring artillery and mortar fire down on us. To the extent that we could, we stayed put during the day and did our moving under cover of darkness.

We knew that we would have to dislodge the Germans from their commanding positions on the heights about half a mile to the north of us, maybe 4,500 feet high. Finally the brigade prepared to attack Mone Camino and awaited the order to move up the mountain. Ours was a motorized infantry brigade, accustomed to the modern style of warfare where speed was the word. This was possible in North Africa because of the open terrain. It was out of the question in the static conditions of southern Italy where mules were more useful than trucks.

We advanced on Monte Camino during the first week in December of '43. Each man was lightly equipped with small arms and with a few days' rations. We followed our officers over various routes toward the base of the mountain which was extremely rough and stony. Eventually we are on the mountainside climbing yard by yard, step by step, foot by foot, until the incline becomes 30 or 40 degrees. We literally crawl up bald slopes and muddy mountain tracks that are too steep even for mules. Silence, quietness is the word. There are possibly two thousand men interspersed at various intervals making their way up this mountain to dislodge the enemy perched atop.

Our first greeting from the enemy was a terrific stonk of mortar shells and even a few shells which I think the Germans were firing from their accurate 88mm guns, positioned possibly two or three miles behind Monte Camino. If they weren't 88 shells, they sure felt like them. The effect of shelling in rocky and mountainous terrain is devastating. Rock does not absorb either the sound or the impact of an exploding shell the way that softer earth does. Instead, there is an amplification and echoing of the sound and a ricochet effect as hundreds of pieces of rock break off and fly through the air.

Our own 25-pounders answered by shelling the top of the mountain. Their fire was so concentrated and heavy that when we finally reached the German positions in the old monastery at the summit of Monte Camino, we found that very few of the enemy were left alive. Those that were still breathing surrendered and were taken prisoner. The monastery was maybe eight hundred years old or more and was built like a fort. The Germans had been lodged in subterranean passages, dungeons, basements, and cells, but the shelling had been too much for them.

We sat up there on Monte Camino for seven or ten days and then were relieved. I remember that it was windy, rainy, and cold; that we did not have blankets or hot meals; and that we could not seek shelter in the monastery because of the bodies piled up inside. Every time someone would try to bury them a shell would hit and dig them all up again.

To give you an idea of how rough the terrain was—full of ridges, jagged peaks, cliffs, and boulders—it took us approximately six hours to make our way down the mountain. I was then given a job as a stretcher bearer with three other men. We went back up the mountain and carried a man down who had been shot in the wrist and hip. He was big, about six foot three, and weighed about 15 or 16 stone (200 pounds). It took us ten hours to carry him down.

Part of our job when not being up in the front line was to function as a carrier party. In fact we became muleteers. Our job was to carry blankets, greatcoats, water, food, ammunition, and other supplies up the mountains practically 4,000 feet high into the positions our men were holding. If you happen to be carrying four-gallon tanks of water, one in each hand, with your own equipment on your back as well as your rifle and your ammunition, and you're climbing a mountain step by step, foot by foot, yard by yard, you know that you're in the army. However, I would cheat a little bit. The mules—those most dextrous portage animals, slender of leg, but great of power—could climb these small mountain tracks, goat tracks if you will, knowing each inch of the way exactly where to step. It used to fascinate me. As I said, I cheated; having dropped off one can of water with some friends who were in need of it, I would then have a free hand with which I'd hold onto the tail of the mule until I got to the top. Sadly, the mules would often be killed along with some of the men when the Germans would open up with a shelling. Or sometimes they'd lose their footing on the narrow and muddy tracks. And of course, by the next day or two, they'd become flyblown and swollen and rather odorous and not too pleasant if the wind was in your direction.

During the first few weeks of January we were wet, cold, muddy, hungry, and tired, but we did get through the Bernhard Line. Our next objective was to get past the Gustav Line. This was another natural barrier, with the fortress of Monte Cassino as its keystone. The line was situated securely on a row of mountains behind the Garigliano and Rapido Rivers. Heavy rains and melting snow had turned these rivers into raging torrents. In addition, the Germans controlled several dams and they used them to flood the lowlands that stretched westward from Cassino to the sea.

The battle to take Monte Cassino and get through the Gustav Line was one of the longest and toughest of the war. The weather and terrain were terrible and the German positions in the mountains were almost impenetrable. So it was decided to try breaching the Gustav Line in the coastal lowlands by crossing the Garigliano and establishing a bridgehead from which to push northward to Rome.

I forget the town where we were preparing to cross the Garigliano, but I do recall that before the attack our engineers were out front sweeping the minefields when the enemy gave us a surprise stonking. It was just around teatime, we were sitting around drinking from our chipped enamel mugs and having a little Spam and bully beef with hardtack, when suddenly the Germans began to shell us. I recall the incident well. I was at the time driving one of our Bren gun carriers. As the shells began to come in we all had to evacuate our positions, hit the road, and advance toward the enemy. I could not start my motor. A sergeant in charge of heavy vehicles had to bring his truck alongside mine with a battery and give me a booster—all this in the middle of a shelling. Luckily, nobody lost their lives and I was able to get my vehicle out of the field where it was lodged. I had to run over a few German bodies to make it over the pontoon bridge across the river. I was given punishment—six drills for idleness and inattentiveness to my vehicle—which I completed at a later time in Florence.

We crossed the Garigliano on January 17 and established a bridgehead which included the coastal town of Minturno. But that's as far as we got for quite some time. Not until May was Monte Cassino captured and the Gustav Line broken. Eventually the infantry began to make its way northward from Minturno up toward Formia, a coastal town where there was some spasmodic fighting and shelling. In fact, one day, near Minturno, I was quite fascinated to sit on the slopes of the coastline falling toward the Tyrrhenian Sea and watch two American ships—my memory is quite clear that the ships were named the *Arkansas* and the *Brooklyn*—sending broadsides into and over Formia to try to rout the Germans out of the town. It's rather strange to be sitting there feeling peaceful while the ships are carrying on a hectic bombardment. All you would see in the distance, maybe six or seven miles out, was a flash of light from the muzzles, a puff of fire, and four seconds later you would hear six- or eight-inch shells humming overhead into the town to help us rout the enemy.

We didn't see much fighting between Formia and Rome, as rather quickly, within weeks, if my memory is correct, the Germans fled to Rome for a last feeble measure of defense. My brigade was resting, or as the Americans say, LOB (left out of battle) for a while.

Rome was a picnic for me. We were there about three weeks or a month, having a good time and bartering the clothes, watches, fountain pens, and other personal valuables that we had taken from prisoners. We felt if we took a prisoner that he was fair game, just as he would have reciprocated had he taken us prisoner.

Of course, right from the beginning, I found all of the Italian people glad that they were out of the war. They helped us at every crossroad and at every village. The partisans, civilians who were out in the line and up front interrogating prisoners for us, were very brave men who put their heads right on the block, knowing that if they were captured it was practically an instant firing squad for them.

From Rome we moved up farther north. This was not too hectic most of the way, stopping for a few days, starting again, stopping, resting, starting. Then, about that time, my battalion, the 6th Grenadier Guards, was disbanded. There were maybe 500 or 600 men left in the battalion. The upper command disbanded the 201st Guards Brigade in Italy and reformed it in the United Kingdom in preparation for D-Day. However, the battalion specialists—the machine gunners, mortar men and Bren gun carrier drivers—were lent to the Welsh Guards who were staying on in Italy. So I found my name not on the roster to return to the UK, but to remain behind in Italy. I was quite dismayed, but reflecting back on it now, I am glad I stayed in Italy.

We soon settled down in our new environment and I found the Welsh Guards to be most enjoyable people. All the Guards Regiments are on a par and equal to each other. We were awaiting another move forward, toward Perugia. My first action with the Welsh Guards was to ride a Triumph motorcycle carrying dispatches back and forth to Rome.

One day, riding not too fast, maybe 50 or 60 miles an hour, I passed an American gun crew that was down in a sunken area when unexpectedly one of their guns fired. It wasn't a blast, it was a sudden shock. I was about a hundred yards in front of the muzzle on an embanked road when the gun fired. The shock managed to veer me and my cycle off the road and I ended up lying under it. The Triumph was a pretty heavy motorbike but I was all right, just a few scratches, scrapes and so on. I got back on the bike and made it back to the Welsh Guards headquarters. But I was a bit dizzy and out of sorts, so instead of going forward to take up positions against the enemy just before Perugia, I was sent backwards.

I was given what they call a nice cushy job. But one cushy job I didn't relish too much, but didn't mind because I figured it was safer, was to go back to a former battlefield where the Welsh

Guards had had a fierce encounter and lost quite a number of men, and serve on a burial detail. I found myself close to the Pioneer Corporal, helping him make very distinguished wooden crosses with the name of the guardsman, his rank and number, and just the simple letters at the head of the cross, "KIA," killed in action. It's been British practice over the years to bury a man where he falls mortally wounded, while the Americans leave their dead in the field and then have their graves recovery unit recover the bodies and move them to a suitable resting place for burial. As the British would bury their dead and recover the bodies at a later date, my job was doing exactly that. We had to dig up bodies and build a makeshift cemetery for them. We lined up the graves, about forty men, and the crosses were left there so that at a later date the bodies could be recovered again and placed in a more suitable cemetery.

After the burial detail we returned to the company. We were going to go forward into the line, and I recall that I wasn't too happy about this. I was detailed to go out on a patrol about six o'clock one evening, just before dusk. We were advancing down a sunken road with embankments on each side, with a respectful five yard distance between each man. What happened, I don't know, but I think the man next to me walked on a mine. I felt a flash in my face and a cascade of mud spattered me and again I found myself in the hospital. I'd been partly blinded in the left eye and the vision was not good in the right eye. Eventually I was taken all the way back to Naples where I underwent treatment for my eyes. Several weeks later, to my great joy, I was aboard a hospital ship bound for England. I was sent to a hospital in Liverpool, which was only a stone's throw from my home. Eventually, treatment and rest for my eyes gave me my full sight back again.

11

EUROPE:
1944-1945

Jerry Carter

As we kept going down, down, down and got closer to the water, my copilot said, "Our engines are on fire." I thought, My God, on fire! In fact, we weren't on fire, we were picking up spray from the North Sea. The props were picking up the spray, and out back it looked like smoke.

—Jerry Carter

Europe: 1944—45

After World War I, the advocates of air power theorized that with enough bombers it would be possible to destroy an enemy's will and capacity to make war and force a surrender, even though its military forces in the field might still be intact. They believed that precision bombing could wipe out an opponent's military, industrial, and transportation facilities without violating the generally accepted view that bombing should not be directed against civilian populations. Air power, it was felt, could achieve victory by itself, without the involvement of conventional land and sea forces, and with a substantial reduction in the number of lives lost.

When World War II began, theories about the effectiveness of air power were a great deal more plentiful than facts. As it turned out, most of these grand assumptions were incorrect and bombers did not live up to their billing as the ultimate offensive weapon. They might have destroyed an enemy's capacity to make war had they been able to fly over hostile territory unopposed, but defensive measures made precision bombing difficult if not impossible. As a result, bombers could not hit strategic targets accurately and had to resort to area bombing. This meant that large residential areas were destroyed and civilian populations suffered heavy casualties.

The assumption that this would weaken civilian morale also turned out to be incorrect. The citizens of London, Berlin, and other heavily bombed cities were proud of their ability to take whatever the enemy dished out. Nor was mass bombing as destructive to manufacturing as originally expected. Despite concerted Allied efforts to knock out fighter production, German industry was turning out far more planes at the end of the war than at the beginning. German bombing did not force the British to their knees at the beginning of the war, nor did Allied bombing force the Germans to surrender later. Throughout the war both the Allied and Axis air forces took and inflicted far higher casualties than had been anticipated.

During the Battle of Britain and the London Blitz, RAF fighters operating with radar ground control shot down so many of the Luftwaffe's bombers that the Germans switched from daylight to night raids in order to reduce their losses. When the British began to bomb Germany, they too opted for night raids. Accurate navigation and aiming over blacked-out enemy territory was extremely difficult. At the outset the RAF assumed that their planes were averaging a bombing error of about three hundred yards. Then reconnaissance photos showed that the error was considerably greater, so the estimated error was revised to approximately one thousand yards—too large to locate and hit targets the size of factories and oil refineries. Further analysis of photos taken during night raids revealed that only one-third of the planes dropped their bombs within five miles of the target (and over certain targets only 10 percent did so). Navigational errors were such that most bombers were not reaching their targets at all.

Just as the RAF bombers were getting better at hitting their targets, German radar-equipped night fighters were getting better at shooting them down. Since they flew at night the British had not equipped their planes to fight. The new German radar made it impossible for them to hide in the darkness. All during 1943 the Luftwaffe took an increasingly heavy toll, and in the five months from November 1943 through March 1944, German night fighters shot down approximately 1,000 RAF bombers. In answer, the British developed ingenious techniques, such as dropping masses of aluminum foil strips to confuse enemy radar.

While the British favored night area raids, the Americans were convinced that daylight precision bombing was possible if their planes were heavily armed and flew in tight defensive formations. They equipped the B-17 Flying Fortress with thirteen 50-caliber machine guns and developed formations that provided intense combined firepower. This worked reasonably well when the B-17's bombed targets within the range of their fighter escorts. But in 1943, when they began to attack targets in Germany well beyond the range of their escorts, they began to suffer very heavy losses.

Committed to daylight bombing, the Americans tried to eliminate, or at least reduce, fighter opposition by knocking out German aircraft production. The Eighth Air Force's B-17's flew a series of missions against aircraft factories deep inside Germany which required them to fly hundreds of miles without fighter cover. Their losses were terrible; so bad, in fact, that in late 1943 the Americans suspended daylight raids until they could provide their bombers with long-range fighter protection.

About this time a fast and highly maneuverable fighter, the P-51 Mustang, was beginning to come off the production lines. With its long-range fuel tanks it could escort deep into and back from Germany. By early March 1944, the Eighth Air Force had enough of these fighters to resume raids over Germany, and Mustang pilots developed new tactics that greatly improved their effectiveness.

Customarily, escort fighters flew along close to the bombers and engaged the enemy only when it attacked. But the Mustangs divided up into relatively free-ranging squadrons, one of which would fly well ahead and above the bombers where it had the advantage of altitude and sun, and could see the German fighters coming up and preparing to attack. The Mustang was a remarkable plane and it ultimately caused air superiority in Europe to shift decisively in favor of the Allies.

In April, 1944, top priority was given to a bombing campaign designed to seal off Normandy in preparation for the D-Day landings. Heavy bombing put the railroads and marshaling yards in northern France out of commission, and by D-Day most of the bridges, engines, and rolling stock in Normandy were destroyed. Of 92 German radar stations in the north of France, only 18 were in working condition on D-Day. Ammunition and fuel dumps, military camps and supply depots were kept under constant attack. In April and May the Allied air forces flew more than 200,000 sorties over France. And while there were fewer Luftwaffe fighters in the air to oppose them, the Germans had improved the range-finding and aiming capabilities of their antiaircraft guns so that flak was taking a heavy toll. In the six weeks between April 28 and June 6, 1944, just under 2,000 Allied planes were shot down and 12,000 airmen lost their lives. But the D-Day landings were made easier by this aerial effort.

In June, while continuing to bomb other targets, the Allies turned their attention to choking off Germany's fuel production. The bomber crews had gained considerable experience by then, and with the Mustangs to ward off enemy fighters, they became increasingly effective at hitting their targets. By the end of 1944 the production of aviation fuel had dropped by more than 90 percent. So even though the German aircraft industry was turning out between 1,000 and 2,000 planes a month, there was not enough fuel to fly them. This meant that the Luftwaffe could send fewer fighters up. Allied air forces became more and more effective, and from late 1944 onward Germany began to be sucked irreversibly downward towards defeat. For the last six months of the war she was virtually defenseless against air attack. City after city was reduced to ashes and rubble, and the economy simply ceased to operate.

The principle that civilian casualties should be avoided was forgotten early in the war. Bombing caused the death of some 300,000 German and 60,000 British civilians. The British government officially estimated that three million homes were destroyed by German bombing (including V-1 and V-2 flying bombs). Aerial warfare killed 500,000 Japanese civilians. Casualties among Allied and Axis airmen were in the hundreds of thousands—far higher than had been expected.

During and after the war many movies were made that helped to create and perpetuate a romantic image of these airmen. True, the men who flew bombers and fighters had a very strong *esprit de corps*; what they did demanded teamwork. They were heroes, but life for the combat airmen was not romantic. They were under tremendous pressure; they had to contend with fatigue as they went on mission after mission, day after day, and they took terrible risks—about one-third of the bombers on every mission were damaged. Often the pilots had no idea how effective they had been at hitting their targets.

Jerry Carter and his B-17 crew arrived in England in the spring of 1944. They participated in raids over German cities, in the softening up of northern France, in missions against German aircraft factories and oil refineries. Jerry Carter's story is not unique. In its essentials it was shared by thousands of pilots, copilots, navigators, bombardiers, and crewmen. Now he is a commercial artist living in Trenton, New Jersey, where he specializes in graphic design and illustration.

Jerry Carter:

I was about to be drafted and I definitely didn't want to go into the ground forces. I wasn't that eager or that brave, I guess. I never cared too much for water, which is a funny thing because I got my share of water later on in the war. But I didn't give the Navy a thought, really. I thought the Air Force was my best bet, so I enlisted with the idea of getting into the flying end of it. When I went in I didn't know one end of the aircraft from the other.

Eventually I made pilot, but you weren't selected for single-engine or multi-engine aircraft until after the advanced training. I liked training. It was exciting. I learned to like flying, and I had no trouble whatsoever. We learned aerial maneuvers, or aerobatics. They put us through extensive aerobatics. The Air Force wanted to save both pilots and aircraft, so they gave us extensive emergency training.

You couldn't get me to do it over again, but at the time I don't think I had any fear whatever. I was just one of a whole bunch. We were like a big family, we were training together, and everything was taken care of for us.

When I became an officer, I was given my choice of becoming a multi-engine pilot or a single-engine fighter pilot. I had no desire to fly singles, because I thought I might want to get into the airlines—the airlines wanted pilots who had been trained by the service because it was a big expense off their shoulders—so I chose multi-engine planes.

Some people think that fighters are more dangerous to fly, but they're not. If you've got nine or ten men behind you in a bomber, you've got a lot more responsibility than having just yourself in the plane to watch out for. If you have any sense of responsibility, you're concerned with the rest of your crew, you worry about their necks as well as yours.

After advanced training about fifteen of us, a handful out of the whole bunch, were selected to go through first pilot training. All the others went out as single-engine pilots or copilots. We spent about three months learning to pilot B-17s and then picked up our crews and trained with them for combat. Then we went overseas.

We flew our own plane over to England, crew and everything, in late April or early May of '44. They assigned us to the 401st bomb group, located in central England, near Kettering. When we got there the big push was on for railroad marshaling yards and oil refineries, and some deliberate retaliation raids, I think, for the buzz bombing of London. We also went after some buzz bomb launching sites. I can recall going on at least one raid, maybe two, where we dropped our bombs from 28,000 to 35,000 feet—once we even dropped from 35,000 feet—that was tough on a B-17, that's as high as they would go with a bomb load. But our normal altitude was around 25,000 to 28,000 feet, and it's hard to find a buzz bomb site from that altitude.

The mission that stands out most in my mind was when we

were hit by antiaircraft fire going to Dessau, which is just south of Berlin—I don't even remember what the target was. We were heading toward Berlin when both our outboard engines were hit by antiaircraft fire. Shortly after that our group was hit by fighters, but we had already been knocked out of the group. On that raid we lost six planes out of eighteen, and five crews. We were picked up later; that's the reason why we didn't lose six crews.

When you get hit you feel it. You can feel a jolt. Our right outboard was hit first, and I couldn't feather it. In fact, the flak must have sheared something, because the engine started to rev up and it just kept on windmilling. As quick as that happened—in a matter of forty-five seconds—the left outboard also was hit, but I was able to feather that one and stop it. I had to drop out of formation, because I couldn't keep up with it. So we just dropped down and pulled out. The men knew that something had happened but they didn't know what. They could see antiaircraft fire coming up and that there were a lot of planes around, naturally, but that was all. The first thing that came to my mind was to worry about enemy fighters, because any time a B-17 was disabled, it was a sitting duck.

The training that we got back in the States was good, because the next thing I thought to do was to take care of the runaway propeller. I was scared, but I wasn't to the point of not knowing what to do. In fact I was reacting better than if I was in normal circumstances. So the first thing I tried to do was dive the plane, drop wheels and flaps—like putting on brakes—and try to pull this runaway propeller right out of the engine, shaft and all. Just pull it off and get rid of it. Because if they do come loose on their own, they can hit the fuselage of the plane and spin right into it, and this can cause you to go down. That was the one fear that was in my mind to begin with, but everything happens so fast.

We were about an hour and a half inland, so we had time to think about what to do. We must have been up at about 25,000 at that time, and we didn't know exactly where to go. We couldn't pull the prop out. It just kept on windmilling, so I slowed the plane down as much as possible to keep the windmilling from just shaking us apart. We couldn't throw our guns overboard, because we expected a fighter attack at any time. We also had a full bomb load. We got completely free and clear of the other bombers on the mission so we wouldn't hit anybody. Our own necks were at stake there, and we were over enemy territory, so we just dropped our bombs. You couldn't worry about where they fell.

We had two engines, both inboard, and I had to set up a gradual descent since we didn't have enough propeller power to keep us straight and level all the way back to England. After a few minutes we knew that we wouldn't make it, and that we were headed to the center of the North Sea between England and the coast of Holland or Belgium. So I said, "What do you guys want to do?" And they asked me what I was going to do. And I said, "I'm going as far as this plane will go. I'm not going to bail out. If you fellows want to get out and take your chances in Belgium, okay. If you're lucky, the Underground and the Belgian people will take care of you, and if not, you'll be POW's."

So they said, "No, if you're going all the way, we want to go with you." We talked it over and we decided what to do. There we were, scared, but talking rationally. Our minds were with us.

We wanted to go out over Belgium rather than the German coast, because the antiaircraft fire was extensive there. As we went over, we were only at about five thousand feet. We were sitting ducks really. The antiaircraft fire came up heavy on both sides of us and I was really frightened then, although we knew what to do because of our training. As we went over the coast the antiaircraft fire was all around but it never touched us. We were later told that we were lucky because the Belgians must have been on the guns. If the Germans had been on them they would have shot us right out of the air.

As soon as we were over the water, we dumped everything. We threw out all of our guns, anything that was loose in the aircraft, anything to get the weight out. We would have been shot down if a German fighter had come along, we were at the mercy of anybody that came along then. When we got over the open water of the North Sea, my radioman got on the "Mayday" air-sea rescue frequency, and started to repeat our problems and our position.

As we kept going down, down, down and got closer to the water—we flew out about sixty miles from the shore—my copilot said, "Our engines are on fire." I remember that so well, and I thought, My God, on fire! In fact, we weren't on fire, we were picking up spray off the North Sea. The props were picking up the spray, and out back it looked like smoke. You have to be mighty close to the water when you start doing that. As we were going down, everybody was joking. The men were joking. They were kids. I had one man that was 35 years old, a waist gunner, but outside of that, at 24 I was about the oldest and I had a tailgunner who was just 19. They were just young guys.

In a B-17 the navigator and bombardier are in the nose. When they went back to position themselves for ditching, the navigator came past me with a deck of cards, and he showed them to me, and said, "Come on back." What else can you say? When ditching, the men squat in position and put their parachutes between them to brace for the impact. You don't practice ditching an aircraft because you just can't do it, you only read about it. So we'd been through the drill, and the night before we'd even talked about it, should we ever need it. Well, there were not many planes that ever needed it, but this one did.

The radio operator stayed right at his post until I told him to get in position. Then I reached down to get my flak helmet—that was procedure too, to wear your flak helmet in case, when you hit the water, you hit something with your head—and I couldn't find it. I don't know where it was. I was bareheaded when we did actually ditch.

When I felt that the plane was going in, I pulled back on the throttles, and the minute it felt like the plane was going to stall I put the tail down, which was according to the book. I felt the tail hit the water and we skipped probably a couple hundred yards. We had about a 90 airspeed at that time. And then the next thing, it hit. People don't realize how hard water is. When you talk about landing a plane in water, they think it's soft. The propellers on that aircraft were bent back over the wings from the impact. Hitting the water was like hitting a solid brick wall. The ball turret was driven right up into the fuselage of the plane.

There was a complete red-out, as they called it. You're jerked forward, and the blood rushes to your head, that's why they call it a red-out. When I came to, we were underwater. I reached up to pull the window open, and if I had, I would have drowned everybody. We were still underwater, and I had the feeling we were going down. Then it stopped, and the plane came back up about half out of the water. It never did come completely out. When we came to the surface, the root of the wing was about two feet under water. I remember I stiff-armed myself when we hit the water, and then I blacked out. I didn't remember anything, for how long I don't know, but as we bobbed to the surface, the next instinct was to get out. So I pulled the window back and swung down on the root of the wing. The plane was floating but the bottom was all ripped out of it and water was rushing in. When I got on the wing I inflated my Mae West—the jacket you wear to keep you afloat—but the air leaked out almost as fast as it came in, and I didn't notice it.

I saw the men getting out of the plane. They had pulled the emergency cords on each side of the B-17 which cause the doors to pop open and the life rafts to flop out and blow up on their own. Well, the rafts popped out, but they just lay on the water like old empty inner tubes. They didn't inflate. As I walked out to the end of the wing I realized that my Mae West was flat, that it hadn't inflated either.

Well, everything happened pretty fast. The plane didn't stay afloat more than half a minute to a minute. We no more than got out as fast as we could move when the weight of the engines flipped the plane right up on its nose with the tail sticking up in the air. It just hung there momentarily, and then it slipped out of sight completely. There wasn't any debris floating around. It was just gone.

Here we were, just hanging onto this loose piece of rubber. There were five of us on each raft. One man had the Gibson Girl radio that he'd brought with him, one man was hurt pretty bad, and some of the others were bruised. My bombardier had gone through the bulkhead into the bomb bay and was out cold. If the navigator hadn't gone in after him and brought him out, he would have gone down with the plane. The men worked with the raft, and suddenly, poof, it just fairly exploded, and there it was. The other raft inflated about the same way at the same time. We tied ourselves together. There we were, right out in the middle of the North Sea, and everything was gone. What to do now?

We started grinding away on the little radio with the Mayday or SOS frequency, hoping that somebody would hear it. We never found it out until later, but they did hear us. We kept flying after we had cut off our transmitter in the plane, so we were several miles from where they thought we were. At the same time, the air-sea rescue PT boat down at the mouth of the Channel had lost one of its engines and was trying to get it repaired, even after they knew they had a pickup in the North Sea above the Channel.

We were cold. The water was like ice. You can't last in it long. It was also rough, about ten-foot choppy waves. We were tied together, and constantly one raft would go up on one side of a wave and we would go down on the other side. (When I landed the plane, I tried to land in a trough and I did fairly well. I could see how to line it up from the air. That's the proper way to do it, you don't get to practice—one time is all.)

So far so good. We took turns grinding the radio, but we were very cold and started to turn a little bit blue. When you're squatted down in a raft and icy water keeps spraying over you, it's terribly cold. It gets to the point that you just don't care. We didn't think that they knew where we were because we didn't see anybody. Finally we saw a plane in the distance. We used to study aircraft silhouettes so we'd be able to identify planes we saw in the distance. It looked like a German Focke-Wulf going back and forth looking for us. Of course, they knew we were out there because they'd been shooting at us as we went over the coast.

That probably scared me the most during the whole thing. I thought this was it. I was saying my prayers. I didn't think we would make it, and, at a time like this, you do a lot of thinking about your folks back home. I was married, and had a new wife back home. When I saw this Focke-Wulf come closer, I thought, What are you going to do, drop over the side? He'll come down and strafe the whole area and there won't be anything left.

And I thought that was the end, but it turned out to be one of our P-47s. He flew back and forth and finally, just before dark, he saw us. And when he did you could just tell that there was something between us down here in these two rafts and that P-47 pilot. He came down over us and his prop wash almost blew us out of the raft. He circled us, just above the water, and you could see him smiling—you could actually see his teeth. I think he was as happy as we were. We had a balloon that went up into the air as our aerial, and after he found us, he came right over the top of us and cut the balloon.

In the meantime he was radioing our location back to air-sea rescue. It was quite a while before they picked us up. It was getting dark when we saw the silhouette of the PT boat coming up over the horizon. Then they came alongside and dropped a net over for us. We couldn't get up. We had been squatting so long we were numb. We couldn't even straighten up. So they dropped the net overboard and scooped us up one at a time. We'd ditched at about 1:00 P.M. and we were picked up the same evening. One afternoon may not seem like very long, because people have been on rafts for days, but when you're in that icy water it's a pretty good feeling to be picked up.

They took us to England and put us in a hospital. I had hurt my back. Outside of that, one fellow had broken his foot, and there were also bruises. We were pretty lucky. They told us back at base that we were the first crew to ditch without losing anybody. In fact, they thought we were gone, and when we got back to the base three days later, the guys had gone through our stuff and divided up our clothes. Our watches and personal things were set to be sent home.

That was my first mission!

My sixth mission was D-Day, the big push. We flew a group lead that day, and we went over about ten o'clock that morning. I can still remember looking down on the action in the Channel. It was in full bloom when we got there. The paratroopers had been going over all night long. You could hear them flying over our airfield, heading for their drop zone behind the German shore defenses. Then we went over and bombed heavy explosives along a smoke line where the German front line was during the D-Day action. We weren't too high that day, I think about 14,000 feet. You could see the battleships and all the other kinds of watercraft down there— you could practically have walked across from England on them, there were so many. Up where we were, the action was panoramic. We didn't have to worry about German fighters, there were none in the area. We just had to worry about collisions with our own aircraft because there were thousands of our own planes up there.

I knew something big was coming up; the rumor was all over that there was going to be a big push of some kind. Then, two or three days before D-Day, I flew one of our commanding officers down to the south of England. I saw hundreds of boats all crowded in there. I never saw so many small craft in my life. They used everything that would float. Every little harbor and nook was just chock-full of these boats. We didn't know for sure until the morning of D-Day. We were briefed about two o'clock in the morning.

There was a briefing before every mission and these briefings were very important. A typical mission would last from eight to eleven hours. They get you up at midnight or 1:00 A.M. First you go to breakfast and then to the briefing room. Lead crews would go first for a special briefing.

I had a tremendous crew. We were a group lead, and it takes a very good crew to be a lead crew. A pilot can fly the plane, but he has to have a good navigator and bombardier to get to the right target and drop the bombs in the right place. All the planes in the group drop their bombs according to the lead crew. That is, the other planes didn't all carry bombsights so they followed us and dropped where and when we did. That's why lead crew briefing is so important.

After the briefing you get your equipment together. All this takes up to two or three hours. Then you go out to the revetment area where your plane is parked, and you wait for takeoff time. It all has to do with fog and different factors. When you see a red flare go up, you hold. When you see a green flare, everybody piles in their ships. And they know their position in the bomb train—or in their own squadron. So they taxi out. I've sat there sometimes for an hour, engines revved up, waiting and waiting and waiting—for a cloud to lift, or maybe for the weather over the continent to clear. Occasionally you're sitting there maybe two, three, or four hours and after all that time you see a red flare go up, and you're scrubbed: you have to go back. It's all over till the next day.

Far more often than not we would eventually take off. It was the nagivator's job to get you where you were going. My navigator was just as good as they come. He was a Georgia boy, and when I first saw him I thought, "What have I got here?" But he was out of this world at guiding us over areas where there wasn't as much flak.

Believe me, there was heavy flak over almost all of Germany and France. Wherever you were they had thousands of antiaircraft guns. You just can't imagine it—literally thousands of guns. Around a big city or an oil refinery there would be five or six hundred guns in one place pumping away at you. They would often knock a lot of planes out of the sky, and there were a lot of planes up there, too. It would sometimes take all the planes in a bomb train two or three hours to form and go in over a target.

I remember a mission to Hamburg. We climbed up gradually over the North Sea to keep away from the guns as we went up around the curve of the continent. We were going to Hamburg, but we made a pass as though we were going to Kiel. But they put a smoke screen right over the city. You could see it starting to blow right over Kiel to obliterate any particular target we might be after. But we circled around and came right down over the oil refineries in Hamburg. It was kind of frightening—you could see planes way in the distance coming right over the target, and a solid box of smoke thousands of feet in the air built up from the antiaircraft guns. The box was a square area of sky just filled with flak that they kept pumping right over the target area. We knew we had to go around and come back right through that. We made our pass and came through it all right.

At the briefing they had warned us not to go over the island of Helgoland because it was heavily fortified. Our group got broken up pretty badly over the target because of the heavy flak, and when we finished our bomb run and were turning off, we were almost on our own. Then I saw the colonel who was leading our group on that mission and I joined up with him. That son of a gun took off and flew right over Helgoland, and sure enough, we got hit. It was the hardest hit we took at any time during the war.

It was as though somebody took a sledgehammer and came right up under that B-17. There was a sudden tremendous jolt. It almost knocked the fillings out of my teeth. It was so solid that it jerked the controls right out of my hands. A shell had gone off right under us, and the guy ahead of us, this colonel in the lead plane, his wheels and flaps were knocked right down.

We recovered from that jolt and one of the men in the back said to me, "Captain, your left outboard engine's on fire." I looked over there and saw that it wasn't smoke, but oil and gas coming out of the outboard engine. You could see the fuel kind of vaporizing and the oil bubbling right out of the top. I feathered that engine as quickly as I could, but we were losing most of the fuel from our outboard tanks.

Our fuel supply was low, and close off to our right we could see Denmark with neutral Sweden just beyond it. We could go over there, or we could try to go all the way home over the North Sea, where there's no flak. But would we make it back to England? We knew that we would be cruising and losing altitude all the way—almost like putting a car in neutral and coasting. But the Germans were very rough on guys trying to get to a neutral country, so rather than take a chance, we decided to go back.

We made it, with our gas tanks measuring empty practically the whole way. We were letting down—cruising. We went back by ourselves, letting down as we went, but we were okay because we were out over the water. We got back with nothing in our tanks but fumes, which are even more dangerous than fuel. We didn't catch fire. We could have, but we didn't.

I was hit by fighters one time severely. We were lagging back in the bomb train—the file of bomber groups going over the target area—usually at about three-minute intervals. Three minutes doesn't seem like much, but there's quite a bit of airspace between you and the other groups if you lag back and get more than three minutes behind.

The German fighters monitor everything. They know what's going on just as well as you do. You're over enemy territory, and you can see them down there if it's a clear day. My copilot nudged me and pointed down, and there was a flight of Messerschmitts coming up at us like bees out of the nest. They just spiraled right up to us and because we were lagging a little bit they zeroed in on my group. Everybody started to tuck in, and I pulled up tight with the group ahead of us in order to concentrate our firepower. I could see the tailgunner of the group ahead of me.

The Germans tried to shoot down the lead ships because they knew that if the lead ship was knocked out on its way to a target, the bomb-sight was gone. The Messerschmitts had 20mm cannons in them, and heavy armament underneath, and they were pretty well fortified. Without our fighter escort we were sitting ducks because the 50-calibers in our B-17's didn't have the range to reach planes with cannons.

One plane kept coming in on our left. He would lay off to the side, and there would be a kind of orange puff whenever his 20mm cannons would go off. He kept coming in after us. We would see this orange puff as he came in on us, and he would pull up and put his armored belly up to us, and then roll out and then come in on another pass again. We were so far in over Germany that our fighter protection had had to leave us, and before our fresh escort could come in, we were without any fighter protection for about three or four minutes.

The German fighters knew that, that's why they came up when they did—they had no one to fight up there. I saw the fighter pilot who was after us get a man over in another group. He hit him right in the cockpit and the plane just stopped in midair and blew up.

When they saw our P-51 fighter escort coming, the Germans just disappeared. They were gone, just that quick. That whole fighter action lasted only two or three minutes at the most. You chew gum as fast as you can and you're thinking, "Get home." Those P-51's were a beautiful sight. They protected us well. But that was one time that I sweated it out, because that plane was after our necks.

We flew an awful lot in a short time. I flew 650 hours in one summer over there, and that's a lot of combat time—with training in between. As a lead crew, we flew every day. We had to practice. We were training new crews from the States.

I flew my missions fast. Once I flew two missions in one day, and was scheduled to go on three in a row. I was so tired I was like a drunk. I didn't care. And the flight surgeon came out to the plane and said, "Carter, you're not going up again. You're going to get some rest." I could get careless and it would be dangerous to the crew.

My closest friend over there was saying, "You're a chicken. How about it?" But on that particular mission he went down. He landed in a potato patch over there and became a prisoner of war.

In England, we flew by instruments because the weather was so bad, and because we did a lot of night flying. I've been lost over there at night when everything was blacked out. You had to do an awful lot by radio, but you had to be careful because of the enemy tuning in on you and your position. I've been lost over there and I've been scared. You actually learn to fly the plane almost by the seat of your pants. In fact, I landed one time with only one wheel. If you get enough combat time in, you're going to have those things happen.

At the end of a mission there were hundreds of planes, all in their own patterns—the airfields weren't too far apart—all trying to get onto the ground. Some were out of fuel, some had injuries on board—they had red flares going up—some had priority over others, and you kept circling and circling. And here's another group right here, circling with you. You'd be surprised at how many times you'd dodge aircraft at the last possible instant.

Sometimes you're hit and you never even know where. In fact, every mission you come back with holes in the skin of the plane from the flak that's flying through the air. Sometimes it would be so thick, you could taxi on it. The German gunners could set their shells to explode at a predetermined height, and on impact. They'd know your altitude, so there'd be millions of pieces of metal flying all over just at your altitude.

One time coming in, we knew that we had possible damage. I knew that we had taken some flak; you can feel the near misses. I put my landing gear down at home base and when we started to touch down I could tell something was wrong. I was talking to the tower, but I never completed my message. I said, "I think we're going to. . . ." And that's all I got out. One wheel was down. The other wheel was there, but it wasn't intact. It wouldn't bear any weight.

I didn't have time to say anything to the men in the plane. Immediately I had that fear of what was going to happen. Almost instantly I felt the wing going down until it hit a concrete runway light. The wing tip caught one of the runway lights and we changed direction about 90 degrees just as quick as you could bat your eye. We were still going about 100 miles an hour, and we headed out across the field and started to spin, and I thought there would be an explosion because when your tanks are full of fumes everything just blows up. And I thought, "My God! What about the men in the plane!" I must have been ashen, because I was afraid even to think what was going on in the nose and in the back of the plane.

My copilot jumped out of his window, and it's a wonder he didn't break his legs. He thought we were going to blow, because of fire and sparks, but I'd told him to cut the switches the minute we touched. It's instinctive, because the instant it happens, the hours of emergency training come back to you. I thought somebody would be killed because of the way we were tossed around. They were shaken up and banged around, but nobody was hurt. That plane was scrapped because everything was bent.

Once when we were loaded with bombs, I had a plane that I couldn't get up off the runway, and we ran out of runway. When I pulled back to lift it up, it dropped back down on the runway again and bounced. I said to my copilot, "Get the wheels up!" And he hit the toggle switch for the wheels to come up.

Just as the plane was lifting off we went through a hedgerow and disappeared out of sight, and the tower said, "Where'd you go? What happened to you?" We were lucky, because we flew hedgerow-high before I could get the thing up in the air. All through that mission I thought the plane behaved very sluggishly, and when we came back we realized that we had leaves and twigs sticking out of our wheel undercarriage.

I formed a kind of superstition as a result of all the experiences I had at that time that I can't get out of my mind really. I'm not afraid of planes, but I won't go up in one unless it's an emergency situation, and so far I haven't had an emergency yet that's required it. If you've ever been in a plane that's falling, it's kind of a funny feeling. When you're coming down you've got to do a lot of thinking. I guess that might have something to do with it. I guess maybe you could say I'm chicken now—I got scared out.

12

NORMANDY:
June 6, 1944

David Stephen Douglass

When we hit the water, I'd say it was chest high. We were about a hundred yards from the beach at this point, but it felt like a lot more than a hundred. The water was cold as hell and there was a lot of surf and you are loaded down with about a hundred and fifty pounds of heavy and cumbersome gear. You can barely move, and they are firing at you. The sandy bottom, which we expected to be fairly level, was very uneven and full of holes kicked up by all of the shells and mines that had exploded. As you're fighting your way through the surf trying to get to the beach, you'd hit one of these holes and stumble ass over teakettle down over your head. Then you'd struggle to get up, and a wave would hit you and you'd go down again. There were bodies all over the place in the water, some floating face up, some face down. The first thing I did was to make for the nearest steel obstacle and hide behind it. This is what most of us did.

—David Stephen Douglass

Normandy: June 6, 1944

The Allies had their backs to the wall in late 1941 and early 1942. The continent of Europe was almost totally under Nazi domination. Rommel had been sent to North Africa and was pushing the British back into Egypt. Malta was under siege. U-boats were sinking an enormous number of ships in the North Atlantic. The Japanese had virtually destroyed the U. S. Pacific fleet, taken Singapore, the Philippines, and a great deal more. And Hitler's invasion of Russia, "Operation Barbarossa," was inflicting huge losses on the Red Army. By the end of 1941 the Russians had lost more than three million men killed or captured, fifteen hundred aircraft, and many thousands of tanks.

Bleak as the situation was, in late 1941 a small group of men in England began to plan for the eventual Allied invasion of Europe. They studied a variety of alternative plans and quickly concluded that a cross-Channel invasion in 1942 or even 1943 would be madness because of the lack of adequate manpower, materials, and shipping. However, Stalin put strong pressure on Roosevelt and Churchill to open a "second front" so that Hitler would be forced to divert some of his divisions and planes away from Russia.

By 1942, conditions on the Russian front were so critical that Roosevelt and Churchill feared the imminent collapse of the Red Army unless something was done to relieve the situation there. So on August 19 a Canadian and British commando force of 6,000 men raided the heavily defended French port of Dieppe. The results were disastrous: 3,500 of the Allied force were killed or captured. But as a result of the Dieppe raid the Germans did move seven divisions from Russia to reinforce the Atlantic Wall. Even more important, the Allies learned that the preliminary bombing and shelling of ports required to assure the success of amphibious operations would render those facilities virtually useless. The experience gained at Dieppe and on similar raids led to improved amphibious techniques and heavily influenced the selection of final invasion landing sites.

Realizing that a "second front" was imperative, but that it would be premature to attempt a cross-Channel invasion, the Western Allies landed a large invasion force in French North Africa in November, 1942. When this force engaged the Germans and Italians in Tunisia, and later in Sicily and Italy, it not only gave the Russians a "second front," but it permitted green British and American troops to get combat training. Events in North Africa and Italy established all too clearly that the Allies needed this combat experience before attempting the assault on Hitler's Atlantic Wall in France.

A few months later, in January 1943, Roosevelt and Churchill met in Casablanca and began planning for a full-scale cross-

Channel invasion, codenamed "Overlord," to take place early in May 1944. An invasion of the size and scope envisioned presented monumental planning and logistical problems. It required the buildup in England of nearly three million men and the supplies and equipment needed to support them as they moved into France. It also involved the accumulation of literally thousands of combat and supply ships and landing craft, as well as months of coordinated Air Force bombing of the Germans' transportation and supply network in occupied France. It was necessary to develop amphibious vehicles and tanks to get men, materials, and firepower ashore, and to build special equipment to break through concrete defenses, minefields and other obstructions. Finally, exact locations and timetables for the landings had to be worked out.

There were about 250,000 American soldiers in England by the middle of 1943, a million by January, 1944, and a million and a half by mid-1944. By the time General Eisenhower arrived to take over as Supreme Commander of "Overlord" in January, 1944, the south of England was crammed full of American, British, and Canadian troops. Every available bit of space was filled with vehicles, munitions, and supplies, and there were ships and landing craft in every harbor, river, and creek.

The invasion plan called for an initial assault by five divisions, each landing in its own area and establishing its own beachhead. In all, eight divisions—nearly 200,000 men—were to be landed on D-Day, along with 14,000 vehicles. A massive buildup was to follow as soon as the beaches were secure, so that 17 divisions would be in France with adequate vehicles, fuel, munitions, and supplies by D-Day plus 3. Weather and tide conditions in the English Channel prohibited more than four consecutive days of unloading reinforcements and supplies without a sheltered harbor. It was doubtful that a French port could be occupied and put into working condition quickly, so the invasion planners constructed hundreds of concrete modules that could be towed over in pieces and assembled into two huge artificial harbors. These "Mulberries" could be secured to the beaches to provide sheltered water and dockside facilities for unloading oceangoing vessels. To ensure that the invasion force got the millions of gallons of fuel it needed, a pipeline, codenamed PLUTO (for PipeLine Under

The Ocean), was built and laid across the bottom of the English Channel.

Extremely tight security was maintained about every aspect of "Overlord" from the earliest stages of planning. Elaborate efforts were made to deceive and confuse the Germans about where landings would take place. These included, among other schemes, the "creation" of nonexistent divisions and the planting of detailed but false invasion plans where German agents were sure to find them. The High Command was greatly concerned that the Germans might learn where the invasion force was headed because surprise is the most important ingredient necessary for success in an amphibious operation. Given twenty-four hours' notice of the invasion site, the Germans could move their reserves into position and throw the attack back into the sea. Forty-eight hours' notice would doom the invasion to certain failure. Considering the number of people involved in the D-Day preparations, it is remarkable that the secret was kept at all. Many millions of maps were printed for "Overlord," twenty thousand men were involved in building the artificial harbors, and hundreds of thousands of people were busy preparing and transporting men and material for the invasion. Yet despite the complexity and vast scale of the operation, security was maintained.

Hitler knew that the Allies would attempt an invasion, probably in northern France, but he didn't know exactly where or when. In November, 1943, he sent Rommel to inspect the French coastal defenses. Rommel reported them sorely inadequate, and in January 1944 was given command of the defense of northern France under Field Marshal von Rundstedt. The Germans were hard pressed to defend the more than six hundred miles of coastline from Brittany to the Dutch border, and Rommel quickly put half a million men to work building landing obstructions and concrete bunkers. His military intelligence led him to conclude that the invasion would come in the Bay of the Seine in Normandy. Von Rundstedt expected the invasion in the Pas de Calais region, owing partly to Allied deception and also because it was the shortest route across the Channel. The generals had other disagreements. Von Rundstedt believed that the best strategy was to conserve his Panzer strike force until after the landing, and then counterattack where and when he wanted. Rommel believed that it was necessary to deny the enemy even an initial foothold, and that if an invasion was to be defeated it would have to be done on the beaches.

Because the Allies had almost complete control of the air, Rommel realized that it would be difficult for reserves to move into action from any distance. He wanted reserve Panzer divisions in his immediate area of operations. Von Rundstedt, with Hitler's concurrence, did not want to gamble on a specific location for the invasion and refused to commit his reserve divisions, keeping them well back. Denied Panzer reserves, Rommel had his men work feverishly through the winter and spring to make the beaches of Normandy an impregnable fortress laced with pillboxes, beach obstructions, mines, and all manner of fortifications.

The Allies chose Normandy as the landing site because, despite Rommel's efforts, it was less heavily defended than the Pas de Calais. During May 1944, Allied bombing and reconnaissance activity increased, as did the volume of radio messages between the French Underground and England. These signs made it clear to the Germans that the invasion would come soon. Both the Allies and the Germans knew that there were only eight days in June when the combination of tide and dawn light would be favorable for amphibious landings, and that if the invasion did not take place on June 5, 6, or 7, conditions would not be suitable again for another two weeks.

On May 30, Von Rundstedt reported to Hitler that there was no reason to believe the invasion "immediately imminent." On June 4, the Luftwaffe's meteorological service advised that because of bad weather no Allied action could be expected for at least two weeks. Rommel—who because of Allied air superiority and the inclement weather had neither aerial nor naval reconnaissance of England—reported that because of a gale in the Channel, the invasion was not imminent. He then left by car for his home in Germany to celebrate his wife's birthday and meet with Hitler about moving the Panzer reserves closer to the coast.

The invasion plan required extraordinarily intricate coordination and timing. Thousands of ships and landing craft had to leave hundreds of harbors and anchorages to arrive, under cover of darkness, at their appointed places off the Normandy coast at just the right time. Meanwhile, on the night before the landings, three parachute divisions were to be dropped behind the enemy beach defenses to secure critical roads, bridges, and rail junctions. A minimum of twenty-four hours' notice was needed for all the elements of the invasion force to get to the right place at the right time. Since everything was to be carried out under complete radio silence, every detail had to be planned in advance. Once the complex invasion process was set in motion, it would be virtually impossible to call it off or to change a detail.

Weather and tide were critical for a successful landing. Ideal conditions would put the sea halfway between high and low tide about half an hour after the first light of dawn. Cloud cover would be light enough to permit bombing, and surface winds light enough to keep the sea relatively smooth. Eisenhower had set Monday, June 5 as D-Day, and the first convoys had started to sail from the most distant ports on June 1. But on Saturday, June 3, Eisenhower's meteorologists reported a marked deterioration in the weather, and Eisenhower called for a twenty-four hour postponement. Planes were sent out to round up and turn back the ships already at sea.

The Germans did not have reliable reports on the weather as it moved from west to east over the Atlantic, but the Allies did. At a weather conference held on Sunday evening, June 4, amid gale force winds and heavy rain, Eisenhower was surprised to hear the meteorologists report that a "pocket" of improved weather— about 50 per cent cloud cover and falling winds—would appear over the invasion area for about 48 hours starting Monday night, and that it would be the best weather of the week. After Tuesday, June 5, it would be another two or three weeks before conditions were right again. Eisenhower knew that Rommel's beach defenses and minefields were being strengthened and extended with great rapidity. He knew, too, that many of his assault troops had already been aboard ship for some days and that to disembark them would damage morale, dull their fighting edge, and increase security risks. In short, further delay would cost more lives. He decided to go for Tuesday, June 6.

The huge invasion mechanism was set in motion, and at dawn on the morning of June 6, more than 1,200 combat vessels and 4,000 landing craft and ships—the largest armada ever assembled—were in position. By 5:30 in the morning the first assault waves were on their way to five separate beaches along a 50-mile stretch of the Normandy coast. The paratroopers were already behind enemy lines disrupting communications and securing key positions. Early on the morning of June 6, the first unconfirmed report of the invasion was broadcast by the American radio networks.

The initial assault, particularly the American landing at Omaha Beach, met with heavy resistance, but for the most part the landings went well. The Allied air forces completely dominated the sky, and under the protective cover provided by 12,000 planes, wave after wave of landing craft unloaded men and equipment on the beaches. By nightfall on D-Day it was apparent that the Germans had been taken completely by surprise and that the Allies were in France to stay. More than 150,000 troops had landed and taken nearly 100 square miles of territory the first day.

Meanwhile Rommel was rushing back to Normandy from his home. He had been right about the invasion's location. He had also been right about the need to commit the Panzer divisions quickly. But the German High Command thought the Normandy landings were just a diversionary attack intended to draw their forces away from the main invasion that would come later, probably across the Straits of Dover. Once they realized that Normandy was, in fact, the main event, the High Command still could not release the powerful Panzer reserves to Von Rundstedt and Rommel without Hitler's permission. But Hitler was asleep, and his staff thought it unwise to disturb him.

The Panzers were not released for action until the afternoon of June 6 and, as they finally began to roll toward the coast, they were exposed to incessant air attack. They continued to move through the night and were still on the road the morning of June 7 when they again came under concentrated attack from the air. By the time they approached the coast, the Panzers had taken heavy losses before even engaging a single enemy tank. Meanwhile, thousands of Allied troops continued to pour onto the beach, applying heavy pressure on the Germans who were trying to hold their ground and wait for Panzer reinforcements. It was more than thirty hours from the time the first Allied troops hit the beaches until the Panzer reserves were ready to counterattack, and by then it was too late for the Germans to regain the initiative. The Allies were firmly ashore and rapidly pushing inland.

The Allies next undertook to build up their reserves of men and supplies and to prepare for deeper penetration into France. By June 12 the five separate landing sites had been linked together into one continuous beachhead forty-two miles long. By June 18 an enormous amount of materiel and more than six hundred thousand men had been put ashore. American forces cut across the Normandy (Cotentin) Peninsula from the beachhead and, after five days of nonstop assault, captured the important Atlantic seaport of Cherbourg on June 27.

Unfortunately for the Allies, the Germans managed to block Cherbourg's harbor and wreck the port facilities; weeks passed before it could be used at all, and months before it was in full operation. Even so, over a million and a half Allied troops were in France before the end of July. But they were bottled up, unable to break out of the beachhead because the Germans were making effective use of the Normandy hedgerows—natural fortifications with solid walls of earth and thick hedges, a difficult obstacle for which the Allies were unprepared.

The Germans fought bitterly in Normandy because they knew that once the Allies broke out of the hedgerow country they would have flat terrain all the way to Paris. Eisenhower became concerned with the failure to gain ground, so he implemented a plan in which General Montgomery, by engaging the Germans at the eastern end of the Allied line near Caen, forced them to put seven Panzer divisions and four heavy tank battalions there to keep the Allies from breaking out. This heavy concentration weakened the rest of the German defense line. In early August, General George Patton broke through these weakened defenses and, in a lightning sweep, hooked around and behind the Germans to envelop their main forces. With Patton completing his end run, Montgomery pushing the Germans from the west, and a Canadian force closing from the north, the Germans defending Normandy were about to be completely encircled near the town of Falaise. Despite the advice of his generals, who saw the encirclement developing and urged withdrawal to the east, Hitler ordered his forces to counterattack. The attack failed and the Allies continued pushing to close the Falaise pocket. Inside the pocket nearly fifty thousand

German troops were killed or captured, but many were able to get away because Montgomery was slow to close the escape corridor. The Germans left a mass of equipment and a great many tanks behind as they retreated across the Seine. The road to Paris lay open.

On August 15 an Allied invasion force landed in the south of France on the Mediterranean coast between Cannes and Toulon. These landings met light resistance. Two days later the main German forces were ordered to retreat northward. Also on August 17, knowing that the Allies were near, the French Resistance began the liberation of Paris from within. A week later the German commander of Paris, disregarding Hitler's order to destroy the city, surrendered it to a Free French division moving east from Normandy. By September 3 the Allied armies moving north from the Mediterranean landing captured Lyon. A week later they linked up with Patton's troops moving east from Normandy and Brittany.

Hitler's world was crumbling. On July 20, a month before the liberation of Paris, there had been an unsuccessful attempt on his life by a group of German Army officers who believed that, with Hitler alive, Germany was doomed to total destruction. In the wake of the assassination attempt Hitler had many of his senior officers executed. Rommel was implicated in the plot, but because he was a national hero he was allowed to take his own life. The propaganda machine claimed he had been killed in an auto accident and gave him a state funeral. The executions led to extensive changes of command, but there was little that the new command could do to stop the Allied armies racing toward Germany.

On September 3, British troops captured Brussels and crossed the Dutch frontier. The next day they took the port of Antwerp completely intact, and immediately began to use it to handle the enormous amount of equipment and supplies steadily being sent from England. In the midst of their rapid advance, debate arose among the Allied generals as to the shape of the final push into Germany. Eisenhower favored the continuance of a broad front, while Patton wanted to lead a rapid thrust in the south.

Montgomery argued for a concentrated pinpoint thrust in the north, under his command. If successful, the benefits of

Montgomery's strategy would include the destruction of the German V-2 rocket launching sites. Since early September these deadly weapons had been hitting England, causing many casualties and much damage. Montgomery's plan would strike at Germany in the north through the Netherlands, outflanking the still heavily fortified Siegfried Line. Using this strategy he would then overrun the Ruhr, a vitally important German industrial center. Eisenhower supported Montgomery's plans, and on September 17 Montgomery launched a daring airborne assault in an attempt to secure footholds on the east bank of the Rhine in the area of Nijmegen and Arnhem.

The plan, unfortunately, did not succeed.

After Montgomery's failure to flank the Siegfried Line, the Allies focused their efforts on resupplying their troops, repairing French roads and railways, and consolidating their positions. Then in October their push resumed and, after three weeks of bitter fighting, American troops broke into Fortress Germany by piercing the Siegfried Line. In November the fight began for that part of Germany west of the Rhine. Though meeting bitter resistance, the Allies slowly pushed the Germans back toward the Rhine.

On the Eastern Front in July, 1943, the Russians had decisively defeated the Germans at Kursk in the largest tank battle in the history of warfare. More than 6,000 tanks were involved in the action on a huge open tabletop plateau. When the battle of Kursk was over, the Germans had in effect lost the war in Russia and it became only a matter of time until they were driven out completely. The Russians followed their victory at Kursk with a winter offensive that began in December 1943. On the northern flank, this offensive led to the relief of Leningrad, which had been under siege for nearly three years, during which time nearly a million of the city's people had been killed, 750,000 of them by cold and starvation. In the south the Russians cut off a German army in the Crimea early in 1944 and forced the remaining German troops to retreat to the Panther Line, part of Hitler's East Wall, a prepared fortification which he planned to hold as his eastern frontier. The Red Army began a new series of attacks during the summer of 1944. The Germans were vastly outnumbered in men, tanks, and air support, and were no longer able to contain the Russian advance. Within three weeks the German Army had lost 350,000 men—it had virtually disintegrated. By the end of 1944 the Red Army was ready to advance into Germany from the east, while the American and British armies were striking from the west.

David Stephen Douglass landed at Omaha Beach on D-Day. As an American footsoldier, he walked most of the way from Normandy across France and into Germany. But his most vivid recollections are of D-Day. Since the war he has been a dishwasher, worked in a gas station, graded psychological tests, been a salesman, a school teacher, and now is a journalist.

David Stephen Douglass:

I was a member of the U.S. First Division. We were known as "The Big Red One" because we wore an arm patch with a big red "1" on it. At the time of D-Day we were considered a veteran division because we had fought in North Africa and been in the invasion of Sicily. So we were shipped over to England as experienced combat troops for the invasion of Europe.

One of the things about the army that you really grow to resent is that the more combat experience you have, the more combat you see. In that sense "there ain't no justice," because after you've been through a few campaigns and survived, you feel that the fresh troops just over from the States ought to take the risks that you've been taking while you get a rest. But that doesn't usually happen. They keep right on using the experienced combat units in every new operation on the theory that they are combat-hardened and less likely to panic in a tight spot. While probably true, this doesn't make it pleasant to be a member of a combat-hardened unit.

In any case, we were sent to the south of England and were crammed into a huge tent city. There were thousands and thousands of troops there—American, British, Canadian, French—and an incredible amount of armor, trucks, jeeps, guns, all kinds of equipment and supplies packed in like sardines in a can.

There was so much war materiel and manpower in the south of

England that people used to joke about how they expected the island to sink under the weight of it all. While we were there, we were going through training exercises and waiting for what we knew was going to be the invasion of Europe. Of course at the time we didn't know where or when the invasion would take place. We spent a good deal of time training and just trying to kill time. I think that for the average G.I. there are three kinds of time: periods of waiting when you have to deal with incredible boredom; periods of movement when you worry about what's coming next; and periods of action, when you don't have time to think, but operate almost entirely on the instinct to survive.

The build-up of invasion forces took some time and we had to cool our heels. The typical enlisted man or noncom doesn't know what's going on. You are just there. Nobody bothers to tell you what's happening, or when it's going to happen, or anything else. I recall that they sealed off the entire south coast of England so that we couldn't go up to London, we couldn't get letters out, we weren't supposed to make phone calls—not that most of us had anybody to call. We were really in a kind of limbo. Obviously this was done for security reasons. You could tell that the tempo of activities was increasing all the time, because the roads were full of all kinds of convoys moving south to the ports: tanks, artillery, trucks full of supplies, vehicle after vehicle, endless numbers of men. As the month of May progressed we knew that whatever was going to happen would occur pretty soon. You could sense it from the increased activity.

In the first day or two of June we were moved out with all our gear and trucked to the embarkation port, where we were ferried out to a troop ship. I remember the harbor was full of ships of all kinds. Some were shallow draft landing craft, some were more conventional ships with assault landing craft on their davits in place of the life boats they would normally carry. There were naval ships all over the place. I remember that as we were going down to the port of embarkation we drove through several towns. In one we happened to pass a nice-looking civilian girl. We knew this was going to be one of the last friendly females we were going to see for a while, if ever again, and the whistling and the catcalls were something fierce. It must have been really embarrassing for her, but she didn't seem to mind. The people we passed must have known where we were going, **and** I remember them throwing kisses and waving to us.

They really packed us in on the troop ship. When we were all crammed together and very uncomfortable, the waiting started all over again. There was a certain amount of letter writing, although we knew that the letters wouldn't be mailed until after the actual invasion. It's an odd feeling to be writing a letter to your family that you know is not going to be mailed until after the invasion takes place, because by then you may be dead. There you were, you were kind of worried, but you just couldn't sit there and stew. So there was a fair amount of card playing and clowning around.

Then, I recall, they briefed us. It was the first time we found out where we were going: a place called Omaha Beach on the Normandy Peninsula. Of course, by that time there was no turning back because once they told us our objective they weren't going to let us off the ship. They certainly didn't want us talking to anybody with the information we had. We were given very detailed maps and shown reconnaissance photographs of the landing site. Essentially, Omaha was a beach area with a fairly high bluff behind it. It looked like a tough spot, because the Germans had gun emplacements up on the heights trained down at the beach. We were told that there was going to be a heavy naval bombardment as well as bombing from the air and that the beach would be pretty well worked over by the time we got there.

I remember, as we sat there being briefed, that I was impressed with the way everything had been worked out in incredible detail—or so it seemed. The maps showed every pillbox, bunker and machine gun nest. They even showed where the minefields were and the location and types of underwater and beach obstacles we would encounter. We knew within a matter of yards where we were to be landed, what our objectives were, and what we were to do when we got to shore. Our weapons were wrapped in waterproof plastic so that, as we came in off the assault craft, they would be protected. We were even issued little vomit bags in case we were to get seasick, which most of us eventually did.

We were on board that ship for three or four days before anything really happened. It was crowded and there weren't enough toilets for the number of men on board, so the toilets backed up. You could smell the backed up toilets and there were just the smells you have from thousands of sweating men being packed in together. All in all, that ship was pretty foul. There weren't enough berths for the number of men on board, so we spent a great deal of time on deck in weather that was generally miserable. When we weren't on deck we spent a good deal of time waiting to use the can or lined up waiting to get chow.

Finally, late in the afternoon on June 5 we upped anchor and very soon found ourselves part of a large convoy: troop ships, LST's, LCI's, supply ships, destroyers, minesweepers and the lot. It was a pretty good sized convoy, and we were soon in open sea—actually the English Channel. Once we were underway I recall a distinct change in mood. The clowning and the card playing stopped. People seemed to become rather quiet. I guess the best way to describe it would be introspective. The ship was such a mess, we didn't want to stay on board any longer than we absolutely had to. On the other hand, none of us were looking forward to what was coming. The guys started to talk, but not about the usual stuff. They talked in a more personal way. Usually the guys in the army are your buddies, but you don't know all that much about their inner thoughts. And I remember that on this occasion it wasn't what you would call the usual G.I. talk.

The crossing was really rough and a lot of us got seasick. I think most of us were aware in some way that we were making history. We had been preparing for months and suddenly all the pieces were coming together. The thousands and thousands of troops and tanks and other equipment that were all over the south of England were now on these ships and moving to France. Everywhere, as far as you could see, there were ships. It was exciting. You never saw so much military power in one place at one time. It gave you the feeling that our side was invincible, but you still felt personally vulnerable.

Nobody seemed terribly frightened when you looked at them, but I was scared to death inside. I'm sure everybody else was scared inside. It was interesting and somewhat comforting to be on deck because there were just masses of ships and you got the feeling that you were not alone in this. After dark, probably around midnight, we heard planes going over. They kept coming and coming, it seemed like thousands of them. Some of them, it turned out, were towing gliders full of airborne troops, others were bombers going over. We had the feeling that there was an endless amount of air power above us. The Channel was rough and there was a hell of a lot of seasickness, but at some point in the early morning—about 2 A.M., maybe earlier, I don't remember—they served what we all called "The Last Supper." It was actually a pre-invasion breakfast. As I recall, they served steak and eggs or something like that. Anyway, most of us weren't very hungry. I tried to eat, but wasn't very interested or successful at it. But there were a few guys packing away second and third helpings.

At about 4 A.M. we assembled on deck by units for a final briefing and began to embark into the assault landing craft. This was done in a variety of ways. Ideally you got onto your assault craft on the deck and they used the davits to lower it into the sea already loaded. Others went down ladders or scrambling nets. The sea was rough and it took longer for loading than I guess they figured. We went down the scrambling nets that were laid over the side of the ship. Let me tell you that's not an easy way to board an assault craft. For one thing you were so damn overloaded with gear that you can barely move. We all had life preservers on, as well as our weapons and backpacks. In addition, we had gas masks, were carrying ration kits, canteens, knives and entrenching tools. Each of us also carried about 200 rounds of ammunition plus grenades.

The Quartermaster Corps, being typically Army, had set up a list of specifications of what you had to carry that exceeded or at least damn near equalled your own weight. You were so loaded down with stuff that you could barely move. The problem was that the sea was fairly heavy and you had to get into a landing craft that was bobbing up and down from a ship that was pitching and rolling, but the two were not necessarily moving in the same direction at the same time. So you went down the scrambling nets hanging on for dear life, and the trick was to try to jump into the landing craft at just the right moment. Needless to say, some guys missed and landed with a hell of a bang, some sprained their ankles, some went into the drink.

Once we were all in the landing craft it pulled away and started circling around the transport. When the whole unit was loaded, the boats stopped circling, fanned out, and started in for shore. I guess the beach was some eight or ten miles away. We felt that just getting into the landing craft and riding it in was as bad as anything that we were likely to encounter on the beach. The spray soaked you incessantly mile after mile. I'd guess we got into the landing craft between 4 and 5 A.M. and we were in it for more than three hours because we didn't come in on the first wave which hit the beach about 6:30, but in the 4th wave which didn't hit the beach until about 7:30.

While we were cruising around waiting for the right timing for our wave to go, we could see and hear the tremendous naval bombardment going on. Thousands and thousands of shells softening up the beach before the first wave went in. Battleships and cruisers and destroyers firing away salvo after salvo. We could hear planes overhead, even though we couldn't see them due to the overcast, dropping their bombs supposedly on the beach. We could see landing ships rigged up with rocket launching devices that fired a hundred rockets or more at a time toward the beaches. All this firepower was very heartening to us.

Our run up to the beach seemed to take forever. I don't know how many miles it was, maybe 10 miles, maybe not that much, but it was a long run, and the sea was heavy, and it seemed to me that we were just wallowing on and on. There were 30 or 40 of us on board and every one of us was sick and wet and cold. Nobody talked because we were too seasick and miserable.

As we got closer to the beach we began to see what looked like utter chaos. There were landing craft all over the place, some at crazy angles, submerged, sinking or sunk. There were a mass of obstructions in the water and on the beach—pointed tetrahedral obstacles, "hedgehogs" that looked like monstrous overgrown jacks, all kinds of stakes driven into the sand so that they would be underwater at high tide. The Germans attached mines and explosive charges to these obstacles so that as we came in our landing craft would be blown out of the water or at least have holes torn in their hulls.

Our final half-mile run up to the beach seemed to take hours. By now there was tremendous fire coming out at us from the German guns on the heights behind the beach and from some cliffs at the far end of the beach. It seemed that all the softening up had done nothing. The Germans were zeroed in on the approaches and the beach and were knocking hell out of us.

There were bodies floating around and parts of bodies and masses of debris in the water. Around us you could see amphibious tanks—they had canvas sides that made them look like boats—being swamped by the heavy seas and going down with the guys inside obviously drowning. You saw the DUK-W amphibious vehicles that we called "ducks" swamping because they were so overloaded they had only a few inches of freeboard and couldn't make it through the chop. As we got close to the beach, one of the landing craft running in with us blew up and literally disintegrated. It either hit a mine or took a direct hit from a high explosive shell. One second it was there, the next it wasn't.

None of this was expected. We had been led to believe that resistance would be fairly light and that the bombing and shelling would neutralize whatever defenses there were. But what actually happened (we found out much later) was that, unknown to our intelligence, a strong German division had been moved into the area facing our objective of Omaha Beach. They weren't expected to be there. It was by sheer chance that they were. And they were really ready for us. Also, either because the weather was bad or because they were being conservative, the bombers which had gone over to soften up the beach had dropped their loads a mile or so behind the beach into the swamp area. They had not hit the German's defensive positions at all. I don't know what happened to the naval shelling and the rockets, but they didn't seem to do it either. The waves that came in ahead of us were absolutely cut down. As soon as the ramps went down the German guns were zeroed in on our guys and they were cut to ribbons. In fact, the landing craft weren't even getting to the beach. They were being hung up on the obstructions and the mines and dumping their men in deep water. It was a carnage. The sea was literally red with blood.

By the time we came in, the beach obstructions were supposed to be cleared but were not. There were landing craft out of commission all over the place and others milling around in total confusion. Anyway, when the guy lowered our ramp we found ourselves right in front of a bunch of steel obstructions, "hedgehogs" sticking out of the water. There were machine guns firing at us and you could see them kicking up little holes in the water all around us. At first, the guys in the front were a little hesitant to get into the water, so the Navy guys, who wanted to get the hell out of there, started yelling to move it and the noncoms kicked a few asses and off we went.

When we hit the water, I'd say it was chest high. We were about a hundred yards from the beach at this point, but it felt like a lot more than a hundred. The water was cold as hell and there was a lot of surf and you are loaded down with about a hundred and fifty pounds of heavy and cumbersome gear. You can barely move, and they are firing at you. The sandy bottom, which we expected to be fairly level, was very uneven and full of holes kicked up by all of the shells and mines that had exploded. As you're fighting your way through the surf trying to get to the beach, you'd hit one of these holes and stumble ass over teakettle down over your head. Then you'd struggle to get up, and a wave would hit you and you'd go down again. There were bodies all over the place in the water, some floating face up, some face down. The first thing I did was to make for the nearest steel obstacle and hide behind it. This is what most of us did.

Some of the guys in the earlier waves had made it to the cover of a seawall about ten or twenty yards up on the beach. On Omaha Beach there was a kind of breakwater that provided some protection if you could get to it, but it was hard to get there. There were a lot of dead and wounded men lying on the exposed sand between the surf and the seawall. So if you were coming in from the water, you made first for the obstacles and hid behind those. Someone who hasn't been through it can't possibly imagine how exposed, how naked you feel in the face of enemy fire. Especially when it's as concentrated as it was on Omaha Beach. That's why your first and only instinct is to find cover and stay there as long as you can. Anyway, the tide was coming in, and, as it did, we kept as little of ourselves exposed as possible and slowly worked our way forward.

It's almost impossible to give an impression of what was happening on that beach. The smell, the noise, the sense of utter and awful and total confusion, the men lying dead and wounded in the water and on the beach. Packs, ammunition, rations, boxes, communications equipment, all kinds of gear strewn all over the place. Wreckage everywhere. You just have no idea of what it was like. It was beyond imagining.

At the time I wasn't thinking in those terms. I was just trying to save my skin and get my ass up into a protected area, working my way up from the surf slowly, trying to stay in the water so as to present the smallest possible target until I could get from one obstacle to the next. I remember resting behind the obstacles and trying to get my bearings. I was very disoriented, partly because of the chaos on the beach, but also because nothing seemed familiar to me. I could not identify any of the landmarks or objectives covered in the briefings. This bothered me a great deal. I couldn't figure out what was wrong with me. Eventually it came to me that we must have landed in the wrong place. That is, in fact, exactly what happened. I remember thinking that if we survived we'd probably catch some kind of hell about it.

There was no sense of order of any kind on the beach. In effect, all the careful planning of who was supposed to go where and take what objective was out the window. It was clear that the German positions were totally intact and that they had us pinned down on the beach and were slaughtering us. We landed right smack in their laps. The softening up had not done its job, and there we were. No one was getting off the beach, and more and more men were crowding behind the little bit of shelter provided by the seawall. Some were wounded, some dead, some were still okay, but nobody was moving forward.

There we huddled without plan, and I would say without any particular leadership, for quite some time. I don't know how long we were there, but by then it must have been mid-morning. The Germans were positioned above us in the dunes so they could cut us down before we could get close enough to knock out their machine guns or artillery.

Finally, some of our destroyers came very close inshore, began firing very accurately on the German positions, and knocked a number of them out. It's much easier to hit a gun position when you can see it firing. During our softening up bombardment the Germans hadn't returned our fire, so the Navy had a hard time getting an accurate fix on them. But now, with the German guns blazing away, our spotters could fix the German positions exactly.

This close naval fire support created a dramatic change on the beach. I don't know if it was morale or a more concrete military thing. But there was less of a sense of hopelessness. By then some tanks and armored bulldozers had gotten onto the beach and one of the bulldozers worked its way up to a bunker and literally buried the occupants under a mass of sand. Soon after that, under cover of the naval shelling, a squad of men rushed a German position and knocked it out.

I know it's a cliché to talk about "the tide of battle," but very, very slowly, almost imperceptibly at first, the hopelessness gave way to a sense that our fate was in our own hands. Then gradually, as we began to isolate and knock out their positions, the intensity of the German firing began to diminish. You could literally feel the initiative shift over to our side. It took us quite a lot longer to get off of the beach, but we were no longer paralyzed, we were moving forward.

As the balance of firepower began to shift in our favor, more and more German positions were knocked out. They lost the advantage of being able to blanket all areas of the beach with crossfire. From then on we took one position after another, either by flanking or by frontal assault. The bulldozers and tanks helped cut paths through the wire and the minefields and by mid-afternoon all resistance on Omaha had ceased. By the end of the day the underwater obstacles and the minefields had been cleared and masses of men and materiel were being put ashore. We dug in in the dunes and were given a rest in anticipation of the massive counterattack that was sure to come, but never did.

13

DACHAU, AUSCHWITZ, RAVENSBRÜCK: 1941-1945

Marie Claude Vaillant-Couturier, Franz Blaha

In block 25, in the courtyard, there were rats as big as cats running about and gnawing the corpses and even attacking the dying who had not enough strength left to chase them away. . . . The work at Auschwitz consisted of clearing demolished houses, road building, and especially the draining of marshland. This was by far the hardest work, for all day long we had our feet in the water and there was the danger of being sucked down. It frequently happened that we had to pull out a comrade who had sunk in up to the waist. During the work the SS men and women who stood guard over us would beat us with cudgels and set their dogs on us. Many of our friends had their legs torn by the dogs. I even saw a woman torn to pieces and die under my very eyes when Tauber, a member of the SS, encouraged his dog to attack her and grinned at the sight.

—Marie Claude Vaillant-Couturier

Then Russian children were brought to Dachau. There were, I believe, 2,000 boys, six to seventeen years old. They were kept in one or two special blocks. They were assigned to particularly brutal people. Those were the so-called professional criminals. They beat these young boys at every step, and gave them the hardest work. They worked particularly in the plantations where they had to pull ploughs, sowing machines, and street rollers instead of horses and motors being used. At least 70 percent of them died of tuberculosis.

—Dr. Franz Blaha

Dachau, Auschwitz, Ravensbrück: 1941–1945

It is difficult to imagine what life was like in occupied Europe and impossible to understand the extent of fear and suffering experienced by those who found themselves singled out for special attention by the Nazis. It is difficult for civilized, rational human beings to comprehend why certain groups were singled out for destruction at all. One cannot make sense out of senseless slaughter, but one can examine the conditions that made it possible. Those conditions began when Hitler first introduced the concept of a "master race" into the receptive minds of the German people.

Hitler was thirty-six in 1925 when Mein Kampf, his statement of political philosophy, was first published. The book is full of flawed observations, grotesque interpretations of history, and distortions of reality resulting from his own enormous prejudices. When the book was first published it made little, if any, impact. In its first year it sold fewer than ten thousand copies, and three years later only three thousand. Had Hitler remained an obscure political malcontent, Mein Kampf would soon have been dismissed and forgotten. But as he and the National Socialists became politically more important the book gained wide readership. More than a million copies were sold in 1933, the year Hitler became Chancellor of Germany. Few may have realized its importance at the time, but Mein Kampf was a blueprint of Nazi tactics and policies, containing the seminal statement and "justification" of Hitler's racist ideas.

Hitler argued the "racial superiority" of the Aryan, granted him mastery over the rest of the species, and asserted the need for him to remain pure and uncontaminated. He also spelled out the relationship which he wanted to exist between the Aryan and "lesser" races and alien ideas.

What his ideas meant in practice was that the German "master race" was to subjugate the rest of Europe and exercise mastery over nations and peoples deemed to be inferior. But the grotesque nature of Nazi racial policy was not limited to the conquered people of Europe. The Nazis perceived that they would need a large number of "racially perfect" Aryans to maintain domination over their subject states. This gave rise to Lebensborn, an officially sponsored breeding policy. Every single German woman of "racially acceptable physical characteristics" who desired a child was encouraged to have one sired by an SS man or other "racially valuable procreation helper," selected on the basis of his Nordic appearance.

Germany's successes in Europe early in the war made it possible for the Nazis to put their other theories of racial supremacy into action as well. They quickly began to create what they called a New Order in Europe. This New Order included the concept of Grossraum whereby conquered lands were made part of a Greater Germanic Estate owned and managed by the Germans themselves. They moved racial and national groups of people around within the "estate" to conform to their political and economic master plan. The New Order assigned menial economic functions to non-Nordic peoples, who were kept subservient and uneducated.

As the war dragged on, more and more German men were taken into military service and it became necessary to bring workers from the conquered nations to maintain war production in Germany's factories. Despite aggressive efforts to attract free foreign labor into Germany, only about 200,000 workers volunteered—far short of the number needed. The shortage was met by using prisoners of war and men, women, and children from German-occupied Europe as forced labor in munitions and other defense industries, often under slave labor conditions. In order to exploit the availability of such labor fully, factories were built close to camps where "inferior" racial and national groups were concentrated. By the end of the war more than 7 million people from occupied Europe and 2 million prisoners of war had been thus exploited in conditions so vile and inhuman that they almost defy description. The victims were crowded into boxcars for shipment to Germany where they were virtually starved, made to live in unsanitary, disease-ridden barracks, and forced to work endless hours.

However, this exploitation of non-Nordic populations did not constitute the entire Nazi plan for the New Order. It also called for elimination of the Slavs, the Gypsies, and the Jews. The scope of the plan was so huge and so monstrous that it included a "reduction" of the Slavic population in Poland and the USSR by 30 million and the transplantation of an Aryan elite into these areas. While the "goal" of eliminating 30 million Slavs was not realized, many millions of Russians were killed, as were some 200,000 Gypsies. But the brunt of Germany's policy of genocide was borne by the Jews.

Jews had lived in Germany continuously and had been persecuted for their religion since early times. This was due in part to the widely held belief that they were responsible for the Crucifixion of Christ, in part to their insistence on a separate Jewish religious and national identity, and in part because they performed such historically unpopular functions as moneylending.

A new wave of anti-Semitism began after Germany's defeat in World War I. When the Weimar Republic was established, Jews, for the first time in German history, were permitted to hold high positions in government. Born out of Germany's defeat, the Weimar government was never popular; the economic collapse and other problems were blamed on the "Jewish government." Also, Germany's Jews were highly visible. Although Jews made up only 1 percent of the population, they constituted 10 percent of the doctors and dentists, 16 percent of the lawyers, and 17 percent of the bankers. Furthermore, the Jews were intellectually and economically progressive, and tended to be agents of change. As such, they were distrusted by the conservative classes—artisans, shopkeepers, farmers, landowners, and the military. In a world that was changing too fast to suit those accustomed to running it, the Jews were made the scapegoats for anything that threatened the established order.

Hitler did not introduce anti-Semitism into Germany; he merely exploited the existing opinion that Jewish influence should be removed from German society. Racism manifests itself by defining the qualities of one people at the expense of another. The Nazis defined "the master race" by glorifying the Aryan and vilifying the Jew as his "opposite." The German propaganda machine presented Jews as subhuman, physically repellent stereotypes. This anti-Semitic message was everywhere—in political cartoons, posters, newspaper articles, films, even children's nursery rhymes.

Such incessant propaganda began to modify the attitudes of

even the most benign citizens. Conditioned to believe that the Jewish presence was inimical to the interests of National Socialism, they were brainwashed into seeing Jews as subhuman and thus did not react to the bestialities inflicted on them by the Nazis. Never in the twelve years of the Third Reich did any civic, academic, or even religious group inside Germany publicly protest the Nazis' anti-Semitic policies.

When there was no protest from any foreign government and no reaction within Germany to the events of *Kristallnacht* in 1938, Hitler construed this lack of interest as a mandate to do as he liked with the Jews. In 1941 he settled on what he euphemistically called the "final solution to the Jewish question," the systematic killing of the entire Jewish population of occupied Europe. Even after this extermination policy became known through official sources in 1942, it was received in the free world with an almost total indifference that was tantamount to complicity. Efforts to save the Jews from Germany and Nazi-occupied Europe were half-hearted and fumbling. Since nobody wanted the Jews and there was nowhere for them to go, Hitler rationalized that he had no alternative but to destroy them.

What made Hitler's anti-Semitic policies different from other persecutions was his perception of the issue as racial rather than religious. When Jews were persecuted on religious grounds it was, at least theoretically, possible to escape death by accepting baptism. But when they were persecuted on the basis of race, religious conviction became irrelevant and death became inevitable simply on the basis of biological parentage.

Originally, Aryan racial purity did not require the murder of the Jews; all it called for was the prevention of social contact. But Nazi racial ideology made extermination inevitable, while circumstances made such a policy both practicable and profitable for the Germans. The conquest of Europe placed large numbers of Jews under Nazi control so that they could be easily rounded up. Every Jew who was killed provided economic benefit to the Germans in terms of property confiscated, slave labor, and even exploitation of the corpse itself: bodies were boiled for soap; hair was used for mattresses; gold fillings were taken from teeth and used as bullion; even eyeglasses, shoes, and clothing were used again. The combination of historical prejudice, virulent propaganda, and the myth of Aryan racial purity created a climate which made it possible for many thousands of Germans to participate in the extermination program and for hundreds of thousands more—who were aware of what was happening—to remain passive.

At first the plan was simply to round up the Jews and drive them into dense population clusters called ghettos. The ghettos were sealed off and manageable numbers of people were taken to killing grounds where they were made to dig trenches, then lined up in front of the trenches and shot. This method was used to kill 33,000 Jews in Kiev in two days and 16,000 in Pinsk in one day. Huge mass graves were dug to hold as many as 100,000 bodies. But this method proved to be too cumbersome and inefficient, so German technology was applied to the problem of mass extermination.

The Nazis had, even in their earliest years, begun to set up concentration camps, the first having been established at Dachau in 1933 and at Buchenwald in 1937. These camps were prisons to which the regime sent political opponents, intellectuals, or those unacceptable on racial or other grounds. Eventually the nature, size, and character of the concentration camps changed as millions of people from all the occupied countries of Europe were sent to them. There were two kinds of camps. Those near important factories were essentially labor camps, though people too old, too young, or too infirm to work were exterminated. Others were established specifically as extermination camps—Auschwitz, Chelmno, Treblinka, Sobibor, and Belsen.

It was in these camps that the grotesque technology of killing was perfected. At Treblinka 6,000 people were gassed and cremated every day. At Auschwitz, where the capacity was 12,000 to 15,000 a day, one million people were murdered in three years. In all, some 10 million people lost their lives in the Nazi camps. Nearly six million were Jews. More than four million Christians lost their lives as well, including at least a half-million Germans who opposed the Nazi regime.

But numbers cannot begin to describe what the camps were like. In the words of Holocaust survivor and author Elie Wiesel: "Auschwitz cannot be explained nor can it be visualized. Whether culmination or aberration of history, the Holocaust transcends history. Everything about it inspires fear and leads to despair: the dead are in possession of a secret that we, the living, are neither worthy of nor capable of recovering."

As the American and British armies pushed into Germany from the west and the Russians moved through Poland from the east, they came upon the indescribable horrors of one death camp after another. These camps became the ultimate evidence of Nazi depravity. The fate of the people incarcerated in them was so horrible and the number who perished so vast as to defy human comprehension. There is just no historical precedent, no frame of reference, to help us understand why and how what happened could happen.

Late in 1945 an international military tribunal met in Nuremberg, Germany, to try major Nazi war criminals for crimes which Chief U.S. Prosecutor Robert Jackson described as "so calculated, so malignant, and so devastating that civilization cannot tolerate their being ignored, because it cannot survive their being repeated." When the trial began, the general public knew very few details about the concentration camps, but as the survivors testified about their experiences the world was struck with inexpressible horror.

Mme. Marie Claude Vaillant-Couturier, a newspaper photographer before the war, was arrested early in 1942 because of her activities as a member of the French Resistance. She spent three years in the concentration camps of Auschwitz and Ravensbrück. Dr. Franz Blaha, a citizen of Czechoslovakia, was the head of a hospital in Moravia when the Germans seized him as a hostage in 1939 and imprisoned him until 1941 for cooperating with the Czech government. He was then confined to the Dachau concentration camp from 1941 until April 1945, when the camp was liberated by Allied forces. While at Dachau, Dr. Blaha performed thousands of autopsies on camp inmates, many of whom had been killed as the result of medical experiments.

Both these people testified as witnesses at the Nuremberg War Crimes Trial. Their experiences must be multiplied millions of times if one is to imagine the full extent of Nazi depravity and contempt for human life. To have endured even one day in the camps took courage; to have come through one day after another for years, as did Mme. Vaillant-Couturier and Dr. Blaha, bears testimony to the human will to survive. It has not been possible to trace what became of them after the war.

Marie Claude Vaillant-Couturier:

I was arrested on February 9, 1942 by Petain's French police, who handed me over to the German authorities after six weeks. I arrived on March 20 at Santé Prison in the German quarter. I was questioned on June 9, 1942. At the end of my interrogation they wanted me to sign a statement which was not consistent with what I had said. I refused to sign it. The officer who had questioned me threatened me. When I told him that I was not afraid of being shot, he said, "But we have at our disposal means for killing that are far worse than merely shooting." And the interpreter said to me, "You do not know what you have just done. You are going to leave for a concentration camp in Germany. One never comes back from there."

I was taken back to the Santé Prison where I was placed in solitary confinement. However, I was able to communicate with my neighbors through the piping and the windows. I was in a cell next to that of Georges Politzer, the philosopher, and Jacques Solomon, the physicist. Mr. Solomon was the son-in-law of Professor Langevin, a pupil of Curie, one of the first to study atomic disintegration.

Georges Politzer told me through the piping that during his interrogation, after having been tortured, he was asked whether he would write theoretical pamphlets for National Socialism. When he refused, he was told that he would be in the first train of hostages to be shot.

As for Jacques Solomon, he also was horribly tortured and then thrown into a dark cell and came out only on the day of his execution to say goodby to his wife, who also was under arrest at the Santé. Hélène Solomon told me in Romainville, where I found her after I left the Santé, that when she went to her husband he moaned and said, "I cannot take you in my arms, because I can no longer move them."

Every time the internees came back from their questioning one could hear moaning through the windows, and all said that they could not make any movements.

Several times during the five months I spent at the *Santé*, hostages were taken to be shot. When I left the *Santé* on August 20, 1942, I was taken to the Fortress of Romainville, which was a camp for hostages. There I was present on two occasions when they took hostages, on August 21 and September 22. Among the hostages who were taken away were the husbands of the women who were with me and who left for Auschwitz. Most of them died there. These women, for the most part, had been arrested only because of the activity of their husbands. They themselves had done nothing.

I left for Auschwitz on January 23, 1943, and arrived there on the 27th. I was with a convoy of 230 French women. Among us were Danielle Casanova, who died in Auschwitz; Maï Politzer, who also died in Auschwitz; and Hélène Solomon. They were intellectuals, schoolteachers; they came from all walks of life. Maï Politzer was a doctor; Danielle Casanova was a dental surgeon and was very active among the women. It is she who organized a resistance movement among the wives of prisoners.

Out of the 230 women, only 49 lived to come back to France. In the convoy there were some elderly women. I remember one who was 67 and had been arrested because she had kept her husband's shotgun as a souvenir. She died after a fortnight at Auschwitz. There were also cripples, among them a singer who had only one leg. She was taken out and gassed at Auschwitz. There was a young girl of 16, a college girl, Claudine Guérin; she also died at Auschwitz. And there were two women who had been acquitted by the German military tribunal, Marie Alonzo and Marie-Thérèse Fleuri; they died at Auschwitz.

It was a terrible journey. There were 60 of us in the car and we were given no food or drink during the journey. At the various stopping places we asked the Lorraine soldiers of the Wehrmacht who were guarding us whether we would arrive soon; and they replied, "If you knew where you are going you would not be in such a hurry to get there."

We arrived at Auschwitz at dawn. The seals on our cars were broken, and we were driven out by blows with the butt end of a rifle, and taken to the Birkenau Camp, a section of Auschwitz. It is situated in the middle of a great plain, which was frozen in the month of January. During this part of the journey we had to drag our luggage. As we passed through the door we knew only too well how slender our chances were that we would come out again, for we had already met columns of living skeletons going to work. As we entered we sang "The Marseillaise" to keep up our courage.

We were led to a large shed, then to the disinfecting station. There our heads were shaved and our registration numbers were tattooed on the left forearm. Then we were taken into a large room for a steam bath and a cold shower. In spite of the fact that we were naked, all this took place in the presence of SS men and women. We were then given clothing which was soiled and torn, a cotton dress and jacket of the same material.

As all this had taken several hours, we saw the men's camp from the windows of the block where we were. We then saw that the camp foremen were returning to the camp. Each foreman was followed by men who were carrying the dead. As they could hardly drag themselves along, every time they stumbled they were kicked to their feet again, or hit with the butt end of a rifle.

After that we were taken to the block where we were to live. There were no beds but only bunks, measuring 2 by 2 meters, and there nine of us had to sleep the first night without any mattress or blanket. We remained in blocks of this kind for several months. We could not sleep because every time one of the nine moved— this happened unceasingly because we were all ill—she disturbed the whole row.

At 3:30 in the morning the shouting of the guards woke us up, and with cudgel blows we were driven from our bunks to roll call. Nothing in the world could release us from going to the roll call; even those who were dying had to be dragged there. We had to stand there in rows of five until dawn, that is, 7 or 8 o'clock in the morning in winter; and when there was a fog, sometimes until noon. The German women guards in uniform came to count us. They had cudgels and they beat us more or less at random. We had a comrade, Germaine Renaud, a schoolteacher from Azay-le-Rideau in France, who had her skull broken before my eyes with a cudgel during the roll call.

On February 5, 1943, there was a general roll call. In the

morning at 3:30 the whole camp was awakened and sent out on the plain—normally the roll call was inside the camp. We remained out in front of the camp until five in the afternoon, in the snow, without any food. Then when the signal was given we had to go through the door one by one, and we were struck in the back with a cudgel, each one of us, in order to make us run. Those who could not run, either because they were too old or too ill, were caught by a hook and taken to Block 25, the "waiting block" for the gas chamber. On that day ten of the French women of our convoy were thus caught and taken to Block 25.

When all the internees were back in the camp a party to which I belonged was organized to go and pick up the bodies of the dead which were scattered over the plains as on a battlefield. We carried to the yard of Block 25 the dead and the dying without distinction, and they remained there stacked up in a pile.

This Block 25, which was the anteroom of the gas chamber, if one may express it so, is well known to me because at that time we had been transferred to Block 26 and our windows opened on the yard of Block 25. One saw stacks of corpses piled up in the courtyard, and from time to time a hand or a head would stir among the bodies, trying to free itself. In the courtyard there were rats as big as cats running about and gnawing the corpses and even attacking the dying who had not enough strength left to chase them away. The rate of mortality in that block was even more terrible than elsewhere because, having been condemned to death, prisoners received food or drink only if there was something left in the cans in the kitchen; which means that very often they went for several days without a drop of water.

One of our companions, Annette Épaux, a fine young woman of thirty, passing the block one day, was overcome with pity for those women who moaned from morning till night in all languages, "Drink. Drink. Water!" She came back to our block to get a little herbal tea, but as she was passing it through the bars of the window she was seen by the *Aufseherin*, who took her by the neck and threw her into Block 25. Two days later I saw her on the truck taking the internees to the gas chamber. She had her arms around another Frenchwoman, old Line Porcher, and when the truck started moving she cried, "Think of my little boy, if you ever get back to France!" Then they started singing "The Marseillaise." All my life I will remember Annette Épaux.

The work at Auschwitz consisted of clearing demolished houses, road building, and especially the draining of marshland. This was by far the hardest work, for all day long we had our feet in the water and there was the danger of being sucked down. It frequently happened that we had to pull out a comrade who had sunk in up to the waist. During the work the SS men and women who stood guard over us would beat us with cudgels and set their dogs on us. Many of our friends had their legs torn by the dogs. I even saw a woman torn to pieces and die under my very eyes when Tauber, a member of the SS, encouraged his dog to attack her and grinned at the sight.

The causes of death were extremely numerous. First of all, there was the complete lack of washing facilities. When we arrived at Auschwitz, for twelve thousand internees there was only one tap of water, unfit for drinking, and it was not always flowing. As this tap was in the German washhouse we could reach it only by passing through the guards, who were German common-law women prisoners, and they beat us horribly as we went by. It was therefore almost impossible to wash ourselves or our clothes. For more than three months we remained without changing our clothes. When there was snow, we melted some to wash in. Later, in the spring, when we went to work we would drink from a puddle by the roadside and then wash our underclothes in it. We took turns washing our hands in this dirty water. Our companions were dying of thirst, because we got only half a cup of some herbal tea twice a day.

Another cause of mortality and epidemic was the fact that we were given food in large red mess tins which were merely rinsed in cold water after each meal. As all the women were ill and had not the strength during the night to go to the lavatory trench (the access to which was beyond description), they used these containers for a purpose other than eating. The next day the tins were collected and taken to a refuse heap. During the day another team would come and collect them, wash them in cold water, and put them in use again.

Another cause of death was the problem of shoes. In the snow and mud of Poland, leather shoes were completely destroyed at the end of a week or two. Therefore our feet were frozen and covered with sores. We had to sleep with our muddy shoes on, lest they be stolen, and when the time came to get up for roll call, cries of anguish could be heard: "My shoes have been stolen!" Then one had to wait until the whole block had been emptied to look under the bunks for odd shoes.

The Jewish internees who came to roll call without shoes were immediately taken to Block 25. They were gassed for any reason whatsoever. Their conditions were, moreover, absolutely appalling. Although we were crowded eight hundred to a block and could scarcely move, they were one thousand five hundred to a block of similar dimensions, so that many of them could not sleep or even lie down at night.

The sores that formed on our feet quickly became infected for lack of care. Many of our companions went to the Revier blocks for sores on their feet and legs and never came back. The Revier was where the sick were put. This place could not be given the name of hospital, because it did not correspond in any way to our idea of a hospital.

To go there one had first to obtain authorization from the block chief, who seldom gave it. When it was finally granted we were led in columns to the infirmary. There, no matter what the weather, even if one had a temperature of 40° centigrade, one had to wait for several hours standing in a queue to be admitted. It frequently happened that patients died outside the door of the infirmary, before they could get in. Moreover, lining up in front of the infirmary was dangerous because if the queue was too long the SS came along, picked up all the women who were waiting, and took them straight to Block 25, that is to say to the gas chamber. So, very often the women preferred not to go to the Revier, and they died at their work or at roll call. Jewish women had not the right to be admitted to the Revier; they were taken straight to the gas chamber.

The only advantage of the Revier was that as one was in bed, one did not have to go to roll call; but one lay in appalling conditions, four in a bed less than 1 meter in width, each suffering from a different disease, so that anyone who came for leg sores would catch typhus or dysentery from neighbors. The straw mattresses were filthy and they were changed only when absolutely rotten.

The bedding was so full of lice that one could see them swarming like ants. One of my companions, Marguerite Corringer, told me that when she had typhus, she could not sleep all night because of the lice. She spent the night shaking her blanket over a piece of paper and emptying the lice into a receptacle by the bed, and this went on for hours.

There were practically no medicines. Consequently the patients were left in their beds without any attention, without hygiene, and unwashed. The dead lay in bed with the sick for several hours; finally, when they were noticed, they were simple tipped out of the bed and taken outside the block. There the women porters would come and carry the dead away on small stretchers, with heads and legs dangling over the sides. During the big typhus epidemics in the winters of 1943 and 1944, the stretchers were replaced by carts, as there were too many dead bodies—250 to 350 dead daily. From morning till night the carriers of the dead went from the Revier to the mortuary.

As to the experiments—I have seen in the Revier, where I was employed, the queue of young Jewesses from Salonika who stood waiting in front of the X-ray room for sterilization. I also know that they performed castration operations in the men's camp. Concerning the experiments performed on women I am well informed, because my friend, Doctor Hade Hautval of Montbéliard, who has returned to France, worked for several months in that block nursing the patients; but she always refused to participate in those experiments. They sterilized women either with injections or operation—there was a very high mortality rate among those operated on—or with rays. The SS said that they were trying to find the best method for sterilizing so as to replace the native population in the occupied countries with Germans after one generation, once they had made use of the inhabitants as slaves.

The Jewish women, when they arrived in the first months of pregnancy, were subjected to abortion. If they came when their pregnancy was near the end, after confinement, the babies were drowned in a bucket of water. I know that because I worked in the Revier and the woman who was in charge of that task was a German midwife who was imprisoned for having performed illegal operations. After a while another doctor arrived and for two months they did not kill the Jewish babies. But one day an order came from Berlin saying that again they had to be done away with. Then the mothers and their babies were called to the infirmary. They were put in a lorry and taken away to the gas chamber.

In principle, non-Jewish women were allowed to have their babies, and the babies were not taken away from them; but conditions in the camp were so horrible that the babies rarely lived for more than four or five weeks.

There was one block where the Polish and Russian mothers were. One day the Russian mothers, who had been accused of making too much noise, had to stand for roll call all day long in front of the block, naked, with their babies in their arms.

At Auschwitz there was a brothel for the SS and also one for the male internees of the staff, who were called *Kapos*. Generally speaking, the SS economized on many of their own personnel by employing internees for watching the camp; SS only supervised. These internees were chosen from German common-law criminals and prostitutes, and sometimes those of other nationalities, but most of them were Germans. By corruption, accusation, and terror the SS succeeded in making human beasts of them. Through fear, and degradation, they were forced to commit acts which made them ashamed of themselves, which resulted in their being no longer human. This was what the SS wanted. It took a great deal of courage to resist this atmosphere of terror and corruption.

When the SS needed servants (for the brothel) they came accompanied by the woman commandant of the camp to make a choice during disinfection, when the women were naked. They would point to a young girl, whom the *Oberaufseherin* [chief overseer] would take out of the ranks. They would look her over and make jokes about her physique. If she was pretty and they liked her, they would "hire" her as a maid with the consent of the *Oberaufseherin*, who would tell her that she was to obey them absolutely no matter what they asked for. The system was identical in all the camps; it was the same thing everywhere. Everything was done to degrade those women in their own sight.

When we left Romainville the Jewesses who were there with us were left behind. They were sent to Drancy and subsequently arrived at Auschwitz, where we found them again three weeks after our arrival. Of the original 1,200 only 125 actually came to the camp; the others were immediately sent to the gas chamber. Of these 125 not one was left alive at the end of one month.

Whenever a convoy of Jews came, a selection was made; first the old men and women, then the mothers and the children were put into trucks together with the sick or those whose constitution appeared to be delicate. They took into the camp only the young women and girls as well as the young men, who were sent to the men's camp. Generally speaking, of a convoy of about 1,000 to 1,500, seldom more than 250—and this figure really was the maximum—actually reached the camp. The rest were immediately sent to the gas chamber.

At this selection also, they picked out women in good health between the ages of twenty and thirty. They were sent to the experimental block; young girls and slightly older women, or those who had not been selected for that purpose, were sent to the camp where, like ourselves, they were tattooed and shaved.

When we worked at the sewing block in 1944, the block where we lived directly faced the stopping place of the trains. The system had been improved. Instead of making the selection at the place where they arrived, a sideline now took the train practically right up to the gas chamber; and the stopping place, about one hundred meters from the gas chamber, was right opposite our block though, of course, separated from us by two rows of barbed wire. Consequently, we saw the unsealing of the cars and the soldiers letting men, women, and children out of them. We then witnessed heartrending scenes; old couples forced to part from each other, mothers made to abandon their young daughters. The latter were sent to the camp, whereas mothers and small children were sent to the gas chambers. All these people were unaware of the fate awaiting them. They were merely upset at being separated, but they did not know that they were going to their death. To render their welcome more pleasant at this time—June–July, 1944—an orchestra composed of internees, all young and pretty girls dressed in little white blouses and navy blue skirts, played during the selection such gay tunes as "The Merry Widow," the Barcarolle from "The Tales of Hoffmann," and so forth. The new arrivals were then informed that this was a labor camp, and since they were not brought into the camp they saw only the small platform surrounded by flowering plants. Naturally, they could not realize what was in store for them. When the Jews arrived they had to leave all their belongings on the platform. They were stripped before entering the gas chamber and all their clothes and belongings were taken over to large barracks and sorted out by a *Kommando* named "Canada." Then everything was shipped to Germany: jewelry, fur coats, et cetera.

Since the Jewesses were sent to Auschwitz with their entire families and had been told that this was a sort of ghetto, they were advised to bring all their goods and chattels along. They consequently brought considerable riches with them. As for the Jewesses from Salonika, I remember that on their arrival they were given picture postcards, bearing the post office address of "Waldsee," a place which did not exist; and a printed text to be sent to their families, stating, "We are doing very well here; we have work and we are well treated. We await your arrival." I myself saw the cards in question; and the *Schreiberinnen*, that is, the secretaries of the block, were instructed to distribute them among the internees in order to post them to their families. I know that whole families arrived as a result of these postcards.

Those selected for the gas chamber, that is, the old people, mothers, and children, were escorted to a red brick building which bore the letters *Baden*—"Baths." There, to begin with, they were made to undress and given a towel before they went into the so-called shower room. Later on, at the time of the large convoys from Hungary, there was no more time left to playact or pretend; they were brutally stripped.

I know these details because I knew a little Jewess from France who lived with her family in Paris. She was called "little Marie" and she was the sole survivor of a family of nine. Her mother and her seven brothers and sisters had been gassed on arrival. When I met her she was employed to undress the babies before they were taken into the gas chamber.

Once the people were undressed they took them into a room which was somewhat like a shower room, and gas capsules were thrown through an opening in the ceiling. An SS man would watch the effect produced through a porthole. At the end of five or seven minutes, when the gas had completed its work, he gave the signal to open the doors; and men with gas masks—they too were internees—went into the room and removed the corpses. They told us that the internees must have suffered before dying, because they were closely clinging to one another and it was very difficult to separate them.

After that a special squad would come to pull out gold teeth and dentures; and again, when the bodies had been reduced to ashes, they would sift them in an attempt to recover the gold.

At Auschwitz there were eight crematories but, from 1944, these proved insufficient. So the SS had large pits dug by the internees, where they burned branches sprinkled with gasoline. Then they threw the corpses into the pit. After about an hour after the arrival of a convoy, we could see from our block large flames coming from the crematory, and the sky was lit up by the burning pits.

One night we were awakened by terrifying cries. And we discovered, on the following day, from the men working in the Sonderkommando—the "Gas Commando"—that on the preceding day, the gas supply having run out, they had thrown the children into the furnaces alive.

Every year, towards the end of the autumn, they proceeded to make selections on a large scale in the Revier. The system appeared to work as follows—I say this because I noticed the fact for myself during the time I spent in Auschwitz. Others, who had stayed there even longer than I, had observed the same phenomenon.

In the spring, all through Europe, they rounded up men and women whom they then sent to Auschwitz. They kept only those who were strong enough to work all through the summer. During that period naturally some died every day; but the strongest, those who had succeeded in holding out for six months, were so exhausted that they too had to go to the Revier. It was in autumn that the large-scale selections were made, so as not to feed too many useless mouths during the winter. All the women who were too thin were sent to the gas chamber, as well as those who had long, drawn-out illnesses. The Jewesses were gassed for practically no reason at all. They gassed everybody in the "scabies block," whereas everybody knows that with a little care, scabies can be cured in three days. I remember the typhus convalescent block from which 450 out of 500 patients were sent to the gas chamber.

During Christmas 1943—when we were in quarantine—we saw, since we lived opposite Block 25, women brought to Block 25 stripped naked. Uncovered trucks were then driven up and on them the naked women were piled, as many as the trucks could hold. Each time a truck started, the infamous Hessler—he was one of the criminals condemned to death at the Lüneburg trials—ran after the truck and with a bludgeon repeatedly struck the naked women going to their death. They knew they were going to the gas chamber and tried to escape. They were massacred. From our own block we watched the trucks pass by and heard the grievous wailing of all those women who knew they were going to be gassed. Many of them could very well have lived on, since they were suffering only from scabies and were, perhaps, a little too undernourished.

Before leaving Auschwitz we were in quarantine for ten months, from the 15th of July 1943 until May 1944—all the surviving Frenchwomen of our convoy. We had heard from Jewesses who had arrived from France in July 1944, that an intensive campaign had been carried out by the British Broadcasting Corporation in London, in connection with our convoy, mentioning Maï Politzer, Danielle Casanova, Hélène Solomon-Langevin, and myself. As a result of this broadcast we knew that orders had been issued from Berlin to the effect that Frenchwomen should be transported under better conditions.

So we were placed in quarantine. This was a block situated opposite the camp and outside the barbed wire. I must say that it is to this quarantine that the 49 survivors owed their lives. It is certain that we could not have survived eighteen months of this regime had we not had these ten months of quarantine.

This quarantine was imposed because exanthematic typhus was raging at Auschwitz. One could leave the camp only to be freed or to be transferred to another camp or to be summoned before the court after spending fifteen days in quarantine, that being the incubation period for exanthematic typhus. Consequently, as soon as the papers arrived announcing that the internee would probably be liberated, she was placed in quarantine until the order for her liberation was signed. This sometimes took several months and fifteen days was the minimum.

Now a policy existed for freeing German female common-law criminals and asocial elements in order to employ them as workers in the German factories. It is therefore impossible to imagine that the whole of Germany was unaware of the existence of the concentration camps, since these women had been released from the camps. It is difficult to believe that they never mentioned them. In the factories where the former internees were employed, the *Vorarbeiterinnen* (forewomen) were German civilians in contact with the internees. The forewomen from Auschwitz had been workers at Siemens in Berlin. They met forewomen they had known in Berlin, and in our presence they told them what they had seen at Auschwitz. It is therefore incredible that this was not known in Germany.

We could not believe our eyes when we left Auschwitz, and our hearts were sore when we saw our small group of 49 women all that was left of the 230 who had entered the camp 18 months earlier. But to us it seemed that we were leaving hell itself, and for the first time hopes of survival, of seeing the world again, were given to us.

On leaving Auschwitz we were sent to Ravensbrück. There we were escorted to the "NN" block—meaning *Nacht und Nebel* (literally "Night and Fog"), that is, "The Secret Block." With us in that block were Polish women with the identification number 7,000. Some were called "rabbits" because they had been used as experimental guinea pigs. The SS selected from the convoys girls in good health with very straight legs and they submitted them to various operations. Some of the girls had parts of the bone removed from their legs, others received injections; but what was injected, I do not know. The mortality rate was very high among the women operated upon. So when they came to fetch the others to operate on them they refused to go to the Revier. They were forcibly dragged to the dark cells where "the professor," who had arrived from Berlin, operated in his uniform, without taking any aseptic precautions, without wearing a surgical gown, and without washing his hands. There are some survivors among these "rabbits." They still endure much suffering. They suffer periodically from suppurations; and since nobody knows to what treatment they had been subjected, it is extremely difficult to cure them.

People were not tattooed at Ravensbrück, but we had to go up for a gynecological examination, and since no precautions were ever taken and the same instruments were frequently used in all cases, infections spread.

In Block 32 where we were billeted there were some Russian women prisoners of war who had refused to work voluntarily in the munitions factories. For that reason they had been sent to Ravensbrück. Since they persisted in their refusal, they were subjected to every form of petty indignity. For instance, some were forced to stand in front of the block a whole day without any food. Others were employed to carry lavatory receptacles in the camp. The *Strafblock* (penitentiary block) and the *Bunker* also housed internees who had refused to work in the war factories.

In the winter of 1944, Hungarian Jewesses who had been arrested en masse arrived at Ravensbrück. There was no longer any room left in the blocks, and the prisoners already slept four in a bed, so there was raised, in the middle of the camp, a large tent. Straw was spread in the tent, and the Hungarian women were brought to this tent. Their condition was frightful. There were a great many cases of frozen feet because they had been evacuated from Budapest and had walked a good part of the way in the snow. A great many of them had died en route. Those who arrived at Ravensbrück were led to this tent and there an enormous number of them died. Every day a squad came to remove the corpses in the tent. One day I passed the tent while it was being cleaned, and I saw a pile of smoking manure in front of it. I suddenly realized that this manure was human excrement since the unfortunate women no longer had the strength to drag themselves to the lavatories. They were therefore rotting in this filth.

There were also executions in the camps. The numbers were called at roll call in the morning, and the victims then left for the *Kommandatur* (headquarters) and were never seen again. A few days later the clothes were sent down to the *Effektenkammer*, where the clothes of the internees were kept. After a certain time their cards would vanish from the filing cabinets in the camp.

The system of detention was not the same as at Auschwitz. In Auschwitz, obviously, extermination was the sole aim and object.

Nobody was at all interested in output. We were beaten for no reason whatsoever. It was sufficient to stand from morning till evening, but whether we carried one brick or ten was of no importance at all. We were quite aware that the human element was employed as slave labor merely in order to die, that this was the ultimate purpose, whereas at Ravensbrück the output was of great importance. It was a clearing camp. When the convoys arrived at Ravensbrück, they were rapidly dispatched either to the munitions or powder factories, or to work at the airfields or to dig trenches.

The following procedure was adopted for going to the factories: the manufacturers or their foremen or other representatives came themselves to choose their workers, accompanied by SS men; the effect was that of a slave market. They felt the muscles, examined the faces to see if the women looked healthy, and then made their choice. Finally, they made them walk naked past the doctor and he eventually decided if a woman was fit or not to leave for work in the factories. Later the doctor's visit became a mere formality as they ended up employing anybody who came along. The work was exhausting, principally because of lack of food and sleep, since in addition to twelve solid hours of work one had to attend roll call in the morning and in the evening. In Ravensbrück there was a factory where telephone equipment was manufactured as well as wireless sets for aircraft. Then there were workshops in the camp for camouflage material and uniforms and for various utensils used by soldiers.

At the workshops where the uniforms were manufactured, two hundred jackets or pairs of trousers were made per day. There were two shifts; a day and a night shift, both working twelve hours. The night shift, when starting work at midnight, received a thin slice of bread—but only after the standard amount of work had been reached. Later on this practice was discontinued. Work was carried on at a furious pace; the internees could not even take time off to go to the lavatories. Both day and night they were beaten terribly, both by the SS women and men. They were beaten if a needle broke or if the machine stopped, or if these "ladies" and "gentlemen" did not like their looks. Towards the end of the night one could see that the workers were so exhausted that every movement was an effort to them. Beads of sweat stood out on their foreheads. They could not see clearly. When the standard amount of work was not reached the foreman, Binder, rushed up and, with all his might, beat one woman after another all along the line, with the result that the last in the rows waited their turn petrified with terror. If one wished to go to the *Revier* one had to receive the authorization of the SS, who granted it very rarely. Even then, if the doctor did give a woman a permit authorizing her to stay away from work a few days, the SS guards would often come around and fetch her out of bed in order to put her back at the machine. The atmosphere was frightful since, by reason of the "black-out," one could not open the windows at night. Six hundred women therefore worked for twelve hours without any ventilation. All those who worked at the *Schneiderei* became like living skeletons after a few months. They began to cough, their eyesight failed, they developed a nervous twitching of the face for fear of beatings to come.

I knew well the conditions of this workship since my little friend Marie Rubiano, a little French girl who had just spent 3 years in the prison of Kottbus, was sent, on her arrival at Ravensbrück, to the *Schneiderei*; and every evening she would tell me about her martyrdom. One day, when she was quite exhausted, she obtained permission to go to the *Revier*; and as on that day the German *Schwester* (nursing sister), Erica, was less evil-tempered than usual, Marie was X-rayed. Both lungs were severely infected and she was sent to the horrible Block 10, the block of consumptives. This block was particularly terrifying since tubercular patients were not considered "recuperable material"; they received no treatment, and because of shortage of staff they were not even washed. We might even say that there were no medical supplies at all.

Little Marie was placed in the ward housing patients with bacillary infections, in other words, such patients as were considered incurable. She spent some weeks there and had no courage left to put up a fight for her life. I must say that the atmosphere of this room was particularly depressing. There were many patients—several to one bed in three-tier bunks—in an overheated atmosphere, lying between internees of various nationalities, so that they could not even speak to one another. Then, too, the silence in this antechamber of death was only broken by the yells of German personnel on duty and, from time to time, by the muffled sobs of a little French girl thinking of her mother and of her country which she would never see again.

And yet, Marie Rubiano did not die fast enough to please the SS. So one day Dr. Winkelmann, selection specialist at Ravensbrück, entered her name in the blacklist and on February 9, 1945, together with seventy-two other consumptive women, she was shoved on the truck for the gas chamber.

In all the Revieren, selections were made and all patients considered unfit for work were sent to the gas chamber, a hermetically sealed building made of boards. The Ravensbrück gas chamber was situated just behind the wall of the camp, next to the crematory, whose chimney rose above the high wall of the camp. At the time of the liberation I returned to these places. I visited the gas chamber, and inside one could still smell the disagreeable odor of gas.

Toward the beginning of 1945 Dr. Winkelmann, no longer satisfied with selections in the Revier, proceeded to make his selections in the blocks. All the prisoners had to answer roll call in their bare feet and to expose their breasts and legs. All those who were sick, too old, too thin, or whose legs were swollen with edema, were set aside and then sent to the Jugendlager—so called because it was a former reform school for German juvenile delinquents—a quarter of an hour away from the camp at Ravensbrück.

In the blocks an order had been circulated to the effect that old women and patients who could no longer work should apply in writing for admission to the Jugendlager, where they would be far better off, since they would not have to work and there would be no roll call. We learned the truth about this later through some of the people who worked at the Jugendlager—the chief of the camp was an Austrian woman, Betty Wenz, whom I knew from Auschwitz—and from a few of the survivors, one of whom is Irène Ottelard, a Frenchwoman living in Drancy, who was repatriated at the same time as myself and whom I had nursed after the liberation. Through her we discovered the details about the Jugendlager.

At the *Jugendlager* the old women and the patients who had left our camp were placed in blocks which had no water and no conveniences; they lay on straw mattresses on the ground, so closely pressed together that one was quite unable to pass between them. At night one could not sleep because of the continuous coming and going, and the internees stepped on each other when passing. The straw mattresses were rotten and teemed with lice; those women who were able to stand remained for hours on end for roll call until they collapsed. In February their coats were taken away but they continued to stay out for roll call and mortality was considerably increased.

By way of nourishment they received only one thin slice of bread and half a quart of soup, and all the drink they got in twenty-four hours was half a quart of herbal tea. They had no water to drink, none to wash in, and none to wash their mess tins.

In the *Jugendlager* there was also a *Revier* for those who could no longer stand. Periodically, during the roll calls, the *Aufseherin* would choose some internees, who would be undressed and left in nothing but their chemises. Their coats were then returned to them. They were hoisted on a truck and were driven off to the gas chamber. A few days later the coats were returned to the *Kammer* (clothing warehouse), and the labels were marked "*Mittwerda.*" The internees working on the labels told us that the place "*Mittwerda*" did not exist and that it was a special term for the gases.

When the Germans went away from Ravensbrück they left 2,000 sick women and a certain number of volunteers, myself included, to take care of them. They left us without water and without light. Fortunately the Russians arrived on the following day. We therefore were able to go to the men's camp and there we found an indescribable sight. They had been for five days without water. There were 800 serious cases; the three doctors and seven nurses were unable to separate the dead from the sick. Thanks to the Red Army, we were able to take these sick persons over into clean blocks and to give them food and care; but unfortunately I can give the figures only for the French. There were 400 of them when we came to the camp and only 150 were able to return to France; for the others it was too late, in spite of all our care.

It is difficult to convey an exact idea of the concentration camps to anybody, unless one has been in the camp oneself, since one can only quote examples of horror. But it is impossible to convey any impression of that deadly monotony. If asked what was the worst of all, it is impossible to answer, since everything was atrocious. It is atrocious to die of hunger, to die of thirst, to be ill, to see all one's companions dying around one and being unable to help them. It is atrocious to think of one's children, of one's country which one will never see again, and there were times when we asked whether our life was not a living nightmare, so unreal did this life appear in all its horror.

For months, for years we had one wish only: the wish that some of us would escape alive, in order to tell the world what the Nazi convict prisons were like everywhere. In Auschwitz as at Ravensbrück, comrades from the other camps told the same tale: of a world governed by the systematic and implacable urge to use human beings as slaves, and to kill them when they could work no more.

Dr. Franz Blaha:

I studied medicine in Prague, Vienna, Strasbourg, and Paris and received my diploma in 1920. From 1920 to 1926 I was a clinical assistant. In 1926 I became chief physician of the Iglau Hospital in Moravia, Czechoslovakia. I held this position until 1939, when the Germans entered Czechoslovakia and I was seized as a hostage for cooperating with the Czech Government. I was sent as a prisoner to the Dachau Concentration Camp in April 1941, and remained there until April 1945.

Until July 1941 I worked in a punishment company. After that I was sent to the hospital and subjected to the experiments in typhoid being conducted by Dr. Muermelstadt. After that I was to be made the subject of an experimental operation and succeeded in avoiding this only by admitting that I was a physician. If this had been known before, I would have suffered, because intellectuals were treated very harshly in the punishment company.

In October 1941 I was sent to work in the herb plantation and later in the laboratory for processing herbs. In June 1942 I was taken into the hospital as a surgeon. Shortly afterwards I was directed to perform a stomach operaton on twenty healthy prisoners. Because I would not do this, I was transferred to the autopsy room where I stayed until April 1945. There I performed approximately seven thousand autopsies. In all, twelve thousand autopsies were performed under my direction.

From the middle of 1941 to the end of 1942 some five hundred operations on healthy prisoners were performed. These were for the instructions of the SS medical students and doctors and included operations on the stomach, gall bladder, and throat. These were performed by students and doctors of only two years' training, although they were very dangerous and difficult. Ordinarily they would not have been done except by surgeons with at least four years' surgical practice. Many prisoners died on the operating table and many others from later complications. I performed autopsies on all of these bodies. The doctors who supervised these operations were Lang, Muermelstadt, Wolter, Ramsauer, and Kahr. *Standartenführer** Dr. Lolling frequently witnessed these operations.

During my time at Dachau I was familiar with many kinds of medical experiments carried out on human victims. These persons were never volunteers but were forced to submit to such acts. Malaria experiments on about twelve hundred people were conducted by Dr. Klaus Schilling between 1941 and 1945. Schilling was personally ordered by Himmler to conduct these experiments. The victims were either bitten by mosquitoes or given injections of malaria sporozoites taken from mosquitoes. Different kinds of treatment were applied including quinine, pyrifer, neosalvarsan, antipyrine, Pyramidon, and a drug called 2516 Behring. I performed autopsies on the bodies of people who died from these experiments. Thirty to forty died from the malaria itself; three hundred to four hundred died later from diseases which were fatal because of the physical condition resulting from the malaria attacks. In addition there were deaths from poisoning due to overdoses of neosalvarsan and Pyramidon. Dr. Schilling was present at my autopsies on the bodies of his patients.

Dr. Sigmund Rascher made exclusively so-called Air Force experiments in the camp. He was a major in the Air Force and was

*High SS rank.

assigned to investigate the conditions to which parachutists were subjected, as well as the conditions of those people who had to make an emergency landing on the sea or had fallen into the sea. According to scientific standards, insofar as I can judge, this was all to no purpose. Like all the other experiments, it was simply useless murder; and it is amazing that learned university professors and physicians, particularly, were capable of carrying out these experiments according to plan.

These experiments were much worse than all the liquidations and executions, because all the victims simply had their suffering prolonged. Various medicines such as vitamins, hormones, tonics, and injections, which were not available for the ordinary patients, were provided so that the experiments might last longer and give those people more time to observe their victims. These experiments were made on Himmler's direct orders. Dr. Rascher had close relations with Himmler. He visited Himmler very often and Himmler visited Dr. Rascher several times.

In 1942 and 1943 experiments were conducted by Dr. Rascher to determine the effects of changing air pressure. As many as twenty-five persons at one time were put into a specially constructed van in which pressure could be increased or decreased as required. The purpose was to find out the effects of high altitude and of rapid descent by parachute. Most of the prisoners used in this way died from these experiments, from internal hemorrhage of the lungs or brain. It was my job to take the bodies out and as soon as they were found to be dead to send the internal organs to Munich for study. About four hundred to five hundred prisoners were experimented on. The survivors coughed blood when taken out; they were sent to invalid blocks and liquidated shortly afterwards. Only a few escaped.

Rascher also conducted experiments on the effect of cold water on human beings. This was done to find a way for reviving airmen who had fallen into the ocean. The subject was placed in ice cold water and kept there until he was unconscious. Blood was taken from his neck and tested each time his body temperature dropped one degree. This drop was determined by a rectal thermometer. Urine was also periodically tested. Some men stood it as long as 24 to 36 hours. The lowest body temperature reached was 19 degrees centigrade, but most men died at 25 or 26 degrees.

When the men were removed from the ice water attempts were made to revive them with artificial sunshine, hot water, by electrotherapy, or by animal warmth. For this last experiment prostitutes were used and the body of the unconscious man was placed between the bodies of two women. Himmler was present at one such experiment. I could see him from one of the windows in the street between the blocks. I was present at some of these cold water experiments when Rascher was absent, and I have seen notes and diagrams on them in Rascher's laboratory. About three hundred persons were used in these experiments. The majority died. Of those who survived, many became mentally deranged. Those who did not die were sent to invalid blocks and were killed just as were the victims of the air pressure experiments. I know only two who survived, a Yugoslav and a Pole, both of whom are mental cases.

Liver puncture experiments were performed by Dr. Brachtl on healthy people and on people who had disease of the stomach and gall bladder. For this purpose a needle was jabbed into the liver of a person and a small piece of the liver was extracted. No anaesthetic was used. The experiment is very painful and often had serious results, as the stomach or large blood vessels were often punctured, resulting in hemorrhage. Many persons died of these tests, for which Polish, Russian, Czech, and German prisoners were used. Altogether about 175 people were subjected to these experiments.

Phlegmone experiments were conducted by Dr. Schütz, Dr. Babor, Dr. Kieselwetter and Professor Lauer. Forty healthy men were used at a time, of whom twenty were given intramuscular injections, and twenty were given intravenous injections of pus from diseased persons. All treatment was forbidden for three days, by which time serious inflammation and in many cases general blood poisoning had occurred. Then each group was divided again into groups of ten. Half were given chemical treatment with liquid and special pills every ten minutes for twenty-four hours. The remainder were treated with sulfanilamide and surgery. In some cases all the limbs were amputated. My autopsies also showed that the chemical treatment had been harmful and had even caused perforations of the stomach wall. For these experiments Polish, Czech, and Dutch priests were ordinarily used. Pain was intense in such experiments. Most of the six hundred to eight hundred persons who were used finally died. Most of the others became total invalids and were later killed.

In the fall of 1944 there were sixty to eighty persons who were subjected to salt water experiments. They were locked in a room and for five days were given nothing for food but salt water. During this time their urine, blood, and excrement were tested. None of these prisoners died, possibly because they received smuggled food from other prisoners. Hungarians and Gypsies were used for these experiments.

It was common practice to remove the skin from dead prisoners. I was commanded to do this on many occasions. Dr. Rascher and Dr. Wolter in particular asked for skin from human backs and chests. It was chemically treated and placed in the sun to dry. After that it was cut into various sizes for use as saddles, riding breeches, gloves, house slippers, and ladies' handbags. Tattooed skin was especially valued by SS men. Russians, Poles, and other inmates were used in this way, but it was forbidden to cut out the skin of a German. This skin had to come from healthy prisoners free from defects.

Sometimes we did not have enough bodies with good skin and Rascher would say, "All right, you will get the bodies." The next day we would receive twenty or thirty bodies of young people. They would have been shot in the neck or struck on the head so that the skin would be uninjured. Also we frequently got requests for the skulls or skeletons of prisoners. In those cases we boiled the skulls or the body. Then the soft parts were removed and the bones were bleached and dried and reassembled. In the case of skulls it was important to have a good set of teeth. When we got an order for skulls from Oranienburg the SS men would say, "We will try to get you some with good teeth." So it was dangerous to have good skin or good teeth.

Transports arrived frequently in Dachau from Struthof, Belsen, Auschwitz, Mauthausen and other camps. Many of these were ten to fourteen days on the way without water or food. On one transport which arrived in November, 1942, I found evidence of cannibalism. Another transport arrived from Compiègne in France. Professor Limousin of Clermont-Ferrant, who was later my assistant, told me that there had been two thousand persons on this transport when it started. There was food available but no water. Eight hundred died on the way and were thrown out. When it arrived after 12 days, more than five hundred persons were dead on the train. Of the remainder most died shortly after arrival. I investigated this transport because the International Red Cross complained, and the SS men wanted a report that the deaths had been caused by fighting and rioting on the way. I dissected a number of bodies and found that they had died from suffocation and lack of water. It was midsummer and 120 people had been packed into each car.

In 1941 and 1942 we had in the camp what we called invalid transports. These were made up of people who were sick or for some reason incapable of working. We called them *Himmelfahrt Kommandos* (suicide squads). About one hundred or so were ordered each week to go the showers. There, four people gave injections of phenol, evipal, or benzine, which soon caused death. After 1943 these invalids were sent to other camps for liquidation. I know they were killed because I saw that their records were marked with a cross and the date of departure, which was the way deaths were ordinarily recorded. This was shown on both the card index and the records in the registry office of Dachau. One thousand to two thousand went away every three months, so there were about five thousand sent to their death in 1943, and the same in 1944. In April 1945 a Jewish transport was loaded at Dachau and was left standing on the railroad siding. The station had been destroyed by bombing, and they could not leave. So they were left there to die of starvation. When the camp was liberated they were all dead.

Many executions by gas or shooting or injection took place right in the camp. The gas chamber was completed in 1944, and I was called by Dr. Rascher to examine the first victims. Of the eight or nine persons in the chamber three were still alive, and the remainder appeared to be dead. Their eyes were red, and their faces were swollen. Many prisoners were later killed in this way. Afterwards they were removed to the crematorium where I had to examine their teeth for gold. Teeth containing gold were extracted. Many prisoners who were sick were killed by injections while in the hospital. Some prisoners killed in the hospital came through the autopsy room with no name or number on the tag which was usually tied to their big toe. Instead the tag said, "Do not dissect."

I performed autopsies on some of these and found that they were perfectly healthy, but had died from injections. Sometimes prisoners were killed only because they vomited or had dysentery or gave the nurses too much trouble. Mental patients were liquidated by being led to the gas chamber and injected there or shot. Shooting was a common method of execution. Prisoners could be shot just outside the crematorium and carried in. I have seen people pushed into the ovens while they were still breathing and making sounds, although if they were too much alive they were usually hit on the head first.

Until the year 1943, Dachau was really an extermination camp. After 1943 a good many factories and munitions plants were established, and then it became more of a work camp. But as far as the results are concerned there was no difference, because the prisoners had to work so hard while going hungry that they died from starvation and exhaustion instead of from beatings.

Many internees came originally from the U.S.S.R. I cannot state exactly how many, only approximately. First, after November, 1941, there were Russian prisoners of war in uniform. They had separate camps and were liquidated within a few months. In the summer of 1942, those who remained—I believe there were twelve thousand prisoners of war—were transported to Mauthausen, where they were liquidated in gas chambers.

Then, after the Russian prisoners of war, Russian children were brought to Dachau. There were, I believe, two thousand boys, six to seventeen years old. They were kept in one or two special blocks. They were assigned to particularly brutal people. Those were the so-called professional criminals. They beat these young boys at every step, and gave them the hardest work. They worked particularly in the plantations where they had to pull ploughs, sowing machines, and street rollers instead of horses and motors being used. Also in all transport *Kommandos* Russian children were used exclusively. At least 70 percent of them died of tuberculosis, I believe, and those who remained were then sent to a special camp in the Tyrol in 1943 or 1944.

Then, after the children, several thousand so-called eastern workers were killed. These were civilians who were removed from the Eastern territories to Germany and then, because of alleged work sabotage, were put into concentration camps. In addition there were many Russian officers and intellectuals.

I believe I am not far from the truth when I say that of all those executed, at least 75 percent were Russians, and that women as well as men were brought to Dachau from outside to be executed. In the summer or late spring of 1944 high-ranking Russian officers—generals, colonels, and majors—were sent to Dachau. During the following weeks they were examined by the political department; that is to say, after each interrogation they were brought to the camp hospital in a completely battered condition. I myself saw and knew well some who for weeks had to lie on their bellies, and we had to remove surgically parts of their skin and muscles which had become mortified. Many succumbed to these methods of investigation. The others, ninety-four in all, were then brought to the crematory in the beginning of Septemebr 1944 on orders from Berlin and there, while on their knees, shot through the neck. In addition, in the winter and spring of 1945 several Russian officers were brought from solitary confinement to the crematory and there either hanged or shot.

It was easy to see that these executions, these transports of invalids, and the way epidemics were dealt with were all part of the general plan of extermination. And particularly, and this I must emphasize, it was always the Russian prisoners who were treated the worst of all.

In 1945, just before the camp was liberated, all "Nacht Und Nebel" (Night and Fog) prisoners were executed. These were prisoners who were forbidden to ·have any contact with the outside world. They were kept in a special enclosure. The people so designated were mostly from the western countries of Europe, particularly Frenchmen, Belgians, and Dutchmen. The Russians—as was the case with the Czechs and also in my own case—frequently had the designation "return undesirable." This actually meant the same. Shortly before the liberation many of these people were executed on the order of the camp commander, that is, shot in front of the crematory. Many of these people, particularly the French and Russians, were serious cases of typhus and with a temperature of 40 degrees centigrade were carried on stretchers to the rifle range.

From 1941 on the camp was more and more crowded. In 1943 the hospital for prisoners was already overcrowded. In 1944 and 1945 it was impossible to maintain any sort of sanitary conditions. Rooms which had held three hundred or four hundred persons in 1942 were filled with a thousand in 1943, and in the first quarter of 1945 with two thousand or more. The rooms could not be cleaned because they were too crowded and there was no cleaning material. Baths were available only once a month. Latrine facilities were completely inadequate. Medicine was almost nonexistent, but I found after the camp was liberated that there was enough medicine in the SS hospital for the whole camp. New arrivals at the camp were lined up out of doors for hours at a time. Sometimes they stood there from morning until night. It did not matter whether this was in the winter or in the summer. This occurred all through 1943, 1944, and the first quarter of 1945. I could see these formations from the window of the autopsy room. Many of the people who had to stand in the cold in this way became ill with pneumonia and died. I had several acquaintances who were killed in this manner during 1944 and 1945.

In October, 1944, a transport of Hungarians brought an epidemic of spotted fever into the camp. I examined many of the corpses from this transport and reported the situation to Dr. Hintermayer but was forbidden, on penalty of being shot, to mention that there was an epidemic. He said that it was sabotage, and that I was trying to have the camp quarantined so that the prisoners would not have to work in the armaments industry. No preventive measures were taken at all. Healthy new arrivals were put into blocks where an epidemic was already present. Infected persons were also put into these blocks. Block 30, for instance, died out completely three times. Only at Christmas, when the epidemic spread into the SS camp, was a quarantine established.

Nevertheless, transports continued to arrive. We had 200 to 300 new typhus cases a day, and about 100 deaths from typhus daily. In all we had 28,000 cases and 15,000 deaths. Apart from those who died from the disease, my autopsies showed that many deaths were caused solely by malnutrition. I believe that two-thirds of the entire population of the camp suffered from severe malnutrition and that at least 25 percent of the dead had literally died of starvation. It was called in German *Hungertyphus*. Apart from that, tuberculosis was the most widespread disease in the camp, and it also spread because of malnutrition. Most of the victims were Russians. The majority of those who died of starvation and exhaustion were French, Russians, and Italians.

The others, the Germans, Poles, and Czechs, who had already been in the camp for some time, had had time, if I may say so, to adjust themselves physically to camp conditions. The Russians deteriorated rapidly. The same was true of the French and Italians. Moreover, these nationals for the most part arrived from other camps suffering from malnutrition, so that they soon fell easy prey to other epidemics and diseases. Also, the Germans, Poles, and many others who worked in the armaments industry had since 1943 been able to get parcels from home. That, of course, was not the case with citizens of Soviet Russia, France, or Italy. These people were just starved to death. At the time of death they weighed 50 to 60 pounds. Autopsies showed their internal organs had often shrunk to one-third of their normal size.

Very many visitors came to our camp, so that it sometimes seemed to us that we were not confined in a camp but in an exhibition or a zoo. There was a visit or an excursion almost every day from schools, from different military, medical, and other institutions. Also many members of the Police, the SS, and the armed forces, and some state personalities came to the camp. Some were inside for half an hour to an hour, some for three or four hours. Many visits, for instance, from schools—from the military and police schools—lasted a whole day. *Reichsführer* Himmler came to Dachau several times and also was present at the experiments. I was present myself on these occasions.

I myself have seen three ministers of state; and from German political prisoners who knew these people I heard that several other personages visited the camp. Besides Himmler there was Bormann; also *Gauleiters* Wagner and Giesler; State Ministers Frick, Rosenberg, Funk, Sauckel; also General of Police Daluege; and others. Twice I also saw high-ranking Italian officers and once a Japanese officer. In my opinion, the people who lived in the area of Munich must have known of all these things, because the prisoners went every day to various factories in Munich and the neighborhood and at work they frequently came into contact with civilian workers. Moreover, the various suppliers and consumers often saw what was done to the prisoners in the German armament works.

Many of these people had access everywhere, in the fields as well as in the various factories, and could observe what life was like in these places. I believe they saw how the people worked, what they looked like, and what they produced there. For instance, I can remember one example quite well. At the time I was working the fields. We were pulling a heavy street roller, sixteen men, and a group of girls passed who were on an excursion. When they passed, their leader said very loudly, so that we all could hear it, "Look, those people are so lazy that rather than harness up a team of horses they pull it themselves." That was supposed to be a joke.

14

THE PACIFIC: 1941-1945

Art Rittenberg

God forbid you lose that rifle. The penalties for losing a rifle were—I don't know—castration. . . .

There was no boredom there, but there wasn't much terror either. I think you get numb. Occasionally you're frightened or startled when somebody or something comes very close to you. But I don't think you can sustain a constant level of terror. I think you'd go mad.

—Art Rittenberg

The Pacific 1941—45

During the months after Pearl Harbor the Japanese achieved a series of military successes unparalleled in modern history. In less than six months they gained an empire in Asia and the Pacific that included the former French colonies of Indochina, the British colonies of Hong Kong, Malaya, and Burma, the Dutch East Indies, the Philippines, and a number of other Pacific islands.

The only break in the flood of news about Allied losses came in April, 1942, when the Americans undertook a daring carrier-launched bomber raid over Tokyo. The raid didn't do much damage, but it gave American morale a lift.

A month later a combined American, British, and Australian naval force turned back a large Japanese invasion fleet in the Coral Sea. The Japanese were attempting to extend their sphere of control to the Solomon Islands and the southern coast of New

Guinea, posing a direct threat to Australia. They were unsuccessful in mounting this invasion, and for the first time their navy suffered some losses. The American carrier *Lexington* was also lost, but tactically the Battle of the Coral Sea was an Allied victory because the invasion force never landed. The Japanese overextended themselves and proved that they were not invincible.

The Coral Sea encounter convinced Admiral Yamamoto that if Japan was to hold its newly acquired Pacific Empire, he would have to destroy what was left of the U.S. Pacific Fleet after Pearl Harbor. He correctly believed that by threatening to attack Midway, the westernmost island of the Hawaiian Archipelago, he could draw the American Navy into an engagement that would make this possible. The Japanese assembled the greatest fleet concentration in the history of the Pacific. Its forward striking force alone consisted of four carriers, two battleships, three cruisers, and eleven destroyers backed up by a large number of additional naval ships and an invasion task force.

Against this strength the U.S. Navy had only three carriers and some support ships. But what Yamamoto did not realize was that his naval code had been broken and that the Americans knew the size of his fleet and exactly where and when it was going to attack.

On the morning of June 4, the Japanese sent more than 100 planes to bomb Midway. While they were returning to their carriers and other planes were being readied for a second Midway raid, American pilots began their attack on the Japanese ships. In the space of five minutes planes from the *Enterprise, Hornet* and *Yorktown* sank three of the Japanese carriers. A short while later the fourth Japanese carrier was sunk. The *Yorktown* went down, but the Battle of Midway was a decisive defeat for Japan. The Japanese lost their four largest carriers, a heavy cruiser, and 322 planes, while the Americans lost one carrier, a destroyer, and 150 planes.

Yamamoto's fleet abandoned their Midway operation and returned to Japan, never again to be a match for the United States Navy. But most important, this was Japan's last major offensive. After Midway, the tide turned and Japan was on the defensive. Nevertheless, it tried to extend its defensive sphere into the Solomon Islands and New Guinea, in order to isolate Australia. The Japanese presence in these islands was a serious threat to troop and supply convoys moving between the United States and Australia. To drive the Japanese out, the Allies mounted their first offensive operation of the war in the Pacific.

On August 7, American Marines landed on the island of Guadalcanal. They quickly established beachheads and occupied the unfinished airstrip. But the Japanese fought back ferociously, by land, sea, and air. Finally, in mid-November, a Japanese naval force was decisively beaten. The Marines held on and early in 1943 the Japanese began to evacuate their troops from Guadalcanal.

The Allies were in the Solomons to stay. From Guadalcanal onward American soldiers and Marines fought their way toward Japan from island to island. In fact, the main objective of the Pacific offensive was to capture certain strategic islands which would enable the Americans to launch heavy air attacks on the Japanese homeland. It was thought that these air raids would eventually bring about a Japanese surrender. The problem was deciding on the best route to Japan.

In the end it was decided that the American offensive should take two routes. General MacArthur was employed in securing a southern route which began by reoccupying New Guinea, while Admiral Chester Nimitz took the more direct island-chain route to Japan. As the forces under Nimitz captured island after island in the Pacific, remote places with obscure names suddenly became household words. They also became the scene of bloody fighting with heavy losses on both sides. For example, Tarawa, in the Gilbert Islands, which was less than one mile square, was occupied by 4,500 Japanese troops ordered to fight to the last man. They did—only seventeen were taken prisoner. It took four days for the Marines to wrest Tarawa from its defenders, and in that time they lost 1,100 men killed and more than 2,000 wounded.

After the Gilbert Islands were secured, the Marshall Islands became the next objective. There the Marines met bitter resistance on Kwajalein. After the Marshalls, the Navy and Marines prepared to attack the heavily fortified and extremely important Mariana Islands, which consisted of Saipan, Tinian, and Guam. The Marianas were vital to the Japanese because Air Force B-29's carried enough fuel to fly from there, bomb Japan, and return. The islands were assaulted on June 15, 1944, by an American force consisting of 535 ships and more than 125,000 men.

The Japanese sent their fleet to intervene. Four days after the Saipan landings a large Japanese carrier force entered the area and a huge carrier battle took place. Although the ships were never in direct contact, the Battle of the Philippine Sea, also known as the "Marianas Turkey Shoot," was perhaps the greatest American air victory of the Pacific war. During a period of eight hours four separate air attacks were launched by the Japanese. They were intercepted by planes launched from American carriers. In this engagement the Japanese lost 346 planes and 3 carriers. The U.S. Navy lost only 130 planes. It was an air battle from which the Japanese never recovered. The American ground forces were also successful in their invasion of Saipan, Tinian and Guam.

But every successful operation presented the Allied High Command with the same question. From what place should the invasion of Japan be launched? The distances in the Pacific were staggering and there were relatively few places with the size, harbor facilities, and other resources necessary for assembling a massive invasion force.

The Marianas were still more than a thousand miles from Tokyo and too small for mounting an invasion of Japan. MacArthur felt the next move should be the liberation of the Philippines—and he eventually got his way. Before the Philippines could be invaded, however, the Palau Islands had to be cleared of Japanese. In mid-September the Palau offensive opened at Pelilu; in a month-long action the Japanese lost 11,000 men killed and the Americans lost 1,800 killed and 8,000 wounded. Finally, on October 20, 1944, MacArthur made good his promise to return to the Philippines as American troops landed on the island of Leyte.

In an effort to stop the American landings on Leyte the Japanese committed more than 70 warships and 700 planes—most of what was left of the Imperial Navy—to the largest naval battle of all time. In the Battle of Leyte Gulf the Japanese opposed a force more than twice its size—166 American warships and nearly 1,300 planes. The battle lasted for four days, from October 23 to 27, and when it was over the Japanese Navy had essentially ceased to exist as a major threat in the Pacific. It had lost one battleship, five carriers, four cruisers, and a number of destroyers and smaller ships.

The Battle of Leyte Gulf was also notable because it was here that the Japanese first used Kamikaze tactics with suicide pilots who flew their planes, armed with heavy bombs, directly into enemy ships. Between Leyte Gulf and the end of the war Kamikaze pilots sank or damaged more than 300 American ships and inflicted 15,000 casualties. It was considered an honor for a Japanese pilot to be sent on a Kamikaze mission, and thousands of young men volunteered.

It took many months of hard fighting to actually complete the liberation of the Philippines. In the end, the Japanese lost nearly 450,000 men killed or captured there. While MacArthur's forces were liberating the Philippines, two other operations were being prepared farther north.

Iwo Jima and Okinawa were needed for air bases before an invasion could be launched against Japan. The amphibious assault on Iwo Jima began on February 19, 1945. The Marines were expected to secure the island in five days. It took more than five weeks and cost 6,000 American and 20,000 Japanese lives. With Iwo Jima in American hands the Japanese lost an air base and a radar station that had been giving them early warning of raids on the home islands and it gave the U.S. air bases less than 800 miles from Japan.

The next objective, Okinawa, was only 350 miles from Japan. It had airfields and good harbor facilities and was an ideal staging area for the final invasion. The Marines landed on April 1, 1945, and met no resistance for five days. But then a large Japanese force unleashed violent air and land attacks. It took 82 days to secure Okinawa and by battle's end 110,000 Japanese and 12,000 Americans were dead.

The island-hopping nature of the Pacific war required vast and highly complex movements of troops and supplies. The men who fought there often describe the experience as "endless periods of boredom punctuated by short moments of utter terror." Art Rittenberg spent 42 months in the Marine Corps, during which time he saw action—at Saipan and Iwo Jima—for only six weeks. But more than 30 years later he describes the invasion of Iwo Jima as "the clearest single event in my life. I can't tell you why it remains so clear in my mind, more clear than things that happened to me a week ago. I think it was probably the sense of trauma."

Rittenberg has been with the publishing house of Prentice-Hall for many years, first as a college traveler, then in a number of editorial capacities, and now as director of general book marketing.

Art Rittenberg:

I graduated from high school in June of 1942 and went to work in a department store as a mailboy. A friend of mine was a stockboy in the same store. One day we were eating lunch on the Boston Common—we brought lunch because we only made sixteen bucks a week and had to pay our own carfare—and he said, "Do you think we could pass the Marine physical? Let's go over and see if we can."

So the next day at lunchtime we went over to the Marine Corps Recruiting Station and we both passed the physical. Since we were only seventeen they gave us papers to take home and get signed. You became subject to the draft at eighteen and there were advantages to enlisting before they drafted you. So we decided we would go in and we would be great buddies. I would be Van Johnson and he would be John Wayne.

So we brought the papers home. My father giggled and my mother said, "Ridiculous." They had no intention of signing those papers. My mother said, "Wait until you have to go." I nagged them and nagged them and they didn't pay much attention. Well, as I started to come close to being drafted I gave them all the recruiting pitches. You know, if I enlist I can pick my specialty and get an education, learn a trade, the whole thing. Finally I wore them down and they signed my papers.

Now my friend's father wouldn't sign his papers and never did sign them. We were going to request service together, but he never did go into the Marines. Instead he was drafted into the Air Corps and ended up with probably the greatest job in the Air Corps. He was in charge of flying pregnant WACS [Women's Army Corps] from Abbadan, Iran, to Karachi. He was in the Military Air Transport—MATS—and that was his job during the entire war. Meanwhile, I was in the Marine Corps because of him. It was his idea.

I remember my forty-two months in the Marine Corps as long periods of absolute boredom punctuated by occasional excitement and a few short moments of utter terror. Mostly we were in training.

It started with basic training, which was one of the most fantastic experiences of my life. I had no idea what it would be like, none whatever. They put me on a train in Boston and 36 hours later they threw me off the train in Beaufort, South Carolina. Here I am, a middle-class kid without any experience. I thought, who the hell are all these people they keep putting on the train?

Finally they throw us off the train in Beaufort. Unbelievable! It was midnight and the temperature must have been 110 degrees. It was early summer—late May or early June. Thirty-six hours on that train sitting up, and we get off dirty, grimy, hungry, and tired. I always felt that they arranged for us to arrive in that condition and at that hour because then your resistance is at its lowest.

Boot camp in the Marine Corps is nothing but basic conditioning. That's what it's all about. Physical conditioning, but more importantly, mental conditioning. So you get off the train and you're standing there looking like hell. You're wrinkled and dirty, and here comes this guy up to you and he's gorgeous. That's the only way I can describe him. He's in khakis starched within an inch of his life, razor creases. He's a handsome guy who looks like he's seven foot two but was probably six feet tall. A slim, beautiful-looking man.

He introduces himself. He says, "My name is Murray Harlan, and I come from Kingston, North Carolina, and I am your D.I." Of course we knew that D.I. meant drill instructor. But he goes on. "Forget that because that's not important. What's important is that I am your god. I am the one god. I am the only god in your life. I hold the power of life and death over you. Do you understand?" Then he says, "Now let me explain something to you. When I give you an order you will jump. When I tell you to shit you will shit and if you can't shit you will strain. But you will stand there until you follow through that order. Do you understand?"

And then he did a very clever thing. He picked out the biggest guy, a guy about six four, 240 pounds, and said, "You come up here." When he came up there, Murray Harlan went eyeball to eyeball with that guy and said to him, "You are in contempt of me." And the guy said, "No I'm not." "Don't speak—shut up! You are contemptuous of me. You don't believe that I am your god, the one god, the true god. You believe that that's just a lot of bullshit, don't you," Harlan said. "I'll talk to you again after five days on bread and water and we'll see whether I am your true god, the one god, the only god." He just tore that guy apart, you see. And that guy disappeared and five days later he came back. Everybody said, "What happened?" He said it was bread and water—one meal a day. This big guy said it was a little cell, like a hot box.

That was all intentional. I'm sure that every time Murray Harlan greeted a new platoon, which was every ten weeks, he did the same thing. It was all part of a concerted, careful campaign to condition you to absolutely fear him. I mean you truly stood in awe of that man. There was nobody else. There must have been a battalion commander, but we never saw him.

One time toward the end of boot camp the adjutant general came to inspect us and Murray Harlan prepped us. The adjutant general, in fact, is a kind of ombudsman for the enlisted men. Murray Harlan said, "This man is going to come, and he's going to talk to you, and he's going to ask you if you're treated well, and the answer is 'Yes sir.' He's going to ask you if the food is good and the answer is, 'Yes sir.' He's going to ask if anybody's been abused and the answer is 'No sir.' "

The adjutant general came and inspected us—we were standing in formation—and he stopped and talked to every man, and Murray Harlan stood right at his left shoulder and looked into your eyes and you looked back at Murray Harlan and you saw the one god, the only god, the true god and you said, "Yes sir, everything's fine, yes sir, yes sir." It was all conditioning.

What Murray Harlan was showing us was that there is no place for you to hide. Very simply, they're trying to get you to take orders. Unreasoning, blind obedience to orders. And the fact is they're right. I mean, forgetting your civil liberties, they are absolutely right. That's the only way to run that kind of outfit.

You were in the Marine Corps. This was the way they built that special esprit de corps. It's real and they build it very simply. And basically what they are trying to do is to make a team in the best sense of that word, absolutely dependent on each other. They say, "Are you going to be the one that lets your buddies down?" Then they tell you the horror stories about the guy that had a dirty rifle and it misfired and as a result the position was overrun and everybody was killed. That guy was never killed, of course. He always survived to live in shame for the rest of his life. "What'll your family say? What's your father going to say when you come home in chains? You'll go to the naval brig in Portsmouth for the rest of your life."

So as a result when you get into physical conditioning you know you're not going to be the guy that quits. You're going to be the guy that climbs the rope, that doesn't pass out on the drill field. Because you're not going to be the one that lets everybody else down. They have all kinds of terms for it, but it's conditioning. Basic conditioning. I bought it absolutely and unquestioningly.

The physical conditioning was devastating. I've never been a sweater, I'd never soaked a shirt. But in the Marine Corps we'd wear green dungarees and they'd be black with perspiration, it was so hot. I played baseball and ran track in high school and I went through a lot of conditioning in track, but I'd never experienced anything like that. I mean, I could do thirty-two push-ups, clap my hands twice and come down again between every push-up. That was just routine. I did those every morning. I was in condition like I don't believe. It was hard work and it was hot, but I liked it. The overpowering impression was one of absolute heat, and they'd say, "This is nothing, wait until you get to Guadalcanal. Yeah—*that's* hot, and we don't have malaria here." In fact, that's one of the watchwords in the Marine Corps: "You think this is tough? Wait till you get to. . . ."

I was proud of the way I developed, not physically now, mentally. I liked the fact that I was a great team player and that I never let down my group—except for one time when we were practicing landings. But that wasn't at boot camp, that was at radio school where one guy from my outfit and I were sent for training. This guy and I stayed together all the way through the service. His name was Riddle.

We were sent to Camp Lejeune, North Carolina, for radio school where we learned code and technical stuff for five or six weeks. While there we were practicing landings. The Coast Guard ran us up to the beach in little LCVP's (small landing craft), and the instructions were very clear: keep your head down because of shrapnel or fire and when you feel the landing craft ground—they run them right up on the beach—and the ramp in front goes down, run and jump as far as you can, because the waves will carry the landing craft up over you and the thing will run you over in the water if you don't. Okay.

So the barge comes in and they're shouting, "Keep your head down! Keep your head down! Keep your head down!" And then it hits with a terrific jar because it's moving, and you kind of stumble around for a minute to get your footing, and down goes the ramp and they're shouting, "Run! Jump! Jump!" And they keep hammering you, "Jump! Jump!" So I didn't realize that the son of a gun had hit a sandbar, and that we were in about eight feet of water and a few hundred yards from the beach. So I jumped. I was in the front of the barge with the radio, I jumped, and I just kept going down. I can swim, in fact I'm a good swimmer. The trouble was that I had a 35-pound radio transmitter strapped on my front and a field pack on my back.

All that gear allows for very little arm movement. Really, about all you could do was dog-paddle. Not only did I have very little arm movement, but all this time I'm trying not to lose my rifle. God forbid you lose that rifle. The penalties for losing a rifle were—I don't know—castration. So the rifle's going down and I'm going down while trying to swim in water well over my head. I don't know how deep it was but it took me a while to sink to the bottom and then after pushing off it took a while for me to return to the surface. That's why I'd guess eight or ten feet.

When the barge hit the sandbar the helmsman was ducking too, you see, so he didn't know what he'd hit. He shouldn't have let the ramp down, he should have backed up and come around the bar to the beach. But he was a rookie, too. By now there were other guys in the water but I had my eyes shut and didn't see anybody. Well, just as I came up to the surface to get a breath, something very large hit me right in the middle of the back. I later found out that it was the two-wheel cart used to string telephone wire—it looked sort of like an ice cream cart. The guys with the cart were in the back of the landing craft and they really took off and jumped.

When the wheel of the cart hit me in the back, it didn't hurt me, but it shoved me all the way back down again. I'd only been to the surface long enough to get a very short breath, so I started to panic because I was running short of air. I managed to come up again, very tired, and having trouble swimming because I was dog-paddling. I swam, and I swam, and I swam. Everything was soaking up water. I was having a hell of a time swimming. I was not terribly buoyant but I had my head up and now the damn helmet strap was down around my Adam's apple and that's tugging at me because—picture it—my helmet's filled with water and it's acting like a sea anchor.

I finally touched ground and I waded in very slowly. I was late, everybody else was in. The rest of the problem was to go up this huge sand dune—it seemed huge to me, maybe it was thirty feet high—and down the other side and set up the radio and establish communication. That was the problem. In those days it took four men to carry all the parts of a field radio. The other three guys are already on the other side of the dune waiting for me.

I tried to get up the sand dune but I didn't have much strength left. I was out of breath. I was tired and the sand kept shifting and I kept slipping and falling and sliding and now the damn sand is clinging to me. I must have gone from 250 to 300 pounds with wet sand hanging all over me. Now a corporal who's wearing nothing but an overseas cap and a .45 is yelling, "Get your ass in there! Get your ass here! You're holding up the team! Get up the dune!"

And I couldn't get up the dune. The more I tried, the tireder I got. You know what it's like to try to run up a sand dune. I just kept sliding. Finally the corporal looks around to see if anybody is looking, sees that there isn't, and says, "Go around." Well, I went around the dune instead of over it and everybody is hollering, "Let's go! Let's go! Let's go!" The point is that we were in a competition and I think everybody else was set up by then and our team came in last. Well, I took a tremendous amount of shit and I was embarrassed and ashamed. I really was.

I was embarrassed for the other guys and they didn't let up on me. Nobody understood. Nobody cared to understand. And I realized the terrible shame of letting your team or your operation or your outfit down. I don't know what I would have done differently. I didn't make excuses for myself, but I was ahamed. It was like, "I'm sorry fellows, I got shot. I let you down. It was my fault. I should have fended the bullet off." I didn't rationalize, "What could I do, the cart hit me, I almost drowned"—I mean, everybody else managed to get in. That's how the Marine Corps builds esprit de corps. It works.

When I finished my training at Camp Lejeune I went to Omaha, Nebraska. It was a fantastic deal. We went to a civilian school that had been taken over and we learned radio repair. It was a sixteen-week course. It was terrific. There were only ninety of us and we lived in the YMCA. When we left there we went to Camp Pendleton in Oceanside, California, for advanced combat training. That was very tough training but we were in great shape. Then, I shipped out and joined the 4th Marine Division. At that point I'd had about a year of various training.

The 4th Division was on its way back to Hawaii from its first operation, which was to secure small islands in the Marshall chain. They were coming back to reform and regroup. Our permanent base was on Maui, one of the Hawaiian Islands. We were very excited about being overseas because Hawaii was considered overseas at that time.

When we got to Maui I was folded into the 4th Signal Company. We were in constant training doing field problems, going out and setting up and fixing equipment out in the field. It was pretty routine.

We took off in mid-May of '44 for Saipan. This was my first combat operation. I came in very late in Saipan and I really wasn't involved in much combat. It was always ahead of me, up further. While we were on the ship to Saipan everybody was given his assignment: "You will go in on such and such a day, such and such a time."

We didn't know where we were going initially. They simply don't tell you. And then you get several days at sea and they start breaking it out. My platoon commander had our assignment. It was all broken down into books. They show you relief maps of the island and give you a lot of briefing. I felt a lot of excitement but I wasn't smart enough to feel anxiety. I didn't understand what it would be like. You know, you never think of them shooting back. It's a big lark.

I think I got that out of my system in Saipan. I saw a lot of casualties. There were a lot of civilians—natives—on Saipan and they took terrible casualties. I began to see a lot of blood and gore and pain and hurt and death and to realize, Jesus Christ, what is this thing? I mean, they never showed that in the John Wayne movies. Oh, sure, a guy got hit in the movies but it was always glamorous. You know, he died well, or he lived beautifully. Of course any fool would have known that isn't the way it is. It's filth and it's pain and lost limbs and lost lives and wasted youth. And you begin to identify with the people who have been hurt. That's when the anxiety begins to grow, because you realize that you have no magic going for you. That stuff is very impersonal. It can happen to anyone.

We took some casualties on Saipan. We had about 25,000 men and I would say we probably took 4,000 or 5,000 casualties dead and wounded. After Saipan we went back to Maui to refit, get replacements, train, and get ready to go again. We were assault troops. Once the islands were secure the army sent in garrison troops. So we went all the way back to Maui and refitted. We had a lot of fixing to do. A lot of stuff was damaged and lost. We were profligate with gear.

We spent a great deal of time in the Pacific aboard troop ships. It took a long time to get anywhere because we were doing a lot of feinting—you know, heading off in the wrong direction and then turning and coming back and forth, so that the Japanese wouldn't know where we were going. This made for very long trips. We must have been aboard ship at least a month going from Hawaii to Saipan.

I was on one of the new transports operated by the Coast Guard. As troop transports go it was a hell of a good ship—it was command ship for that convoy. But even the best troop ship is pretty awful. You're bunked in the bowels of the ship. It's so hot and crowded that you can't stay down below. We were in the Central Pacific where it's very hot anyway. You're in a steel ship and it's like an oven. Everyone wants to be topside, so there's no room on the deck. Most of the fistfights start because somebody steps on someone trying to get through. People get edgy.

You have absolutely nothing to do, and they're trying to occupy you with a little physical training. How much of that can you do? There's very little room on deck—or anywhere else—and you don't want to sit out in the sun because it's so damn hot. So everybody is trying to get the little bit of shade that's on one side of the ship or under the boats. You spent most of your time standing in the chow line. Not because you got there any faster, but because there's nothing else to do. The chow line is wrapped around the ship, the fistfights start when you try to crash it. The techniques were few in number and transparent as hell: you'd stop to talk to a guy and the next thing you know you're in line. They only fed you twice a day and that was tough. But the food was okay and there was plenty of it. Besides, what else was there to look forward to? It was the high spot of the day.

I read a lot and I played a lot of bridge. I got to be a pretty good bridge player. There was a lot of gambling. I got in with some good players who taught me. We had one guy who used to knit sweaters and then take them apart, roll the yarn up and knit something else again. You had so much time that it was boring. Just boring.

That was boredom of a variety that I don't think I've ever experienced and there was no end to it. We didn't know how long we would be at sea. They never told us the date when we would get where we were going. We asked the sailors when are we going to get there, but they didn't know any more than we knew. Anybody who knew didn't talk. Anybody who talked didn't know. That was the byword. What they call scuttlebutt goes around. A scuttlebutt is a drinking fountain and that's where the gossip always was since everybody went to the drinking fountain.

Life on a troop transport is strange. I think you could lose your grip on reality. You could go a little mad, it's a little like being a man without a country, you know, forever at sea. There's nothing to see, of course, but water. You occupy yourself by doing your laundry. You get a line from the crew, tie your stuff to it, hang it overboard, and let it slap along in the wake and that would clean it. It would come out salty and kind of hard and crusty. But what you would do then was wear your clothes in the shower and rinse them in fresh water. Wash them in fresh water with soap and rinse them fast, take off your stuff, wash your body and get out! Because everybody's pulling at you and yelling at you to get out. The salt water showers are on all the time but you can't wash in salt water, all you get is itch after a while. They turn the fresh water showers on one, maybe two hours a day. There were battles to get in the shower if some guy stayed in longer than he should have. You're living in close quarters and guys would get very tough on people that didn't take regular showers because they'd stink up the whole area.

We used to fight with the sailors. I was not, myself, much of a fighter and I don't think I ever picked a fight. But we had guys who picked fights just from sheer boredom. The movies were a high spot. We had them every night in the mess hall—there would be seven sittings. We could sit on deck as much as we wanted, but we couldn't smoke at night. You couldn't show a light. You couldn't sleep on deck because if there were general quarters the Navy had to be able to get to its guns. There was a nice breeze on deck, especially at night, so we stayed up there even though we weren't allowed to sleep.

Our next major action was Iwo Jima. It took us a long time to get there—five weeks, maybe even six. Thankfully, I didn't go into Iwo Jima on the first day because it was a terrible time. When the first men got to the beach they took tremendous fire. And then the ocean got rough and the waves became so large we couldn't get reinforcements and more ammunition in. Those guys were pinned on the beach with no place to hide. They took terrible casualties the first day. It was lucky they held the beachhead.

I knew more about what was going on than most guys because I had duty as a communications runner. I would run messages from the radio room to the Marine Corps strategy group where a brigadier general was directing the assault. The messages were written, and even though we weren't supposed to, I'd read them as I walked them up to the commander. I couldn't always understand them, but I'd read them. Then I'd hang around the radio room. By staying in the radio room I'd hear transmissions coming in and going out.

I knew that the 23rd Marines, an infantry regiment, was pinned down and that their commander was getting all kinds of shit. "Move! Move! Move!" They were hammering at him to move and he was saying, "I can't move, I can't get out of here. I need support,

I need artillery, I need planes, I need rockets." And they were saying, "Get up, get out. The fire is coming from above you. We can't get at it." And he was saying, "I need help." Boy, they were coming down on him.

We landed more or less in the middle of the island. Actually, more toward the mountain, Mt. Suribachi, which was the high point. The island was pear-shaped and we came in toward the narrow part of the pear. The mountain was at the stem. There were heights at either end of the island and the Japs pouring fire down on us from both ends. We couldn't come in at the heights because it was a sheer cliff. The Navy was just pounding the hell out of that constantly with all kinds of stuff. They had rocket launchers mounted in tiers and they were just pounding that stuff in. The big battleships were sitting way out and pounding away with 16-inch shells. My God! Pounding, pounding, pounding, pounding. Trying to soften up. But that island was volcanic stone, and the Japanese were in caves. So all of that softening up wasn't very effective.

I know the reconnaisance was bad, and I'll tell you why. They told us that the operation would take four days. Afterwards, they told us that we were supposed to have come back aboard ship and gone directly on to Okinawa. We were not supposed to go back to Maui, as we actually did; we were supposed to go on to Okinawa. We went into Iwo Jima on February 19 and, if I remember correctly, forty days later Okinawa started. Well, there's your recon. They said four days, but we didn't get off that thing until March 17—it was nearly a month. No way could we have been at Okinawa by April 1. And we never even got to Okinawa. We had 25,000 men in the division and I think we had 20,000 casualties. It was terrible. There were over 5,000 killed alone.

On the ship that first day I was watching the bombardment and reading these messages and in my heart of hearts I was glad I wasn't there. I was glad somebody else was there. By the time I went in we still did not have a hell of a lot of island. We had reached the first airstrip only. I mean, we were pounding it out inch by inch. This was combat in the truest sense. The island is so small that there's no place to hide. It was only two and a half miles long. You could hit anybody on the island with a mortar shot. I had a lot of anxiety going in. They were plopping mortars onto the landing craft coming in. So even the landing wasn't very safe, and then they would get you off the beach fast.

People have always had the greatest admiration for the beachmasters. They were the Navy people who ran the beach. Unbelievable! The enemy is homing in on the beach because that's where the supplies are coming in and they want to hit them there while they're all bunched. The beachmasters were unbelieveable. I don't know where they put their emotions. I don't know how they stood it. The fatality rate among the beachmasters had to be terrible. The beach was awful.

Anyway, I finally hooked up with my outfit. And all the guys immediately start to tell you, "Oh boy, it was bad, you're lucky you weren't here. This happened and that happened and this happened." And then, of course, very quickly you fall into your routine. It's a different routine than you're accustomed to, but I think it's human nature. You must have a routine. We started doing our work fixing gear. Then one of the radio operators got hit, and I was sent up to work with the battalion commander as his communicator. He gets a lot of communication. In other words, I was with him, literally. It was my job to stick to him like glue.

We had the SCR-300 Signal Corps standard infantry radio. It went on your back and you talked into a telephone. The thing I didn't like about it was it had a big long very flexible antenna sticking up and people didn't want to be around you because they were always sure that the antenna would draw fire. As a matter of fact, I don't think the antenna could be seen very far because it was so thin. But people were always moving away from you, you were a leper.

I just sent the colonel's messages, almost by rote. He would speak to you and you would concentrate very carefully on what he said. Occasionally, he would hand you something in writing if he wanted a record, but mostly it was "Send to division the following message," and he would say, "Need artillery fire coordinate such and such." That was always the breakdown. The battalion commander's not exposed much of the time. He's dug in and he's getting reports from the companies. I didn't handle those reports from the companies, I only handled division communications for him. He would just tell me what to send. There was no small talk.

It was all business. Once in a while he'd look at me and say, "Did you eat?" And I'd say, "No sir," and he'd say, "Eat." That's about as much communication as we ever had. I slept right beside him. I was with him twenty-four hours a day.

There was no boredom there, but there wasn't much terror either. I think you get numb. You go into a state of semi-shock. I think your system adjusts to it. Occasionally you're frightened or startled when somebody or something comes very close to you. But I don't think you can sustain a constant level of terror. I think you'd go mad. You're busy all the time, busy with the routine. Occasionally you go up and peak, but you come right back down again. There's no way you can sustain that.

I have very few recollections. I was constantly busy with the same things, with the routine. Once in a while the colonel would grab the phone away from me and say to the other operator, "Put your commanding officer on." I'd stand there and cringe and he would just chew that guy out. Usually, of course, he had just been chewed out himself. So he'd pass it down the line to the company commander, who'd be a captain probably. He'd say, "I don't want any of your excuses. You take it, you take it. I have no help for you. No. You do it! Do it now! I want a report from you at 0100 hours. And the only report I want to hear from you is you took it. That's all."

It was tough. But I don't know how else you'd do it. You sure aren't going to have meetings all the time to discuss whether it was possible. It just comes right down the chain of command. It's utterly impersonal and it must be, because otherwise they'd lose their minds. They took the casualty reports and they immediately were trying to see where they could get replacements.

There were no clichés about kids, people, husbands and brothers. How else could it be? They have to develop that kind of detachment. They give orders that they know are sure death for a certain number of people. They assign ten men and know there's no way that five of them are going to come back. They did it—and what's so crazy about it is that's the way they had to do it. I think they were decent, rational people. They had an assignment to do. It was an utterly rational assignment in an utterly irrational context.

Through the whole experience of the war—whether in training

or in action or just waiting—the one event that made the deepest impression on me was Cecil B. Penn's death. Cecil B. Penn was a guy I was in radio school with and then stuck with all the way to Iwo. There were four of us, in alphabetical order: Penn, Riddle, Rittenberg, Stein. They broke us off alphabetically and we four eventually went from Camp Pendleton to the 4th Division. We were all friends and we saw each other all the time. Then Penn got killed on Iwo Jima. We had heard he was killed, Archie Stein told us. And we went to find him. We saw his body lined up with others before they buried them. Penn was the same age as me—we were all about nineteen. I thought he was a hell of a guy. I liked him and I respected him. I thought he was a tough guy. It was just one of those freak things, you know. A shell came in and killed him. And Riddle and Stein and I used to talk about it all the time.

It haunted me for years. And I still think of him occasionally. Someone will mention Texas—he was a Texan—and I'll think of Cecil B. Penn. Other guys, whom I knew less well, were also killed. But when I saw that body lying there—and it had started to swell from the heat—it was a terrible thing. That pungent odor is something you'll never get out of your mind as long as you live. I can smell it now, you know. You can almost taste it. I'll never forget those things. And I'll never forget that the guy was a friend of mine and that it could have been me.

In the happy periods of my life I've always thought of how C. B. Penn could never again experience these things. The happiness that my parents felt, his parents never felt. That to me is an overriding tragedy. That's a very powerful memory to me. It brought home my own mortality more forcefully than anything I've ever experienced before or since. Probably the only other thing that brought that home as forcefully was when my own father died. I mean, if I am the flesh of someone who was mortal then I must be mortal.

On Iwo I thought about C. B. Penn's death and I knew that it didn't make sense except that humankind has not figured out a way to handle things like violence or insults to national honor. We haven't worked out a system yet. So—yes, it makes no sense, and yes, it makes a lot of sense.

After Iwo we went back to Maui. We were decimated. We'd lost a lot of troops and most of our gear. We were in bad shape and we took a tremendous number of replacements and we started to refit again. We'd missed Okinawa and everybody knew what had to be next. All you had to do was look on a map. You see, there were stepping stones right across the Pacific. What's the next step? It's got to be the Japanese home islands. There was nothing else left.

You could read it in the press. I used to get *Time* Magazine's overseas edition. It explained how we had isolated a lot of the Japanese-held islands, like Truk, without even bothering to take them. We just shut them off and let them rot. That was the only sensible thing to do. There was no point in invading islands you didn't need because you had something beyond them. We knew it was going to be the home islands and that was scary.

Make no mistake about it, the Japanese were great fighters and everyone respected the hell out of them and feared them. They fought like hell for Iwo and what the hell was Iwo, a two-and-a-half-mile long piece of volcanic sand and rock. What are they going to fight like in the home islands? There were at that time 60 or 80 million civilians. There were a few civilians on Saipan and a few on Okinawa, but we had never really been involved with civilians before. That was a whole special problem.

In April, while we were refitting on Maui, two things happened in rapid succession. Roosevelt died. That was very sad. He was a father figure, a god. He'd been with us since most of us were babies. I think that everybody felt a very personal sense of loss. The war in Europe also ended in April. We figured, now they're going to bring all those guys over here and it'll be wham, bam, thank you ma'm and the end.

As a matter of fact they didn't bring them over. Instead they dropped the atom bomb on Hiroshima. We're still on Maui but the gear's all packed and stenciled now. And we know we're going. We were about to load up and board ship. No question in anyone's mind then. We're going to the home islands. And then they drop the bomb. Holy Toledo!

We had access to the news magazines and the Honolulu papers so we knew what happened. Then they dropped the second bomb at Nagasaki. Of course we knew that Truman had said unconditional surrender only. And we said, "Right, unconditional only, don't let them up."

Then the war was over and we never did go. Great relief, great relief. By that time everyone was sick to death of the Pacific, and the Japanese, and the islands, and the war, and everything else. Everyone had been in too much by then. We gave no thought to the effect of the bomb on the Japanese. None at all. We felt they started it, they asked for it. We had no sympathy for them. None whatever.

Of course, our attitudes were affected by our own propaganda. It heavily influenced the way we viewed the Japanese. I never thought of them as people like myself who had gone to high school, who had gone to a dance, who had friends, who had parents. They were "the Japs." They were cast in a role that was essentially subhuman. They were a bunch of monkeys. I think that was a very serious mistake on our part, because at first we underrated them. Towards the end we didn't underrate them any more because they were awfully good at what they were doing. There were more of us and we outmuscled them, but we never outfought them.

At that time we didn't know about the effects of the A-bomb either. But I think that even if we had known we'd have felt that it was better their lives than ours. After all, they dragged us into it because they bombed Pearl Harbor, we didn't bomb them. I can't ever remember anybody saying, "Oh, my God, what must that have been like?"

Of course, we were already firebombing the Japanese cities before that. Those B-29 saturation bombing raids were terrible. Had there ever been an invasion of the home islands, the lives lost—military and civilian—would have been unbelieveable. If that invasion were handled the same way as the operations I was in, how could it have been otherwise?

In retrospect, cruel and horrible and grotesque as it was—and difficult as the decision must have been for President Truman—I suspect that quantitatively, in terms of lives on both sides, dropping the A-bomb was the best way. If you can reduce it to how many people are going to be killed this way versus another way, I don't think there is any contest. If we had continued with saturation bombing of those cities and naval bombardment and an invasion assault, the slaughter would have been even more horrifying. You must remember, of course, that both sides were involved in inhuman acts all along. If one kind of killing is inhuman, so's another kind. It's a self-cancelling kind of thing. When is war not inhuman?

Well, shortly after the bomb was dropped, Japan surrendered. The division packed up and almost everyone went home. I was shipped all the way to Okinawa to help set up a communications network for the military government. I had the seniority to go home but because I had some special expertise I was "frozen" and couldn't go. I stayed on Okinawa for five months, and when they finally did let me go they stuck me on the slowest ship in the Navy—an LST that made 8 knots—and it took thirty days to get home. That was the final irony.

In all, I spent 42 months in the Marine Corps and during that time I was in actual combat situations for a month and a half or two months. That means I spent 95 percent of the time training, drilling, doing routine jobs; and only 5 percent of the time actually doing what I had been trained to do. Of course, you tend to think about the two months you were in action, and not all those other months of boredom. They were nothing. There's nothing to remember. What did I do? What's to remember?

15

HIROSHIMA:
August 6, 1945

Miss Palchikoff

The burns the people had were a dark color. People just turned the color of Negroes. That's the nearest I can get to it. And the skin would just peel off—some would peel off very thickly and some very thinly—and the thicker the peeling, the worse the wound, of course. On some of them you could see the bones. The eyes closed, and the nose bled, the lips swelled and the ears swelled, and the whole head started swelling by about two or three hours. Then there were patients with other kinds of wounds. These were fractured arms and legs, and huge water blisters which had to be punctured. Then there were split stomachs—the intestines would come out—and fractured skulls.

—Miss Palchikoff

Hiroshima: August 6, 1945

Early in 1945 the military situation began to deteriorate rapidly for Japan. The war in China had dragged on for years, sucking up large amounts of manpower and material, and when the Japanese had no more troops to spare, Mao Tse-tung's and Chiang Kai-shek's armies began to liberate territory that the Japanese were spread too thinly to defend.

The border between Japanese-held Manchuria and the Soviet Union had been quiet during most of the war because Japan and the USSR were busy fighting elsewhere and had observed a truce. But as the war against Hitler drew to a close, Soviet forces—with Allied encouragement—threatened to attack occupied Manchuria, and Japan, already overextended, had to maintain sizable forces there. In the Pacific, Japan's fleet had been destroyed and could no longer prevent the free movement of Allied ships, while her land forces were being driven from the Philippines, Iwo Jima, and Okinawa.

Major cities on the home islands were being systematically gutted by relentless incendiary raids that turned crowded residential and industrial areas into raging conflagrations. On the night of March 9, Tokyo was being buffeted by high winds when more than three-hundred B-29's dropped their napalm-like bombs on the city and created a firestorm that left 100,000 people dead, 125,000 wounded, and more than a million homeless. This was the most destructive bombing mission ever to have taken place, but similar raids were carried out over Kobe, Osaka, and other cities.

As Japan's vulnerability increased, it became apparent that the invasion of the home islands was imminent. There were very few other military objectives left. Yet such an invasion promised to be a bloodbath. The Japanese soldier had proven an effective and tenacious combatant when fighting on Pacific atolls thousands of miles from Japan. He was likely to be even more determined when defending his home ground. The Japanese had not lost a war since 1598, and while the Navy knew it had been defeated because its ships were gone, the Japanese Army felt that it had never really been defeated in this war. In fact, the bulk of the Army's land forces were very much intact—there were still millions of armed men in the home islands, on the Chinese mainland, and in Manchuria—and there were some five thousand planes ready to be used as Kamikazes for the home defense.

Thus the invasion of Japan appeared inevitable, and there seemed to be no way to avoid the slaughter on both sides that would accompany such an event. But there was a way that few could have imagined. It began in the late nineteenth century, when British physicist J. J. Thompson first suggested a relationship between mass and energy that culminated, after years of concentrated scientific effort, with the atomic bomb.

The scientists who explored the relationship between mass and energy did not set out initially to build an atomic bomb. They believed, in the words of Dr. Arthur Compton, that ". . . atomic energy would eventually become one of the greatest gifts that science could ever provide ... [that] the bomb was only the wartime aspect of a much greater vision." The men and women who pursued this vision came from many countries. They demonstrated that science has no nationality, but flourishes wherever and whenever minds are free to question, to challenge, and to move beyond conventional ideas.

In the last few months of 1941, a team of scientists was organized to consider the practicality of an American effort to develop an atomic bomb. They recognized that a bomb was possible in theory but that the technical problems in actually making one were almost insurmountable. Ernest Lawrence of the University of California theorized that an effective bomb could be made using less U-235 than had been thought necessary. He also suggested that the element plutonium, newly discovered in his laboratory and more easily obtained than U-235, could be used for making an atomic bomb. Even with Lawrence's "shortcuts," Nobel Laureate Arthur Compton concluded that a bomb would require three or four years of all-out effort and would cost roughly a billion dollars. At the time developing an atomic chain reaction was only an idea on paper. On December 6, 1941, Compton reported to President Roosevelt that the bomb might be decisive in the war. A report received from British scientists said much the same thing. Roosevelt urged that all possible effort be put into the project. The following day the Japanese bombed Pearl Harbor.

A huge undertaking was begun, in complete secrecy and under the innocuous title of "the Manhattan Project," to make the materials needed for the bomb. Uranium 235 and plutonium were essential; massive, complex facilities were built in Oak Ridge, Tennessee, and Hanford, Washington, in order to produce even small quantities of the substances. The project was carried on with such secrecy that most high officials knew nothing about it. Vice-President Harry S. Truman only learned of it when he became President after Roosevelt's death. Just the words "Manhattan Project" were enough to produce even the scarcest war materials because they carried the highest priority for personnel or materials. The whole project was divided so that those working on it usually knew just one phase of it, and from no single phase could they guess the ultimate objective.

The force and destructive capacity of the atomic bomb remained only a theory until July 16, 1945, when the first atomic device was tested in the New Mexico desert. Scientists erected a steel tower and suspended the bomb from it, then moved ten miles away and detonated it. The blast was heard for hundreds of miles. A great ball of fire many times brighter than the midday sun billowed skyward. The steel tower was vaporized. All that was left was a great smoking crater. A massive mushroom cloud surged skyward, reaching the stratosphere in about five minutes. It had cost two billion dollars and monumental effort, but the United States had its atomic bomb.

President Truman was quickly informed of the successful test. On the following day he met with Churchill and Stalin at Potsdam, Germany, and told them that the new weapon was ready for use. On July 26 an ultimatum prepared at Potsdam was sent to Japan, warning that it faced utter destruction if it did not surrender.

Unfortunately the Japanese interpreted the Potsdam Ultimatum as being no different from the propaganda that had been directed at them throughout the war. President Truman regarded the atomic bomb as a military weapon and never had any doubt that it should be used. On August 6 the bomb was dropped on Hiroshima.

Even then the Japanese refused to surrender. Three days later Truman warned of the consequences of carrying on the war. Still the Japanese ignored the warning. So a second atomic bomb was dropped, this time on Nagasaki. It was the last bomb the Americans had. The next day Japan's Supreme War Council met, but still the generals and admirals could not agree to surrender. Finally, saying, "I cannot bear to see my innocent people suffer any longer," Emperor Hirohito announced that he felt compelled to accept the surrender terms. On August 14, 1945, the Japanese officially accepted the terms of unconditional surrender. On September 2, aboard the USS Missouri anchored in Tokyo Bay, the surrender documents were formally signed.

Truman's decision to drop the atomic bomb is perhaps the biggest unresolved question of World War II. It did more than hasten the downfall of Japan and mark the beginning of the nuclear age: it started an unending debate about the wisdom and morality of using nuclear weapons. Viewed with the benefit of more than thirty years' perspective, it might seem easy to say that Truman was wrong. But at the time, and in context of the war, this was not clear. In the words of Art Rittenberg, "If it was inhuman to drop the atomic bomb, then it was inhuman to carry on saturation raids with incendiary bombs. We were bombing those cities anyway. Bombing is inhuman. War is inhuman. When is war not inhuman? We were totally in favor of the A-bomb if it was going to end the war and keep us from getting killed."

Of course, it is impossible to imagine the awesome reality of being on the receiving end of an atomic bomb. A survivor of the Hiroshima bombing, known only as "Miss Palchikoff," was an eyewitness to the explosion. The daughter of foreign missionaries or educators, she lived with her family in Hiroshima throughout the war. Several months after the Hiroshima bombing, she was interviewed by an investigating team of the United States Strategic Bombing Survey. Her first name was not recorded. Typical of the victims of the blast, she searches, often in vain, for a rational explanation—an understanding—of the suffering and devastation wrought by the single explosion. There is no record of what became of her after the war.

Miss Palchikoff:

The bomb was dropped at about a quarter to eight in the morning. It was just a flash, and I didn't have time to notice what it was all about. You see, when the flash came, the house tumbled down on us. We had no time to flee to the air raid shelters, or even to dugouts. My mother called to us—my father, my brother and me. When we found that everybody was safe, we rushed outside to see what it was all about.

Our home was approximately three kilometers from the center of the bomb. When we went outside we looked around our house. There were people starting to come out, some bruised, some wounded, some burned. Then we looked down toward the town and we saw it flaming. Then my father asked us what we would like to do, as he didn't know what the bomb was like and he thought it was just an ordinary bomb. Then mother said, "Well, we'll leave it to fate and just follow the road." And so we took a little bag where we had our bandages and medicine and a bit of rice. That was all we had with us.

We started up the road toward the mountain. Hundreds of people came after us. But to our astonishment, we looked at them and we saw Negroes, just Negroes. They weren't Japanese—they were Negroes. I asked them: "What happened to you? What's the matter with you?" And they said: "We saw the flash and this is the color we turned." Well, I didn't take time to ask how it all happened. We went further, and there were people wounded, very badly wounded. And I heard someone screaming from under a house. I tried to pull her out, but I couldn't. I just saw a hand, and I knew it was a woman's hand. I couldn't get her out. It was just too hard with so much on top of her. It was impossible.

Then we started up the mountain. We didn't follow the road because it was too crowded with people and we couldn't really move on it. The mountains were starting to burn all around and the city was ablaze. Well, anyway, we walked for about two hours. On the way we met many people suffering, dying. Finally we reached a military hospital. It was supposed to be just a school, but it was used as a military hospital in case of heavy air raids.

My head was aching like anything because a beam had fallen on me, and there was a big scar, and blood falling over my face. Mother's shoulder was wounded too. My father and little brother weren't wounded at all. But we were terribly tired, just all-out fatigued, so we decided to take a rest.

But I couldn't rest. There were people whining, groaning, asking for help. I thought it was my duty to help them. I stayed and helped at the hospital for two days. I went over to the doctors and nurses who were very few, of course. And they said, "What kind of medicine do you think we should put on? We don't know what it's all about. All we've got is castor oil and mercurochrome." So they smeared mercurochrome over those burns and then they smeared castor oil. The reason they smeared castor oil was because they thought these were just ordinary burns. The doctors and nurses didn't give anybody any water, even though people asked and even begged for water. Some people gave water to the wounded, and as soon as they drank they vomited it all out and they'd keep on vomiting until they died. Blood would rush out and that was the end of them. So the doctor said not to give water under any circumstances.

The burns the people had were a dark color. As I said, people just turned the color of Negroes. That's the nearest I can get to it. And the skin would just peel off—some would peel off very thickly and some very thinly—and the thicker the peeling, the worse the wound, of course. On some of them you could see the bones. The eyes closed, and the nose bled, the lips swelled and the ears swelled, and the whole head started swelling by about two or three hours. Then there were patients with other kinds of wounds. These were fractured arms and legs, and huge water blisters which had to be punctured. Then there were split stomachs—the intestines would come out—and fractured skulls.

On the first day we dressed as many of these wounds as we could. On the second day the wounds, especially the burns, became very dirty and they smelled very bad. Even the air around the hospital smelled very bad. The wounds became yellow in color and they'd go deeper and deeper. No matter how much you tried to take off the yellow rotten flesh, it would just go deeper and deeper. The people that were very badly burned turned a greenish yellow color and vomited all the time, absolutely without intermission—vomited and vomited so they couldn't take in any water, or even ice.

The fingernails of the burned people just—I think that if you pulled them they'd come off. I didn't have the chance of ever trying to do anything like that. They bent outward. The skin was all off and I think that if I tried to take them off, they'd just come off. And their fingers weren't straightened out. It was as though they were holding something very hard—all the people. You tried to straighten up the fingers—that's what hurt them very much, and the fingers would click, so I think the inner bones were burned too.

And there were cases of many people burned through their clothing, without their clothes themselves having been burned off. I know of a surgeon who was doing an operation, and he had his back toward the center of the place where the bomb dropped.

And he had on that big officer's uniform, that thick uniform, and the whole of his back from the head down was burned right through the uniform and he died in three days. There were also cases in which clothing actually was burned off the people who were not in a fire—people who were out in the open. Their clothing burned off from them. I think woolly and heavy things burned faster than just cotton.

There were about four different kinds of patients: The ones that died off within two or three days—they died because of heavy burns. If people were burned on more than one-third of the body, most of them died. Then there were the patients who lived for maybe a week. They died from inhaling the gas, I think, and their heart weakened, and they died of exhaustion, I should say. Then there were the ones who lived through the burns—their burns got well, but in a month's time they'd find their hair falling out and have a very high temperature, and their throats would become very sore and they'd turn pale green and then they'd die. And then there's a fourth category. They say that people who were in an area within two kilometers in circumference of this bomb cannot live more than three years. I don't know whether it's just a rumor or fact, but the Japanese police said that people with burns on their faces or hands or anywhere would not live more than three years even though the burns got better.

People presumed that the bomb gave off some kind of gas. That is how they explained its effects. But some doctors said that it was interaction of the uranium with the sun's rays which passed through the body that would poison all the bones and everything inside the bones. That's how they explained it.

When the people at the hospital died, there were no priests— there was nothing, nothing at all. They'd be piled—the bodies would be piled just one on top of another—big sort of mountain pile, outside where you walk. There were so many flies on the piles. When I was in Hiroshima in the middle of September, I couldn't walk without a mask because the flies covered me. Oh, they sit on you. I couldn't eat or anything downtown.

Right after the bombing the people on the road were terribly panic-stricken. Not in the way Western people are, you know. The Japanese keep everything in their hearts, so they had their heads down and were just walking away. They didn't know where they were going or what they were going to do. They didn't care about anything anymore. They just said, "Everything's gone." And about losing their children, they said: "We couldn't get the child out, it was crushed under our house," and they'd grin. The Japanese when in sorrow show it with a smile, and when a girl is a bride she has her head down and doesn't smile at all; she keeps a straight face—just the opposite from us.

The Japanese thought it was queer that there wasn't one foreigner killed in Hiroshima. Everybody was safe. There were two German missionaries who were badly injured: one had an artery cut and he bled for eight hours, and then there was another man who had his hand or foot fractured and I think he was not coming along very well. And then there was another, Father Aruppe—he's Spanish, I believe. This young man was a surgeon, he went right in and helped very many Japanese. He believed in cutting off the arm if it was badly burned. The Japanese tried to scrape off the rotten flesh and everything, but he believed in cutting the arm off and he saved very many Japanese by doing that.

The Japanese knew that we were foreigners and they thought that the Americans dropped the bomb so not one foreigner would be killed. They said, "Why on earth are you safe? Why weren't you burned?" They looked at us with jealousy, and I didn't go downtown because I was afraid that they might kill me. Even among the Japanese there was antagonism among the people that were burned toward the people that weren't burned. Even now, the last time I went to Hiroshima, I was there from September 11th to the 19th, there were very many people who were burned, and they'd look at me with very bad eyes.

The people in Hiroshima didn't think that they would be bombed. The city had been bombed before just once; one incendiary bomb was dropped. We heard that Hiroshima would be left alone, because Hiroshima was such a beautiful place. That was the propaganda in our city anyway, but people from Tokyo, the burned-out people, would come and they'd say: "You'd better not play with fire."

The fire lasted in Hiroshima from half past eight to, I think, the next morning. Early in the morning about six o'clock it ended. People who were already encircled by the fire tried to save themselves. They jumped into the rivers. There are seven rivers in Hiroshima and they were just full of people. I know of a Russian gentleman who stayed in the water for seven hours. He'd come out of the water for a little while to get a breath, and then he would go in again. He was in the water nearly all the time—seven hours, and it was so hot that he said he was afraid the water was going to boil. On both sides the fire would just get fiercer and fiercer. Doctors were so panicky they forgot the patients that were lying around.

I was looking directly towards the city when it happened—when the bomb dropped. I saw the light very close to me. I thought it was on me, and I felt the hot waves too. I thought it was very hot. Yes, I felt uncomfortable. It was all in one flash. I never heard the explosion. I suppose there was an explosion—a big sound—but I never saw it. I just saw the house tumbling down, and I believe that it was all dark. That is all I remember. Everything in darkness for about two or three minutes. I think it was just dust, because my eyes—I couldn't clear out my eyes for about two or three days. They were full of little bits of sand and glass, I suppose. Everything. Very painful.

My brother had been playing outside. When he saw the flash, he just lay flat on the ground. He was completely in the open, with nothing to protect him. But he was not burned. No burn—nothing at all. The children who were playing with my brother were burned. They didn't lie down on the ground. They were little, little children. They got burned and they died soon after.

I didn't see it myself, but I heard that the wooden buildings burned immediately with the flash. The brick buildings were all destroyed, and they fell on top of the people and injured them. Many, many people were killed by big buildings like this—from seven to eight stories high falling down and becoming one story high. And then they'd never come out.

All services were out. Absolutely. In the police station—it was kind of in the suburbs—only about two policemen were left in the whole staff. You see, everything went back to ruin, absolute ruin.

After the bomb fell, people said that it was very inhuman. They said: "I suppose that we'll lose the war." And they said: "Perhaps all the Japanese are going to be killed. But we're going to live in the dugouts and not give up because of this." They were all of various opinions. There were people who right from the beginning said, "We shouldn't have fought with the Americans. We shouldn't have fought with foreign people anyway."

There were many criticisms of the Japanese government. They said that the radio locators didn't work very well, because the airplane would fly over and then the sirens would go. On the day the bomb was dropped, there were no sirens whatsoever. There was always a B-29 or two flying about and no sirens. They blamed the people who were supposed to take care of telling us when the enemy plane would be over, and they blamed the government for not paying much attention to that. The whole of Japan—I mean, all during the war there was criticism—especially of the military folks.

The government did take steps immediately following the bombing for rehabilitation. From other towns there were policemen, nurses, doctors, and engineers. But the only thing they took care of was the food, nothing else: no bandages, no clothing, absolutely nothing. No Red Cross. They were not able to come down there. Everything was smashed.

They didn't bury people—they didn't even burn them. There were just thousands and thousands of soldiers and people who dug up a big, big hole in front of the Regimental Headquarters. There was a big field where the soldiers march and have parades, you know. They'd dig a big hole there and throw the bodies in there and cover them. And they did it about five times.

Many months before the bomb we were supposed to evacuate. We had a command from the government saying that we had to evacuate Hiroshima by the 25th of February and people started going to the country. But the country people started saying: "You didn't pay much attention to us when times were good. Now that you are asking for help, well, we won't let you in." And, you see, they made all sorts of excuses, saying that there was a sick person, or the house is too small. So, even if the city people went to relatives to live, they'd come back with nervous breakdowns, saying: "I'd rather be killed by bombs than live in a house where they don't want you." So then many people came back.

After the atomic bomb fell, oh, then they sympathized, at least they sympathized with us, even though we were foreigners. They acted very nice to us. But, in general, the Japanese were so astonished. Everybody was out of their wits. Everybody had a girl or a boy wounded or a husband killed, and they went downtown to hunt for their husbands, wives, or children. They had to hunt for three or four days before they found even traces of the bones. They had no time to eat or talk or anything. They were just so tired out hunting. They'd go on hunting for weeks, and they wouldn't find anybody so they'd give up. And when they'd talk about it, they'd say, Shikataganai, and they'd laugh away. Shikataganai means "we can't do anything about it."

INDEX

Lolling, Dr., 214
London Blitz, 79–86, 151
Luftwaffe, 73, 79–80, 142, 151–52
  D-Day and, 172
  withdrawal from North Africa of,
    125
Lüneburg War Crimes Trials, 206
Luzon, Japanese invasion of, 110

MacArthur, General Douglas, 110,
  122, 226–28
Maginot Line, 62
Majdanek Concentration Camp, 44,
  51
Malaya, 105, 106
  Japanese capture of, 110, 224
Malta, 124
  siege of, 168
Manchuria, Japanese occupation of,
  246–47
"Manhattan Project," 249
Mao Tse-tung, 246
Mareth Line, 133, 135, 137, 138
Mariana Islands, 226–27
Mastrangello, Tom, 87, 89–104
Maui, 235, 236, 243
Mauldin, Bill, 115
Mauthausen Concentration Camp,
  217, 219
Medical experiments in concentra-
  tion camps, 201, 203, 207–8,
  213–18
Mein Kampf (Hitler), 189
Merchant ships
  armed guards on, 96–103
  escorts of, 92–95
Merdinger, Charles, 105, 107–9
Messerschmitts, 164
Midway, Battle of, 225
Military Air Transport (MATS),
  229–30
Minturno bridgehead, 147
Missouri (ship), 250
Monte Camino, Allied assault on,
  144–45
Monte Cassino, Allied capture of,
  129, 143, 146
Montgomery, General Bernard, 126,
  129, 135–38, 175–77
Morocco, 133

Allied landing in, 127
Muermelstadt, Dr., 213, 214
"Mulberries," 170
Munich, concentration camps near,
  223
Mussolini, Benito, 124, 127, 128
Nacht und Nebel prisoners, 207, 220
Nagasaki, bombing of, 243, 250
National Democratic Party (Poland),
  35, 38
National Socialists, see Nazis
Naval warfare, see U. S. Navy
Nazis
  concentration camps run by,
    189-223
  consolidation of power of, 23–26
  domination of Europe by, 168
  in occupied countries, 30–31
  persecution of Jews by, 19–22,
    25–28, 39, 51–52, 190–93
  racist policies of, 189–90
  reannexation and, 29
  rise to power of, 13–14, 17–19
  See also Germany
Netherlands, see Holland
Nevada (battleship), 107
New Guinea, 224–26
New Order, 190
Newspapers
  Nazi control of, 21, 24
  in occupied Poland, 45
Nimitz, Admiral Chester, 226
90th Light Division (Germany), 139
Nisei, 114–15
NKVD, 32
Normandy, Allied invasion of,
  171–76
  See also D-Day
North African campaign, 124–27,
  130–41, 169, 178
Norway, German invasion and
  occupation of, 30, 62, 95
Nuclear fission, 248
Nuremberg War Crimes Trials, 194

Office of Strategic Services (OSS),
  122
Okinawa, Battle of, 228, 239, 243,
  247
Oklahoma (battleship), 107

	DATE DUE	
OCT 28		
	MAR 1 8 1994	
MAR 13 1987		
DEC 4 1992		
APR 29		
MAY 28		